D1203517

WORDSWORTH AND COLERIDGE

WORDSWORTH
AND
COLERIDGE

Studies in honor of
GEORGE McLEAN HARPER

EDITED BY EARL LESLIE GRIGGS

:

ESSAYS BY ÉMILE LEGOUIS · RAYMOND
D. HAVENS · OSCAR JAMES CAMPBELL
NEWTON P. STALLKNECHT · ERNEST DE
SELINCOURT · LESLIE NATHAN BROUGHTON
M. RAY ADAMS · SAMUEL H. MONK · GERARD
HARTLEY BUCHANAN COLERIDGE · B. R.
McELDERRY, JR. · EARL LESLIE GRIGGS · CLARENCE
DeWITT THORPE · EDITH J. MORLEY

:

AN APPRECIATION BY J. DUNCAN SPAETH
A BIBLIOGRAPHY BY EVELYN GRIGGS

NEW YORK
RUSSELL & RUSSELL · INC
1962

PREFACE

•

THE editor has left to Dr. J. Duncan Spaeth the privilege of writing
in a personal way upon the character and attainments of his friend
and colleague, Professor George McLean Harper, in whose honor these
studies have been prepared, and it is a great pleasure to thank the scholars
who have so generously contributed to this volume. Acknowledgment is
also extended to the editor of the *London Mercury* for permission to
reprint Miss Edith J. Morley's article dealing with Coleridge in Germany.

In selecting contributors the editor has endeavored to include persons
who for one reason or another feel particularly indebted to Professor
Harper. It has seemed wise, therefore, to include not merely Words-
worthiana but also studies relating to Wordsworth's contemporaries.
This is especially fitting, inasmuch as Professor Harper's own researches
cover far more than his *magnum opus* upon Wordsworth.

It is the unhappy duty of the editor to note the death of Professor
Émile Legouis. Professor Legouis would have welcomed an opportunity
to read the proof sheets of his contribution, a task which his son has
generously undertaken.

The editor takes this opportunity gratefully to acknowledge the
assistance on the part of Princeton University, members of the Class
of 1884 (Professor Harper's class in Princeton), and other friends of
Professor Harper, in helping to defray the cost of publication of this
volume. Without their cooperation these studies could never have been
offered to the public.

E. L. G.

CONTENTS

•

•

PART TWO

PART ONE

SOME REMARKS ON THE COMPOSITION
OF THE *LYRICAL BALLADS* OF 1798

ÉMILE LEGOUIS

•
•

THE *Lyrical Ballads* of 1798 being an epoch-making book and generally considered as the initial date of English romantic literature, it is natural that they should have been almost exclusively studied and searched for the new elements of thought, feeling and form they contain. There lies without doubt their essential interest. Yet, the very fame of the collection can also invite one to examine it as a whole, such as it is: a somewhat random and incongruous assemblage of short poems connected by a preface that was an afterthought.

The origin and growth of the little volume have been amply told by the authors; none could have been more humble and matter-of-fact. It was born not of a concerted plan of poetic reform but of a need of money. Coleridge and Wordsworth on leaving Alfoxden on November 12, 1797, with the latter's sister to visit the Valley of Stones, agreed to cover the expense of the trip by writing a poem for which they might obtain £5 from the publisher of the *Monthly Magazine*. Coleridge proposed a ballad, ballads then being the fashion, and himself being at the time under the spell of Bürger's *Lenore*. Thus was begun *The Ancient Mariner*. Wordsworth almost at once withdrew from the undertaking "upon which he could only have been a clog." His genius was not fitted to the fantastic and Coleridge alone chanted the adventures of his "old navigator." As the ballad was finished no less than four months later, in March 1798, it could not serve its original purpose. This was no great inconvenience for Coleridge, who very soon after the excursion was offered by the Wedgwoods a generous annuity of £150 which he accepted.

No longer goaded by necessity, and moreover deterred from his ballad-writing by the composition of political odes on present events, he could not find it in himself to bring to a conclusion two other poems, more or less akin to ballads, *The Two Graves* and *Christabel*, which he began immediately after *The Ancient Mariner*. On the other hand, Wordsworth, who remained as poor as ever, tried to make money by some verse he had in manuscript and Coleridge helped him by an introduction to the Bristol publisher Cottle, with whom he was on friendly terms. Wordsworth first thought of giving Cottle his *Salisbury Plain*, including *The Tale of a Woman* (later called *The Female Vagrant*). In this choice he was again directed by pecuniary motives. He would not offer to Cottle his tragedy of *The Borderers*, no more than Coleridge would offer him his tragedy of *Osorio*, because the two authors calculated that they would make much more by their plays if they chanced to be staged. For his *Salisbury Plain* Wordsworth expected to receive £30. He reiterated his offer to Cottle on May 9, 1798, but added in the same letter, "I have been lately busy about another plan which I do not mean to mention till I see you." In the interview that immediately followed, Cottle informs us "that it was determined that the volume should be published under the title of *Lyrical Ballads* . . . , that this volume should not contain the poem of *Salisbury Plain* but only an extract from it; that it should not contain the poem of *Peter Bell* but consist of sundry shorter pieces more recently written."

The reason for this change of design is well. known. Wordsworth, whose vein had been stopped at first by his inability to cope with Coleridge, had suddenly found his lips unsealed and produced several poems in quick succession in the spring of 1798. In fact, only three of those offered to Cottle could be properly called ballads, viz. *Goody Blake and Harry Gill*, *The Idiot Boy*, and *The Thorn*. Though very different from *The Ancient Mariner*, for whose fantastic and remote theme they substituted humble incidents from present ordinary life, though they drew their inspiration not from the German *Lenore* but from the more familiar tales in Percy's *Reliques*, they were genuine ballads with their short verse and spirited gait. That they also deserved the epithet "lyrical" is not so evident as it is for Coleridge's *Mariner*. There is an air of defiance, and almost of parody, in the word "lyrical" when applied to the ride of poor idiotic Johnny. If the epithet was retained it must have been owing to Wordsworth's determination to assert the right of the meanest subjects to rank beside the most exalted in poetry. But, though Wordsworth seems to have thought otherwise, none of the other poems in the collection can be denominated ballads, not even *Simon Lee, The Last of the Flock*, or *We Are Seven*, which come nearest to the preceding ones in outward appearance; these are mere moral anecdotes like the one called by the poet *Anecdote for Fathers*. Some pieces are simply songs, e.g. *The Mad Mother* and *The Complaint of a Forsaken Indian Woman*. Several short poems, e.g. *Lines Written in Early Spring, Expostulation and Reply, The Tables Turned*, etc., are direct effusions of the poet himself, lyrical but without any relation to the ballad genre. It is superfluous to exclude Coleridge's *Nightingale*, called by the author a conversation poem, or Wordsworth's *Old Man Travelling* which is undertitled a sketch, or the extracts from the tragedy of *Osorio*, or the reflective poem of the *Yew-tree Seat*. To be true to its contents, the title of the volume ought to have been, not *Lyrical Ballads with a Few Other Poems*, but rather *A Few Ballads with Sundry Other Poems*.

The selection made by the two poets among the pieces they had ready in May 1798 may well surprise us. It is as difficult to account for the rejection of some as for the admission of others. Wordsworth could have given the masterpiece he had in manuscript and which he called either *The Story of Margaret* or *The Ruined Cottage*; he does not even mention it to Cottle. After some hesitation he also rejects *Peter Bell* which would have been an important addition to his few ballads. He seems to have kept both out, on account of their length, for higher destinies. He did not wish to risk all his productions in a single venture and declined Cottle's proposal to publish two volumes instead of one. Yet the one volume, for want of the pieces expected from Coleridge and left in abeyance, being decidedly too thin—and also perhaps because Wordsworth had formerly promised the whole *Salisbury Plain*—he inserted the extract from it named *The Female Vagrant*, the language of which clashed with the doctrine he had now arrived at and was to set forth in the Preface.

This particular poem belonged to a time when he thought of a social, not a poetical reform. It had been written at least five years before—even seven years, if we credit the Fenwick note of 1842. The tale was begun at the time of *The Evening Walk* or of *The Descriptive Sketches*. It presents the same characteristics of a pseudo-poetic diction as these early poems. Though described as "an artless story" told by a poor woman in low life, it abounds with the most notorious instances of the language condemned in the Preface. She calls her sheep "her fleecy store," spring "May's dewy prime," the fisherman her father "my active sire," her cottage "my native bowers." She does not say that twenty years passed away, but that

> The suns of twenty summers danced along.

Instead of "when June came" she says:

> When jocund June
> Rolled fast along the sky his warm and genial moon.

She calls the ocean "the illimitable waters" and uses the highest-flown language either to depict a tempest:

> The equinoctial deep
> Ran mountains-high before the howling blast,

or calm at sea:

> Peaceful as some immeasurable plain
> By the first beams of dawning light impress'd,
> In the calm sunshine slept the glittering main.

She has the most refined turns of phrase, the least expected from her station. She speaks of swans "spreading their snowy pride"; of her dog's "starts of furious ire." The free life of the vagrants and robbers that saved her from starvation is thus defined:

> For them, in nature's meads, the milky udder flowed. . . .

She is no less equipped with subtle phrases when she analyzes her own feelings:

Yet does that burst of woe congeal my frame. . . .
Dizzy my brain, with interruption short
Of hidden sense. . . .
. . . I have my inner sense abused,
Foregone the home delight of constant truth. . . .

We recognize in those instances the most striking and some of the worst features of Wordsworth's juvenile style. The surprise here is in their admission at a time when he had repudiated and in a volume destined to expose them. They are as far removed as possible from "the language of conversation in the middle and lower classes of society," which he declared in the Preface to be "adapted to the purposes of poetic pleasure." They are redolent "of the gaudiness and inane phraseology of many modern writers" which he condemned in the same Preface. He could not be unconscious of the discrepancy between the style of *The Female Vagrant* and that of *Goody Blake* which immediately follows. He was indeed careful to say that his observations on style only applied to the *majority* of the poems in the volume. But he was also probably blinded by paternal love of a tale which he was still proud of and which had been highly praised by Coleridge. Thus were past and present strongly mixed up in the *Lyrical Ballads* so as to puzzle and disconcert their first readers.

There was another cause of surprise for them in the innate difference between the style of Coleridge and that of Wordsworth, the volume being anonymous and supposed to be the production of a single author. Though the two friends agreed in the condemnation of the artificial and effete language of late eighteenth century poetry, and in the desirability of using the simplest, most familiar words and phrases in verse, they drew very different effects from their application of this principle. *The Ancient Mariner* is only distinguished from the rest in the Preface as being imitative of the elder poets and admitting some archaic phrases. But there was much more than that to set it apart from the other ballads. Coleridge, as Wordsworth recognizes elsewhere, had the ear of an Epicure which Wordsworth had not. His simplest lines are raised to special beauty by an undefinable harmony which is felt even when they are separated from the context:

> 'Twas sad as sad could be. . . .
> That ever this should be . . .
> He cannot chuse but hear . . .
> We could not speak no more than if . . .
> We had been choked with soot. . . .
> The ice was here, the ice was there,
> The ice was all around . . . ; etc.

On the contrary there is a crudity and a flatness in Wordsworth's lines of corresponding simplicity:

> 'Twas all in vain, a useless matter. . . .
> And all who see him say 'tis plain. (*Goody Blake*)
> What must be done? what will betide? . . .
> But yet I guess that now and then
> With Betty all was not so well. . . .
> And Betty sees the pony too. . . . (*The Idiot Boy*)
> I cannot tell; I wish I could,
> For the true reason no one knows. . . . (*The Thorn*)
> Few months of life has he in store
> As he to you will tell. (*Simon Lee*), etc.

Not that Wordsworth is devoid of the power of coining verse of searching melody, but he can attain this only when his feelings are roused. Coleridge seems to be unable to utter a single syllable that has no music in it. There is nothing in the Preface to suggest this exquisiteness which makes his *Mariner* the gem of the little volume.

Yet language and verse are not all, though the Preface lays all the emphasis on them. *The Lyrical Ballads* have a philosophical undercurrent. It is now admitted (and I am partly responsible for the admission) that they hold a protest against the out-and-out rationalism of the day, and more particularly against the form it had assumed in Godwin's *Political Justice*. That many poems of the collection are so directed can scarcely be questioned, and this protest was and remains the chief inner novelty of the book. But it is no less true that almost as much is retained in it of Godwin's social doctrine as is repudiated of his one-sided and short-sighted psychology. The contemporary reviewers were justified in pointing out the revolutionary tendency of several poems. Professor Harper in his masterly *Life of Wordsworth,* while he duly vindicated Godwin from the wholesale depreciation of Tory critics and paid a deserved homage to that which was sane and noble in his teaching, has rightly asserted that Wordsworth was still under the influence of Godwin in 1798. We know by Coleridge's testimony that his friend was then a semi-atheist, and that he remained an obstinate necessitarian even some years more, though already dissatisfied with Godwin's simplified conception of human nature. It is a fact that attacks against the injustice of the existing order are diffused throughout *The Lyrical Ballads,* which is the more striking as the authors were at some pains to avoid what might shock the readers' political ideas. They decided that the volume should be published anonymously because they knew that they were marked out as Jacobins and that their names stank in the nostrils of the conservative public. The same reason may partly account for the omission of *Salisbury Plain,* a poem that surely was in its early form (now lost) much more aggressive than when it was printed in 1842. Yet, *The Female Vagrant* retains much of Wordsworth's reforming spirit with its fierce denunciation of war and warriors

> . . . the brood
> That lap (their very nourishment!) their brother's blood.

or of the iniquitous distribution of wealth in society:

> And homeless near a thousand homes I stood,
> And near a thousand tables pined, and wanted food.

More charity is said to be found among robbers than among the rich:

> The wild brood saw me weep, my fate enquired,
> And gave me food, and rest, more welcome, more desired.

Two new poems, one by Coleridge, *The Dungeon,* and the other by Wordsworth, *The Convict,* are similarly inspired, the former with its reprobation of prison life, and chiefly the latter with its onset against

capital punishment. *The Convict* introduces us to a criminal on the eve
of hanging. It contrasts the concert of praise offered to a king after
victory with the misery of a solitary man fettered in gaol for a single
murder before being sent to death:

> When from the dark synod, or blood-reeking field,
>   To his chamber the monarch is led,
> All soothers of sense their soft virtue shall yield,
>   And quietness pillow his bed.

The just punishment of the convict ought to be transportation, as
Godwin proposes:

> My care, if the arm of the mighty were mine,
> Would plant thee where yet thou might'st blossom again.

In a less tragic way several other poems censure the harshness of the
social law or the lack of fellow-feeling among men. Goody Blake can
make no fire in the coldest winter unless she steals sticks from the hedge
of her hard-hearted neighbor Harry Gill. Poor Martha Ray is got with
child and forsaken by Stephen Hill; she kills her babe and becomes half-
witted. In *The Last of the Flock* we are asked to pity a father of ten
reduced by poverty to sell all his sheep one by one.

Even in poems dedicated to nature we find hints at the deplorable
condition of society. In *Lines Written in Early Spring* the poet contrasts
the happiness and beauty of a grove with "what man has made of man."
In *Tintern Abbey* his thoughts occasionally turn from the harmony of
Nature to listen "to the still sad music of humanity" and count among
the evils of this world "the sneers of selfish men."

In this condemnation of present society Wordsworth still agrees with
Godwin, though he sets his hope of redress on love and charity rather
than on the progress of reason. The woes that Godwin tries to cure by
appealing to the intellect, Wordsworth strives to alleviate by refining
the sense of pity. Sensibility stands with him in the place of mere logic.
He fights for the same cause as Godwin, but his weapons are feeling and
"the language of the senses." It is hard at times to disentangle the God-
winian and non- or anti-Godwinian elements in the same poem. Both,
for instance, are at one in deploring the unreasonableness of gratitude.

Both believe there would be no room for it in a perfect world. Godwin declares that gratitude is wrong because "it makes one prefer one man to another for another consideration than that of his superior utility or merit." Wordsworth is made sad by the profuse thanks of poor old Simon Lee for a trifling help that has cost the poet no trouble. This absurd gratitude is a proof of the dearth of charitableness in everyday life. Such assistance as he has given to Simon Lee ought to be of common occurrence and worth no notice. Where Godwin is coldly indignant, Wordsworth is deeply moved:

> I've heard of hearts unkind, kind deeds
> With coldness still returning.
> Alas! the gratitude of men
> Has oftener left me mourning.

His poem is a development or a complement of Godwin's position rather than an attack against it.

In other pieces we have of course a decided revolt from the rationalism of philosophers, on which it is needless to insist here, since it has been dealt with at some length elsewhere. But it must be acknowledged that the *Lyrical Ballads* show many a trace of the passage from an earlier to a maturer mood. The transition is perceptible not only in the style but in the thought also. This is to a certain extent owing to the somewhat haphazard gathering of the contents. It must not be forgotten that the greatest of Wordsworth's poems in the series, *Tintern Abbey,* was written at the last hour, while the book was printing. It has but little connection, as regards verse and manner, with the rest. It was an unpremeditated addition.

The preceding considerations, if they tend to impair the unity of the glorious little volume, may add to its interest for the critic or biographer.

SOLITUDE, SILENCE, AND LONELINESS IN THE POETRY OF WORDSWORTH

RAYMOND D. HAVENS

•
•

IN Wordsworth's temple of Nature the ministering spirits are Solitude, Silence, and Loneliness. The three are sisters and the function of each is the same: to give the devotee the fullness of what the goddess has to offer. Wordsworth was no hermit but a family man, affectionate, keenly interested in the affairs of his country, one who condemned "the heart that lives alone . . . at distance from the Kind," and who made the Solitary not the hero of *The Excursion*, but an example of "self-indulging spleen." Yet, as it is recorded of the great Friend of Man that when by force they would make him king "he departed again into a mountain himself alone," so Wordsworth filled the hidden springs of his being from lonely places, in solitude and in silence. It was within the solemn temple of mountain solitudes that he received his earliest visitations.[1] The wayside brooks and flowers, birds and their songs, clouds and sunshine—the things for which his sister Dorothy had so exquisite a discernment and which mean most to the usual lover of nature—also delighted him, but when he speaks of "the passions that build up our human soul," of the "fellowship" Nature vouchsafed to him with no stinted kindness, he mentions

> November days,
> When vapours rolling down the valley made
> A lonely scene more lonesome . . . woods,
> At noon and . . . the calm of summer nights,

[1] *Prelude*, xiv, 139-41. Unless otherwise noted all references in this essay are to *The Prelude*. An A after the number of the book refers to the 1804-1805 version.

When, by the margin of the trembling lake,
Beneath the gloomy hills homeward I went
In solitude.   (i, 407-24)

Likewise the incidents in his early years that he dwells on as the most delightful and the most significant usually occur in lonely places, in solitude, and in silence. The same is true of his account of the Wanderer's boyhood, "that lonesome life" which is a kind of idealized autobiography; hence it was that the youth

> was o'erpowered
> By Nature; by the turbulence subdued
> Of his own mind: by mystery and hope. (*Excursion,* i, 282-4)

Indeed it is to these features that the events of the Wanderer's youth and many of those narrated in *The Prelude* owed their impressiveness. The mountain would not have "strode after" the young Wordsworth with "measured motion like a living thing" if he had "borrowed" the boat on a sunny afternoon at Cambridge, and there would have been no dedication if he had returned from the dance with a group of noisy companions.

It is lone individuals, furthermore, who call forth his imaginative power: the discharged soldier,[2] the shepherd in the mist, the Leech-

---

[2] In the account of the meeting with the discharged soldier silence, solitude, and loneliness are emphasized. Wordsworth begins by referring to the pleasure he finds in a

> public Way, when, for the night
> Deserted, in its silence it assumes
> A character of deeper quietness
> Than pathless solitudes. (iv, A, 365-8)

Later this was changed to:

> When from our better selves we have too long
> Been parted by the hurrying world, and droop,
> Sick of its business, of its pleasures tired,
> How gracious, how benign, is Solitude. (iv, 354-7)

Then he tells of stealing along a "silent road . . . from the stillness drinking in A restoration . . . all was peace and solitude . . . the solitude . . . was heard and felt" (A, 385-91). Instead of these last lines the final text has

> All else was still;
> No living thing appeared in earth or air,
> And, save the flowing water's peaceful voice,
> Sound there was none—but, lo! an uncouth shape. (384-7)

gatherer, the Solitary Reaper, the Solitary, the Wanderer, Margaret, the Forsaken Indian Woman, the Old Cumberland Beggar (whose days pass in a "vast solitude"), the persons described in "Lucy Gray; or Solitude," "The Last of the Flock," "The Affliction of Margaret," "The Sailor's Mother," "The Thorn," "To a Highland Girl." The work which was to include both *The Prelude* and *The Excursion* was entitled *The Recluse*. Michael is in the main a solitary figure, his sheepfold is built in "an utter solitude"; Peter Bell's crisis comes when he is alone in a lonesome spot, and Newton is "a mind for ever Voyaging through strange seas of Thought, alone." This preference extends to animals: the single wren of Furness Abbey, the horse standing alone, motionless in the moonlight,[3] the white doe of Rylstone, and "The swan on still St. Mary's lake." Concerning this last Wordsworth remarked:

The scene when I saw it, with its still and dim lake, under the dusky hills, was one of utter loneliness: there was *one* swan, and one only, stemming the water, and the pathetic loneliness of the region gave importance to the one companion of that swan, its own white image in the water. . . . Had there been many swans and many shadows, they would have implied nothing as regards the character of the scene; and I should have said nothing about them.[4]

It will be recalled that "one coy Primrose to that Rock The vernal breeze invites," that Lucy is

> Fair as a star, when only one
> Is shining in the sky,

and that to the loud voice of the Vale but a single "star upon the mountain-top Is listening quietly."

Turning again to A:
> He was alone,
> Had no attendant, neither Dog, nor Staff,
> Nor knapsack; in his very dress appear'd
> A desolation, a simplicity
> That seem'd akin to solitude . . . at his feet
> His shadow lay, and mov'd not. (A, 415-25)

[3] Passage in manuscript W, later omitted. *The Prelude*, ed. Ernest de Selincourt, Oxford, 1926, p. 601.

[4] Aubrey de Vere, "Recollections of Wordsworth," *Prose Works*, ed. Grosart, iii, 487-8.

In the account of his tramp through France and Switzerland the incident most fully described is the visit to the convent of Chartreuse,

> an awful *solitude:*
> Yes, for even then no other than a place
> Of soul-affecting *solitude* appeared
> That far-famed region.   (vi, 419-22)

The summary narrative of his later college years pauses for a somewhat extended description of how he frequented the college groves by night "through hours of silence" or loitered "on calm clear nights Alone" gazing at a single tree. Even in his picture of London the silent, deserted streets in the moonlight or late on winter evenings when "rains Are falling hard" are a memorable feature, and it is the "silent, bare" city that inspires his great sonnet on Westminster Bridge. No wonder he wrote, "spells seemed on me when I was alone."[5]

It is surprising to find that Wordsworth uses "alone" in the sense of "solitary" some one hundred and fifty times in his poetry; "solitary" (excluding The Solitary in *The Excursion*), about seventy-five times; "solitude" or "solitudes" about one hundred and five times; "lone," "lonely," "lonesome," "loneliest," "loneliness" approximately two hundred and fifteen times, but employs "silent" or "silence" some three hundred and fifty times.[6] His sensitiveness to silence might be expected from his keen awareness of sound, but emphasis such as these figures imply is suggestive of the importance he attached to solitude and loneliness as well as the mystic significance he found in darkness. For "The silence that is in the starry sky"[7] is more than mere privation of sound, so too is "the silence of the seas Among the farthest Hebrides," the silence of the patient, despoiled trees in "Nutting," the silence upon

---

[5] vi, 66-94; vii, 654-68; iii, 232.

[6] Compare these with the following approximate figures: "rejoice," etc., eighty-five times; "sorrow," "sorrowful," and the like, two hundred times; "glad," "gladness," and the like, two hundred times; "hope," etc. (omitting "hopeless"), six hundred times; "stream," "streams," "streamlet," three hundred; "soul," "souls," etc., five hundred and thirty times; "sky," "skies," three hundred times.

[7] "Brougham Castle," 163. In *The Recluse*, I, i, 129-33, "the voice Of lordly birds" admonishes man "Of solitude, and silence in the sky"; in "The Idiot Boy," 245-6, the town "Is silent as the skies"; in "A Volant Tribe," 14, the sky is "more than silent."

which the Woman in *Guilt and Sorrow* "fed." For does not the "lengthened pause Of silence" which baffled the best skill of the boy of Winander "plant, for immortality, conjoined impressions of sound and sight in the celestial soil of the Imagination"?[8] Are we not told that in silence there is "Music of finer tone [than in sound]; a harmony . . . though there be no voice. . . . A language not unwelcome to sick hearts"? that a certain peak "often seems to send Its own deep quiet to restore our hearts"? that star-gazers feel "a grave and steady joy" which is "not of this noisy world, but silent and divine"? that in periods of insight

> Our noisy years seem moments in the being
> Of the eternal Silence?[9]

These last lines recall the phrase "Helvellyn, in the silence of his rest" and Nature's promise when she makes Lucy her own: "hers shall be . . . the silence and the calm Of mute insensate things." To Wordsworth silence was a Power; it partook of the nature of the permanent; in a

---

[8] Preface of 1815 (*Prose Works*, ed. Knight, London, 1896, Vol. II, p. 215). This passage was omitted by Wordsworth in the 1845 and later editions of the Preface and is not to be found in the editions of Hutchinson and Grosart. The passages referred to just above are from "The Solitary Reaper," 15-16; "Nutting," 52-3; *Guilt and Sorrow*, 341.

[9] *Excursion*, ii, 710-16; "There is an Eminence," 7-8; "Star-gazers," 26-8; "Ode, Immortality," 158-9 (cf. "On the Power of Sound," 217-18,

> O Silence! are Man's noisy years
> No more than moments of thy life?).

In *The Excursion* we read that a man on a mountain top is privileged

> To breathe in solitude, above the host
> Of ever-humming insects . . .
>   murmur of the leaves
> Many and idle, visits not his ear:
> This he is freed from, and from thousand notes
> (Not less unceasing, not less vain than these,)
> By which the finer passages of sense
> Are occupied; and the Soul, that would incline
> To listen, is prevented or deterred. (ix, 72-80)

Two of the four sonnets written at Dover are devoted to the spiritual ministry of silence, the latest having the lines:

> Ocean's o'erpowering murmurs have set free
> Thy sense from pressure of life's common din.

world of flux it belonged with those "eternal things" wherein only we can find the joy and rest for which we were created.[10]

At the close of a description of the country round about Dove Cottage, Wordsworth "boldly" asserted that "solitude," that is lonesomeness in the usual sense of the term, "is not Where these things are." "He truly is alone," that is, lonesome, he continues,

> He of the multitude whose eyes are doomed
> To hold a vacant commerce day by day
> With objects wanting life, repelling love;
> He by the vast Metropolis immured.   (*Recluse*, I, i, 592-7)

This passage is one of the few in which Wordsworth touches on the loneliness of the human spirit. As a rule, whether speaking of himself or of others—Milton, Chatterton, and Coleridge, for example—he seems unaware of "The unplumb'd, salt, estranging sea" that flows between each man and his fellows. He was naturally too independent and he had learned too well "The self-sufficing power of Solitude" to feel any deep need of other persons. Coleridge, who craved affection, remarked: "Of all the men I ever knew, Wordsworth has the least femineity in his mind. He is *all* man. He is a man of whom it might have been said, —'It is good for him to be alone.'"[11] Yet for Coleridge, for a small group of friends, and especially for his family Wordsworth cared deeply and upon them he leaned, in certain respects, heavily. For one of his temperament his lot in life was eminently fortunate: what he lacked he did not need, a host of friends and supporters; what he needed he was richly blessed with, the constant companionship of those he loved. Except for two periods, one of which lasted only three or four months, he spent his entire life with or near some one—usually several persons— of whom he was very fond and to whom he was very dear. At Hawkshead there were his brothers and the friend "passionately loved"; at Cambridge, Jones, Mathews, and Wrangham; later there was Annette; then Coleridge; then wife and children. Only when in London and

---

[10] "To the Clouds," 92-4; cf. i, 409. The passages quoted just above are from viii, 14, and "Three years she grew," 16-18. Others that might be added will be found in *Excursion*, iv, 414-15; "Yew Trees," 27; "Personal Talk," i, 9-10.

[11] *Table Talk*, ed. T. Ashe, 1903, p. 339.

Paris did he live remote from the objects of his affections,[12] and the emotional isolation of these periods undoubtedly affected his opinion of city life. In addition to association with those he loved he enjoyed, after 1795, sympathetic understanding and companionship in the things dearest to him: nature, his way of life, his work. If the general public was indifferent or scornful, Dorothy and Coleridge were a host. No wonder there is little in Wordsworth's poetry of that craving for affection, sympathy, and understanding which is one of the most universal and poignant of human feelings.

Wordsworth was, however, conscious of the isolation of genius, for he remarked: "Possessions have I that are . . . shared by none, Not even the nearest to me and most dear."[13] And in speaking of imagination and the higher love he declared:

> no Helper hast thou here;
> Here keepest thou in singleness thy state . . .
> The prime and vital principle is thine
> In the recesses of thy nature, far
> From any reach of outward fellowship,
> Else is not thine at all.   (xiv, 210-18)

Yet it is noteworthy that in neither instance nor, so far as I know, elsewhere does Wordsworth refer to this isolation as unpleasant. For him also solitude, physical as well as spiritual, and lonely places doubtless had their dark side; but he who wishes to see the stars does not complain of the night.

Yet we have seen that Wordsworth uses the words "lone," "lonely," "lonesome," "loneliest," "loneliness" over two hundred times in his poetry, more often than "sorrow" and "sorrowful" or "glad" and "gladness." His use of the terms is distinctive since he commonly applies them to places or natural objects, but rarely to states of mind and almost always to suggest something that is desirable. A typical instance is the

---

12 To be sure, Wordsworth was not in London all of the two and two-thirds years between his second return from France and his settling at Racedown, but much of the time when he was absent from the metropolis he spent with Jones, with Dorothy, and with Raisley Calvert.

13 *Recluse*, I, i, 686-8.

November mists which "rolling down the valley made A lonely scene more lonesome." Here, as in the reference three lines later to "gloomy hills," nature is thought of as attractive because lonely. So the "sweet Recess . . . Of hidden beauty" in which the Solitary immured himself is "lonesome" but "Not melancholy."[14] Inversneyde, which inspired the lines "To a Highland Girl," is described as a "lonely place" almost too lovely to be real—"Like something fashioned in a dream." Indeed, Wordsworth's conception of perfect bliss is living with the maid one loves "in some lonely spot."[15] Such was the happiness Ruth dreamed of sharing with the Youth from Georgia on the "lonesome floods, And green savannahs" of the new world; such the idyllic life of the Solitary and his bride upon the "lonely Downs."[16] The idealized Indian is pictured as "Free as the sun, and lonely as the sun" and the loneliness of the Wanderer's youth—which is conceived as a kind of Spartan ideal—is repeatedly insisted on.[17] There are a number of references to the pleasure the poet found in lonely roads and one notable sonnet on his delight in "Long, barren silence" by his cottage fire.[18] His sister also wrote, "we shall then in right earnest enjoy winter quiet and loneliness."[19]

Dorothy's realization of the part loneliness played in her brother's spiritual life seems to be indicated in her naming after him a "lonely Summit," "The loneliest place we have among the clouds."[20] Raisley Calvert likewise, the poet tells us,

> deem'd that my delights and labours lay
> Among the lonely places of the earth.[21]

Yet, as Wordsworth's admirers have often overlooked the part lonely places had in his development, it may be well to recall how many of the notable incidents recorded in *The Prelude* owe much of their

[14] i, 416-18; *Excursion*, ii, 349-55. A later reference to the same spot mentions "The loneliness of this sublime retreat" (iv, 372).

[15] xiii, 120-7, with A²C variant of A, 131-2. The final text has "in some lone nook."

[16] "Ruth," 110-14; *Excursion*, iii, 532.

[17] *Excursion*, iii, 941 (cf. *Prelude*, vii, 745-7), i, 126-31, 219, 262, and especially 100, "The feeling pleasures of his loneliness."

[18] iv, A, 363-99; xiii, 117-19, 162; "Loud is the Vale," 11-12, "Personal Talk," i, 10.

[19] Letter to Lady Beaumont of November 29, 1805.

[20] "There is an Eminence," 17, 13.

[21] Y variant of xiv, A, 362-5.

significance to the loneliness of their setting: the robbed trap, the stolen boat ride, bird-nesting "on the lonesome peaks," standing, "If the night blackened with a coming storm, Beneath some rock," the first circuit of the lake after returning from Cambridge, the encounter with the discharged soldier, the passage through the "gloomy strait" in the Alps, the night after leaving Gravedona, the coming upon the place of the gibbet, the watch for the palfreys to take him home, the vision of the Druids on Salisbury Plain, the ascent of Snowden. But his gratitude for the "intercourse" that had been his in loneliness was probably less for these incidents than for innumerable occasions when there had been nothing to record save that the austere beauty—beauty which often had terror in it—of solitary tarns, uninhabited valleys, bare mountain sides half hid in mists was borne in upon him and ministered to his spirit. Hence it was that Wordsworth thought of the "high-souled Bard" as "trained in lonely woods," that when speaking of the ministry of Nature he invoked the "Visions of the hills! And Souls of lonely places," that the "fellowship vouchsafed" so richly in his youth immediately suggested "a lonely scene [made] more lonesome."[22]

This added lonesomeness was achieved, it will be recalled, by November mists, which may direct our attention to another feature common to many of the incidents just enumerated—bad weather. Wordsworth has warm praise for the pastoral life described by Latin poets and for that he observed himself on the endless plains of the North, but he adds:

> Yet, hail to you
> Moors, mountains, headlands, and ye hollow vales . . .
> Powers of my native region! Ye that seize
> The heart with firmer grasp! Your snows and streams
> Ungovernable, and your terrifying winds,
> That howl so dismally for him who treads
> Companionless your awful solitudes!   (viii, 215-22)

Even Green-head Ghyll and the fastness of the Solitary smiled and grew friendly in the sunshine; for perfect loneliness one needed the mists and winds that are the usual play-fellows of mountains. Hence

22 "To Enterprise," 91-2; *Prelude*, i, 464-6, 415-18.

in offering his thanks to nature as the source of whatever is best in him, he addresses

> Ye mountains, and ye lakes
> And sounding cataracts, ye mists and winds
> That dwell among the hills where I was born, (ii, 424-6)

and he speaks of the "Genius" that dwells in the mountains and "can subdue" the ephemeral products of the plain as "Most potent when mists veil the sky."[23]

Clouds and mist, wind and rain were dear to Wordsworth not merely because he was accustomed to them but because they reinforced and concentrated what lonely places had to offer, just as loneliness and silence made more potent the ministry of solitude, and all four when united gave to mountains their supreme impressiveness and mystery and, on especially fortunate occasions, prepared the way for supreme experiences akin to the mystic. Accordingly, Wordsworth's love of solitude and lonely places has none of the self-conscious and self-admiring sentimentalism of the eighteenth century graveyard poets, the wistful backward glance of the picturesque travellers, or the introspective exhibitionism of later romantics who nourished their morbid egoism with the untamed wildness and sublimity of mountain solitudes. Behind the sonorous periods of Byron's

> There is a pleasure in the pathless woods,
> There is a rapture on the lonely shore,
> There is society, where none intrudes,
> By the deep Sea, and Music in its roar,

we catch echoes of the less sincere "I have not loved the World, nor the World me."[24] When Wordsworth climbed to the lonely Grisedale

---

[23] "The Pass of Kirkstone," 33-8.
[24] *Childe Harold*, III, cxiii. Indeed the stanza preceding the one quoted above (*ibid.*, IV, clxxviii) has the lines:

> Oh! that the Desert were my dwelling-place . . .
> That I might all forget the human race.

What is said here of Wordsworth refers to his maturity. In his youth, as he himself confesses (vi, 547-61), "Dejection taken up for pleasure's sake" was a mood not unknown; see vi, 171-8; it is certainly present in *Descriptive Sketches*.

Tarn or descended the mist-filled Kirkstone Pass his meditations were not of himself or of the world. Werther and Manfred sought solitude to feed their melancholy; Wordsworth to feed his "lofty speculations." The Spirit of Nature as he had come to know it among the mountains was not one of lawlessness but of "Composure, and ennobling Harmony"; in waste places he did not see his own ego writ large; he was conscious of "the one Presence," "the Upholder of the tranquil soul."[25] Thus he is classical in his disapproval of melancholy and virile in his love of lonely mountain retreats.

In a revealing comment on his life at Cambridge he explains:

> Yet could I only cleave to solitude
> In lonely places; if a throng was near
> That way I leaned by nature; for my heart
> Was social, and loved idleness and joy. (iii, 233-6)

The early books of *The Prelude* certainly bear out this characterization: as a boy and young man Wordsworth loved companionship and sports and was alone by chance rather than choice. It was on this account that he needed lonely places. His palms, like those of most strong men, were doubtless not so easily won as we think. He knew it was the hills from whence came his strength but he did not always look up unto them; in consequence he was

> thankful, even though tired and faint,
> For the rich bounties of constraint;
> Whence oft invigorating transports flow
> That choice lacked courage to bestow!
> ("Pass of Kirkstone," 57-60)

His first year at the university illustrates his need of the help the lake region had given him. Cambridge afforded no mountains and few lonely places without which there was for him no real solitude; as a result he filled his life with trivial things—

> To the deep quiet and majestic thoughts
> Of loneliness succeeded empty noise.[26]

[25] vii, 766-71; iii, A, 130, 120.
[26] iii, A, 210-11. Even if the "visitings of the Upholder of the tranquil soul" (119-20)

And he was happy; not until his return to Hawkshead did he sense what
he had missed. But on a cold, raw evening when once again he made
the circuit of Esthwaite,

> a comfort seemed to touch
> A heart that had not been disconsolate:
> Strength came where weakness was not known to be,
> At least not felt; and restoration came
> Like an intruder knocking at the door
> Of unacknowledged weariness. (iv, 153-8)

The ministry of lonely places was in part purely negative; they
isolated him, physically and spiritually, from worldly concerns; they
"subdued" the trivial and the transitory. Such service was particularly
valuable to one whose mind was not quick or brilliant but was given
to brooding for long periods over profound problems. Waste places
turned his thoughts to such problems and stimulated his meditations
upon them. They also uplifted him, bringing tranquil restoration, "the
deep quiet and majestic thoughts Of loneliness" and giving new energy
and vitality to old convictions. Among the mountains, as the Wanderer
found, "all things"

> Breathed immortality, revolving life,
> And greatness still revolving; infinite:
> There littleness was not; the least of things
> Seemed infinite; and there his spirit shaped
> Her prospects, nor did he believe,—he *saw*.
> What wonder if his being thus became
> Sublime and comprehensive! (*Excursion*, i, 226-34)

As Professor Bradley remarks, "To call a thing lonely or solitary is,
with him, to say that it opens a bright or solemn vista into infinity";[27]
and it will be recalled that

described in iii, 90-169 took place during this first year and not later, the general character
of the year, as Wordsworth repeatedly insists, was idle amusement. In London, Paris,
Orleans and Blois he saw equally little of lonely places, and this fact may explain in part
why the years spent in these cities were relatively barren of the sublunary things so richly
bestowed during the brief tramp through the lonely Alps.

[27] A. C. Bradley, *Oxford Lectures on Poetry*, 1923, p. 142.

> Our destiny, our being's heart and home,
> Is with infinitude, and only there. (vi, 604-5)

Again, lonely places, particularly mountains, which furnish a spectacle of rugged endurance under circumstances usually adverse, bred an austerity, a self-reliance, a preoccupation with the permanent; in them "appear Most obviously simplicity and power" whence "Attention . . . comprehensiveness and memory flow";[28] they contributed notably to the ministry of fear—indeed, they furnished much the same ministry in a less intense form; they deepened the sense of mystery and wonder on which the spirit of man is nourished.

Perhaps the best evidence of how deeply Wordsworth drank of solitude, silence, and loneliness is his power of describing them:

> he had been alone
> Amid the heart of many thousand mists,
> That came to him, and left him, on the heights.
> . . . they
> Who journey thither find themselves alone
> With a few sheep, with rocks and stones, and kites
> That overhead are sailing in the sky.
> ("Michael," 58-60, 9-12)

> Yon star upon the mountain-top
> Is listening quietly. ("Loud is the Vale," 7-8)

> There sometimes doth a leaping fish
> Send through the tarn a lonely cheer;
> The crags repeat the raven's croak,
> In symphony austere. ("Fidelity," 25-8)

---

[28] vii, 740-4; note viii, 599-600, "seeking knowledge at that time Far less than craving power." Hazlitt wrote: "There is little mention of mountainous scenery in Mr. Wordsworth's poetry; but by internal evidence one might be almost sure that it was written in a mountainous country, from its bareness, its simplicity, its loftiness, and its depth!" (*Spirit of the Age, Works,* ed. Waller-Glover, Vol. IV, p. 274.)

> The silence that is in the starry sky,
> The sleep that is among the lonely hills.
>   ("Brougham Castle," 163-4)

The authentic, the essential Wordsworth, one is tempted to say, is here; at least his peculiar power is nowhere more fully revealed than in lines like these which deal with some of the chief sources of that power: solitude, silence, and lonely places.

WORDSWORTH'S CONCEPTION OF THE ESTHETIC EXPERIENCE

OSCAR JAMES CAMPBELL

.
.

I

THE term "esthetic experience" never appears in Wordsworth work. It would doubtless have sounded pretentious and queer to his ears. Yet he thought long and deeply about the function of poetry and expressed his ideas on this subject with memorable eloquence. These conceptions have been repeatedly analyzed and restated by the critic so that the chance of illuminating them further seems slight. Yet it is only the social and linguistic aspects of Wordsworth's controlling idea that have been adequately examined. The revolutionary psychological significance of his theories has remained obscure. Yet to the present writer the essence of Wordsworth's view was that poetry should produce in both author and reader what we now call the esthetic experience.

Wordsworth's idea of this psychological phenomenon is not easy to simplify. In the first place, his notions on the subject, as indeed on almost every other, changed greatly during the course of his long poetic career. In the second place, the conception which he held at any one time was never simple. His experience with beauty always produced an intricate mental pattern, formed of almost every thought and feeling which agitated his mind at the moment. I shall not attempt to describe in this essay every modification which the poet made in his views on this important subject; I shall be content first to explain the conception of the esthetic experience which Wordsworth held consistently from 1798 to 1805. Then I shall show how under the influence of various sorts of emotional crises this idea was superseded by a substantially different one, under the influence of which he wrote *The White Doe o*

Rylstone, the *Sonnets to the River Duddon,* and the *Ecclesiastical Sonnets,* three works which represent most clearly his later achievements.

Throughout all the changes in his theories, Wordsworth as an esthetician attached himself to one school of eighteenth century critical thought and ignored the tenets of all the others. He was attracted only to the so-called "School of Taste," the central doctrine of which was that beauty in all of its manifestations was a psychological experience. This assumption clearly captured Wordsworth's imagination. It is more difficult to determine the specific authors from whom Wordsworth derived his knowledge of this principle. However, certain recent critics believe that they have discovered the sources of his esthetic system. They assume that it was a simple compound, one-half the psychology of David Hartley,[1] and one-half Alison's esthetic ideas as expressed in his *Essay on Taste* written in 1790. Dean Sperry expresses this simple view in his *Wordsworth's Anti-Climax.*[2] He believes that Wordsworth accepted from Hartley the notion that all the higher complexes of the mind are grounded in simple sensation. On this base the processes of association, operating automatically and mechanically, build up from the memories of earlier sensation which are regarded as simple ideas, complex ideas; and it is these which form the content of mature thought. Alison founds his esthetics squarely upon this associationistic psychology. He assumes that if an individual's mind remains passive and vacant, these complex ideas will associate themselves in the mind. If they are of the right sort, that is, based in each case upon a pleasurable primal sensation, the resultant complex will arouse a particular sort of excitement, half emotional and half intellectual. In this state imagination is aroused. Then the esthetic experience is in full flower, whether or not artistic creation takes place. Wordsworth states that the object of his poetry is the production of this form of excitement. It is the result, then,

[1] Wordsworth probably read the abridgment of Priestley in its second edition: *Hartley's Theory of the Human Mind on the Principle of the Association of Ideas,* 1790. The first edition had appeared in 1775. Professor Arthur Beatty in his *William Wordsworth,* Madison, 1927, pp. 38-127, gives the account of Wordsworth's relation to Hartley to which all subsequent students of the subject are greatly indebted.

[2] Willard L. Sperry, *Wordsworth's Anti-Climax,* Cambridge, 1935, in his chapter called "The System," pp. 122-43.

not of "gross and violent stimulants" but of sensations derived from
"great and permanent objects" which alone can serve as the constituent
elements of those complex ideas which arouse esthetic pleasure.

Many of the most famous pronouncements in Wordsworth's Prefaces
are obvious echoes of formative ideas of Hartley's psychology and
Alison's esthetics. But other ideas expressed either in Wordsworth's
poetry or in his prose show that he based the principles derived from
these masters upon certain metaphysical affirmations of which they were
innocent. However, these doctrines were implicit in the work of
eighteenth century critics who accepted the classical tradition in esthetics.
They preserved the notion that beauty was in essence the apperception
of proportion or harmony in Nature or in human nature. Then it was
an easy step for a deistical esthetician to regard the entire scheme of
things as unified by a similar harmony. To Shaftesbury, as well as to
many members of the school of taste, this vivid feeling of metaphysical
concord stimulated a sense of a first or archetypal beauty. This conception was nearly related to Plotinus's predication of a world-soul
wherein all individual souls are united. Haunted as they were by forms
of Platonic thinking, many of Wordsworth's critical predecessors thus
associated the experience of beauty with definite metaphysical conceptions and with wide human sympathies.

Another development of Plotinus's thought in this school of taste
carries us closer to the naturalistic esthetics of Wordsworth's early
career. The neo-Platonists thought of Nature and the soul as being a
twin-birth. Hence beauty and the instinct in man that senses it are in
vital, if hidden, correspondence. For example, Akenside in his *Pleasures
of Imagination* (1744) explains the reason for the resemblance of certain
aspects of Nature to the very quality of the human mind, by asserting
that the universe of ear and eye and man's mind are parts of the same
Idea of God.[3] Sir Joshua Reynolds expresses approximately the same
ideas in more concrete form in his famous Seventh Discourse. He begins
by saying that the imagination of men is affected by causes which

---

[3] An excellent exposition of Akenside's relation to this neo-Platonic tradition appears in
Margaret Sherwood's *Undercurrents of Influence in English Romantic Poetry*, Cambridge,
1934, pp. 78-87.

exist in Nature and proceeds to the more sweeping statement that "the real substance, as it may be called, of what goes under the name of taste, is fixed and established in the nature of things."[4] Therefore, "Whatever pleases has in it what is analogous to the mind, and is, therefore, in the best and highest sense of the word, natural."[5] But the most remarkable of his utterances is the one in which he expresses a philosophical view of Nature far in advance of his time. Nature, he says, "comprehends not only the forms which she produces, but also the nature and internal fabric and organization of the human mind and imagination."[6] To this extensive body of doctrine which regarded beauty as essentially an effect of the mind and one involving definite metaphysical concepts, Wordsworth could turn for suggestion and guidance.

He wrote his earlier long poems, such as *Guilt and Sorrow* and *The Borderers,* before he had developed any clear conception of the essential function of poetry. The esthetic assumptions on which the tale of terror depended or those involved in the poems preaching sentimental morality he regarded merely as convenient conventions. They offered him the form in which he could most effectively embody the ideas and emotions which then animated him. His systematic explanation of the esthetic experience appears first two years before in the Preface to the 1800 edition of *The Lyrical Ballads.* However, in *Tintern Abbey,* employing the direct method of art he carries his readers into the heart of this exalted mental state.

Wordsworth's conception proves to be a direct product of a metaphysical affirmation similar to those which have just been quoted. Like Sir Joshua, he believes that the most important structural principle of the world is a functional relationship between Man and Nature. It is the one condition essential to all human experience. Wordsworth saw the ethical and metaphysical importance of this fact, but showed his originality in realizing its great esthetic significance. The phrases in which he expresses this idea most effectively appear in the additions

[4] Sir Joshua Reynolds, *Discourses,* ed. Roger Fry, London, 1905, "The Seventh Division," p. 210.
[5] *ibid.,* p. 197.
[6] *ibid.,* p. 193.

made to the Prefaces in the version of 1802. They are familiar to all
students of Wordsworth. Quotation of a few of the best known of them
will recall their substance. A poet is "a man pleased with his own
passions and volitions . . . delighting to contemplate similar volitions
and passions in the goings-on of the Universe." He regards man and
Nature as essentially adapted to each other and the "mind of man as
naturally the mirror of the fairest and most interesting qualities in
Nature." The "primal sympathy" which such passages express is something more intrinsic to psychological experience than a realization that
the elements of all higher mental complexes are simple sensations of
natural objects. The intense feeling of pleasure which Wordsworth
believed to be the essence of the esthetic experience is caused not by
constant recognition of the operation of a psychological system, but by
the "holy passion" aroused by the consciousness that man is an intimate
and essential part of this world's scheme of being. This ecstasy suffuses
the complex of ranging ideas and feelings and unifies them into a
single phenomenon.

If this be a just exposition of the matter, Wordsworth's early preoccupation with natural objects assumes a different significance from that
usually assigned to it. In a world metaphysically integrated no sensation
is an isolated fact to be cherished merely as a constituent element of
later and more complicated mental experiences. On the contrary, every
object that meets the mature eye or ear assumes its place in an intricate
pattern of sensations, memories, and ideas. Sensation thus becomes
transmuted into insight and past experiences into vision. The meanest
flower that blows, if it but sojourn with memory and contemplation,
thus becomes a center which radiates passion through all the channels
of a lively apprehension of multitudinous relationships. The power of
nature, thus operating through the senses and the metaphysical imagination, fecundates the higher mental life and enables it to transmute past
experience into communicable beauty.

This discussion of these theories of Wordsworth has sought to show
what he believed to be the proper content of the esthetic experience. The
nature of the emotions which this congeries of mental phenomena

hould arouse can be best revealed by a brief analysis of *Tintern Abbey*. The real subject of this poem is the esthetic experience. It is not usually o interpreted. The work has been regarded primarily as an impassioned lescription of the poet's attitudes toward Nature which were later to :ulminate in orthodox transcendentalism. Thus conceived, it is a con- ession of faith, a recognition of the existence of mystical sanctions to aatural morality.

Professor Beatty would have us believe that the poem is psychological autobiography expressed in the terms used by David Hartley to describe he growth of the mind. Wordsworth's main interest in this system was :he process by which the automatic machinery of association trans- formed sensations and strong feelings into serene and stable states of mental equilibrium. The object of the poem, thus conceived, was to present systematically certain psychological concepts and to illustrate them by pages torn from the personal history of the poet. It is true that n *Tintern Abbey* Wordsworth traces the psychological history of the individual and emphasizes the mind's dependence upon sustenance con- tinuously drawn from communion with natural objects. But this purely intellectual conception is presented as subordinate to some presiding emotional attitude. Otherwise the work would be a mere versified psychological treatise. The poem is filled with emotional excitement, but it is not generated by Wordsworth's mere contemplation of the mysterious way in which simple sensations flower into the highest human faculties. It is rather aroused by the experience which comes to the poet when he realizes the central place which the mind occupies in the all-embracing unitary system of nature and the vast mental riches which such a relationship reveals.

Wordsworth attains the first eminence of rapture in the poem when he finds himself in the state of energetic quietude which sensations and emotions derived from nature have precipitated after they have been transformed by the alchemy of memory. Spiritual impulses germinate secretly here until they suddenly flower into a moment of vision. Then comes a flash of insight which reveals the essential nature of man's place in the entire scheme of being. Wordsworth calls this experience

> . . . that serene and blessed mood,
> In which the affections gently lead us on,—
> Until, the breath of this corporeal frame
> And even the motion of our human blood
> Almost suspended, we are laid asleep
> In body, and become a living soul:
> While with an eye made quiet by the power
> Of harmony, and the deep power of joy,
> We see into the life of things.

The poet experiences his second moment of ecstasy at the moment of his reassertion of the delight which captures his soul when it feels itself interfused with the entire Universe

> . . . And I have felt
> A presence that disturbs me with the joy
> Of elevated thoughts; a sense sublime
> Of something far more deeply interfused,
> Whose dwelling is the light of setting suns,
> And the round ocean, and the living air,
> And the blue sky, and in the mind of man:
> A motion and a spirit that impels
> All thinking things, all objects of all thought,
> And rolls through all things.

This is a mystical experience. But in *Tintern Abbey* Wordsworth celebrates not the grandeur of the conception, but the emotional radiance with which it suffuses the individual. In this light his mind assumes a new amplitude and is quickened with new energy. Thought and feeling join in vital union to produce insight. Then he can penetrate to truths which disclose the heart of the universe. At this moment of revelation he loses none of the identity of his individual soul; on the contrary, he feels an awakened and intensified consciousness of self.

> Gently did my soul
> Put off her veil, and, self-transmuted stood
> Naked, as in the presence of her God.

This becoming one with the whole means to Wordsworth "not mystical annihilation, loss of identity, but . . . greater life, Nature in that profound union summoning him to deeper individuality."[7] This adventure, shared by all the higher powers of one's being, it is the function of poetry to produce. It is the archetype of all human situations in which man and the objects among which he lives act and react upon each other.

This brief exposition of Wordsworth's conception of the esthetic function of poetry at the time when he was composing his most celebrated works is merely a restatement of familiar critical views. It has been presented here again that it may serve as a background against which to set the esthetic theories illustrated in *The White Doe of Rylstone* and the two sonnet sequences with which the poem has been associated earlier in this essay.

II

Wordsworth did not long remain satisfied with a naturalistic basis for his philosophy and his esthetics. As early as 1802, when he probably wrote part of the *Ode on the Intimations of Immortality,* he begins to suspect that the world of eye and ear gives an unsatisfactory answer to the two questions which increasingly trouble his peace. They are "What is Man's Origin?" and "What is Man's Destiny?" The pleasures of her own with which earth fills her lap do not combine to create in man's mind a high complex of metaphysical certainty. This should have come to pass if Locke's psychology had performed the services of which Coleridge and Wordsworth believed it capable. Instead natural phenomena seem to lead man along a primrose path at the end of which lies neglect and forgetfulness of the central problems of existence.

In the third book of *The Excursion* these intimations of dissatisfaction become clear and articulate. It appears in the Solitary's account of his futile efforts to relieve his despondency through a trial of all the advertised comforts of naturalism, including association with "Primeval Nature's child." But none of the tenets of this creed dispelled his

[7] Margaret Sherwood, *Undercurrents of Influence in English Romantic Poetry,* Cambridge, 1934, p. 187.

anxiety, for he realized that everything in nature was impermanent subject to ceaseless change which ended in death.

> For mutability is Nature's bane;
> And slighted Hope *will* be avenged; and, when
> Ye need her favours, ye shall find her not;
> But in her stead—fear—doubt—and agony![8]

No central peace now remains subsisting at the heart of the endless flux which agitates the world of eye and ear. Wordsworth's faith in Nature as a congeries of vivid and beautiful sensations was thus wrecked on the rock of mutability.[9] When this foundation crumbled, the structure reared upon it inevitably also fell.

The most important of these rejected doctrines was his belief in the functional unity of Nature and the mind of man and the naturalistic esthetic which was the response of Wordsworth the artist to the delight of dwelling in a universe thus supposed to be perfectly adapted to his emotional comfort. To a man with as deep a philosophic concern with the proper function of poetry as Wordsworth maintained, a fundamental revision of his metaphysical system inevitably effected a corresponding change in his conception of the esthetic satisfaction which he desired to have his works produce.

The death of Wordsworth's brother John in a foundering of the ship *Abergavenny* on February 5, 1805, of which he was captain, convinced Wordsworth once for all of the inadequacy of his natural-

---

[8] *The Excursion*, Book III, 458-61.

[9] S. G. Dunn denies that Wordsworth had any interest in the problem of man's origin and his destiny ("A Note on Wordsworth's Metaphysical System" in *Essays and Studies by Members of the English Association*, XVIII, 1933, p. 101). Wordsworth's problem the author avers "was to find a way out of Pantheism while retaining his conviction of a life in things, a soul divine in which we participate." To prove that Wordsworth considered the question whither or whence of no importance, he quotes a passage from *The Excursion* (III, 234 *ff*.) in which Solitary explicitly denies such an interest. The text of the speech is

> Here are we, in a bright and breathing world,
> Our origin, what matters it?, etc.

It is almost impossible to determine the date at which this passage was written. The idea is one characteristic of Wordsworth's period of naturalistic enthusiasm. But to use these lines as evidence of settled unchanging belief of the poet is to neglect chronology in the study of Wordsworth's development and to ignore many passages written from 1805 on in which he implicitly rejects the doctrine confidently presented in the third book of *The Excursion*.

stic philosophy. In this loss mutability donned for the poet her tragic mask. She assumed the guise of an implacable foe to that serenity which Wordsworth throughout his life believed to be the only state of mind in which authentic poetic impulses could originate. Death became monstrous to him as the destroyer of "the thinking principle." He believed that the only way to preserve the dignity and the authority of the human mind was to deny the reality of death by supposing the existence of another and better world undisclosed to the senses.

In his essay, "Upon Epitaphs," published in *The Friend* of February 22, 1810, he goes much further, asserting that the development of the most specifically human qualities of man's nature is dependent upon a belief in its survival. The mind would, in fact, be barren soil for the growth of the most generous of human feelings unless even before they had been planted there it had received intimations of spiritual realities that transcend time. He writes, "It is to me inconceivable that the sympathies of love towards each other, which grow with our growth, could ever attain any new strength, or even preserve the old, after one had received from outward senses the impression of death—if the same were not counteracted by those communications with our internal being, which are anterior to all these experiences, and with which revelation coincides, and has through that coincidence alone (for otherwise it could not possess it) a power to affect us."[10] The fundamental need for a belief in immortality led him eventually to accept all the doctrines of the English church. This surrender of his personal convictions to those of an institution, according to one group of critics, marked the end of his artistic distinction. Henceforth, they say, he kept his intellect and his emotions stiffly confined within the unyielding moulds of dogma. In other words, religious orthodoxy permanently stifled Wordsworth's native artistic impulses.

The "new" or "psychographic" critics have found a reason for the so-called decay of Wordsworth's poetic powers in his psychological escape from uncomfortable emotions. For example, H. A. Fausset believes that Wordsworth, in order to defend himself from the remorse

---

[10] "Upon Epitaphs," *The Prose Works of William Wordsworth,* ed. by A. B. Grosart, London, 1876, Vol. II, p. 29.

caused by his desertion of Annette Vallon and their baby, built up a Pharisaical attitude of self-righteousness. Such moral and emotional hypocrisy smothered every sincere emotion within him and so destroyed at its source true artistic expression.[11]

Other critics suggest that his decline was the result of his lapse into extreme political conservatism.[12] His Toryism was of a sort to make him suspicious of mankind, contemptuous of other individuals, and inhospitable to any but the most conservative political, moral, or esthetic ideas. Herbert Read believes that this stubborn reactionary mood had its origin in a kind of double transference of emotion. The thought of Annette Vallon brought a sense of guilt; therefore he acquired a positive distaste for her. Then he transferred to the French Revolution, with which she was associated in his mind, and to all its liberal ideas the hostility which was in truth directed against his cast mistress.[13]

It is salutary to turn from these ingenious explanations of Wordsworth's sudden artistic deterioration to one which remains consistently upon an esthetic plane. For such is the method of Dean Sperry's analysis presented in his interesting *Wordsworth's Anti-Climax*.[14] He maintains that this anticlimax was the inevitable result of the limitations of the poet's psychological-esthetic "system." This had restricted the subjects which he believed suitable for poetry to remembered sensations, particularly to those received in childhood, when the eye and ear were particularly keen. To him these sensations had come from natural objects and from incidents in the monotonous lives of the dalesmen of Westmorland. These sources of poetry he soon exhausted. In his young manhood he had spent his artistic patrimony like a prodigal. When that was gone, he found himself possessed of nothing to take its place. That is, he had used up all the emotionally charged memories which his mind held. He therefore pursued the only course that his system permitted. He began to search deliberately for new sensatory experience in which poetry might germinate. Such self-consciousness of one's esthetic appa-

---

[11] Hugh I. Anson Fausset, *The Lost Leader*, London, 1933, *passim*.

[12] cf. G. McL. Harper, *William Wordsworth*, New York, 1916, Vol. II, pp. 323-5.

[13] Herbert Read, *Wordsworth*, London, 1931, pp. 206-14.

[14] Willard L. Sperry, *Wordsworth's Anti-Climax*, Cambridge, 1935, especially in Chapter VIII, pp. 122-43.

ratus must of necessity defeat its natural functioning. In other words, Wordsworth became a doctrinaire psychologist and esthetician watching the decay of his powers, and assenting to it as a convincing illustration of his theories.

The weakness of this explanation, like all the others which have just been presented, is that it assumes that Wordsworth during his entire career maintained allegiance to the theories which he held during his great decade and that to the end of his life he made futile efforts to write poems based on a naturalistic esthetic. This is, I believe, a false assumption. When Wordsworth realized that the essential law of Nature was change and that mutability destroyed man's most precious beliefs, he sought not only a religion but also an esthetic norm beyond nature—one that might produce in him through its permanence and stability unchanging peace. This feeling had been an essential part of the esthetic experience as he first conceived it. Indeed, it was its final stage or culmination. Nature, viewed down long corridors of memory, reconciled present personal disharmonies. Thus sublimated it produced first ecstasy and then opened ways beyond that feeling of excitement into deep peace, that "Central Peace subsisting at the heart of endless agitation." But by 1805 Wordsworth began to seek permanence and quietude directly, and devised an artistic procedure by which he could attain that end through his poetry. He discovered a principle of thought that triumphed over time and a poetic process that would enshrine it in a work of Art. His philosophy was a kind of Platonism and his form symbolic art.

In the *Ode to Duty* (1805) Wordsworth renounces his unchartered freedom, his reliance upon chance guidance from Nature and the esthetic creed founded upon the recurrence of ecstatic moments of insight. He seeks instead a principle of thought and feeling independent of sensation, anterior to it—a law of the Universe in whose will he can find peace.

> My hopes no more must change their name,
> I long for a repose that ever is the same.

The poem summons the individual to a conscious submission to a system of thought and feeling that will insure him mental and emotional stability. The Solitary in the third book of *The Excursion* defines the end sought by his acquiescence. It is

> The universal instinct of repose,
> The longing for confirmed tranquillity,
> Inward and outward; humble yet sublime:
> The life where hope and memory are as one;
> . . . And heaven revealed
> To meditation in that quietness![15]

It is the monastic brother who is here described as having attained the "prime object of a wise man's aim." But this fact is of secondary importance. His is only one of the ways in which man can secure that peace which is the "central feeling of all happiness," and particularly that supreme satisfaction which the esthetic experience generates.[16] The poetic procedure which Wordsworth devised to serve as an effective artistic expression for his new philosophy was a kind of symbolic art. It assumes different, but closely related forms in three considerable poems: *The White Doe of Rylstone* (1807), *The River Duddon* (1820), and the *Ecclesiastical Sonnets* (1821). Each of these works in its own way establishes an atmosphere of peace in which the spirit of beauty may soar quietly. On occasion this instinct for repose is spiritual indolence. More often it is a call to subjective activity, a summons to the soul.

Wordsworth's fear of mutability was clearly the initial cause for his devising a form of symbolic art. But the direction of this process was partly determined by his simultaneous retreat from objective reality to deeper and deeper recesses of subjectivity. In a letter written to Sir

---

[15] *The Excursion,* Book III, 397-400.
[16] In his later work Wordsworth secures this serenity through a devout Christian submission of his will to God. The following stanza from "Near the Spring of the Hermitage" (1818) is typical:

> Troubled long with warring notions
> Long impatient of thy rod
> I resign my soul's emotions
> Unto Thee, mysterious God.

George Beaumont on October 17, 1805, he confesses that all he would say
about "taste in natural beauty" would begin and end in the human
heart, as under the direction of the "Divine Nature" it confers "value on
the objects of the senses."[17] He came to regard his early delight in pure
sensation as a pleasure extrinsic to the mind. But by the time that he
described his life in London in the seventh book of *The Prelude*[18] he
realized that objective facts, provided that they had been assimilated to
the texture of mind by the operation of memory and meditation, could
give one's personality an habitual tone. The spirit thus produced was so
strong that even amid the trivial objects of the city

> The soul of Beauty and enduring Life
> Vouchsafed her inspiration, and diffused
> Through meagre lines and colors, and the press
> Of self-destroying, transitory things,
> Composure and ennobling harmony.

It will be remembered that the harmony which Wordsworth felt when
he stood a creative soul in the presence of beautiful natural objects
aroused ecstasy. But the harmony which the spirit, ennobled by remembered intercourse with majestic nature, imposes upon objects, in themselves trivial and essentially meaningless, produces composure. Wordsworth's bent to subdue all objective facts to the quality of his own mind
has here triumphed. The gradual growth of this subjective encroach-
ment upon the domain of the senses is familiar to all students of Wordsworth. However, its bearing upon the appearance of his new art has not
before been remarked. Yet in a letter written to Francis Wrangham in
January 1816, the poet explains that the essential quality of *The White
Doe of Rylstone* has been established by this transcendence of the mind
over the objects brought into it by sensation. He writes:

Throughout [*The White Doe*] objects [the banner, for instance] derive
their influence, not from properties inherent in them, not from what they are

---

[17] *Letters of the Wordsworth Family*, ed. by William Knight, London, 1907, Vol. I,
p. 205.
[18] Much of this book, including the passage quoted, was written during the final month
of 1804; see Ernest de Selincourt's edition of *The Prelude* (1926), pp. xxxviii and xxxix.

actually in themselves, but from such as are bestowed upon them by the minds of those who are conversant with or affected by those objects. Thus the poetry, if there be any in the work, proceeds, whence it ought to do, from the soul of man, communicating its creative energies to the images of the external world.[19]

In this poem, then, Wordsworth embarks upon a quest for a new esthetic experience, one that will be less involved in mutability than his earlier, naturalistic view and one more free from the tyranny of the senses. In searching human life for experience independent of flux and change he discovers suffering and devotes his work to its endurance and its apotheosis. His preface to the poem are lines he had written in *The Borderers*.

> Action is transitory—a step, a blow,
> The motion of a muscle—this way or that—
> 'Tis done; and in the after vacancy
> We wonder at ourselves like men betrayed;
> Suffering is permanent, obscure, and dark
> And has the nature of infinity.[20]

Efforts to escape from suffering are futile. The poet must therefore learn how to sublimate it and to release the spiritual radiance lying implicit in it.

A quotation from Lord Bacon, also prefaced to the poem, suggests that the way is that of Christian orthodoxy: "They that deny a God, destroy Man's nobility; for certainly Man is of Kinn to the Beast by his Body; and if he be not of Kinn to God by his Spirit, he is a base, ignoble creature." This idea brings us to the esthetic center of the poem, the white doe itself. The most important fact about this animal is that its significance does not lie in its life as a natural creature. It does not act at all like the Pet-Lamb at its potations. It is described as "a child of the eternal prime." Wordsworth himself reminds his readers that none of the surface aspects of the poem are of any importance. And he adds, "The anticipated beatification, if I may say so, of her [Emily's] mind and the apotheosis of the Companion of her solitude, are the points at

---

[19] *Letters of the Wordsworth Family*, Vol. II, p. 68.
[20] ll. 1539-1544, Act III, sc. v.

which the poem aims." The white doe is thus a symbol of a great spiritual truth. It does not restore Emily in its capacity as a benignant natural object; for the deer as a companionable animal does not bring her the desired repose. Only when, after prolonged contemplation, Emily ventures to read:

> Of time, and place, and thought, and deed,
> Endless history that lies
> In her silent Follower's eyes,

does she understand that the white doe's importance to her lies in the authentic tidings of invisible things that it bears. This message is that Emily and all other human beings have been granted as guideposts in their march through Time, definite assurances of an eternal principle which quietly dominates all that is temporary and transitory in their nature. These spiritual certainties enable Emily to pass through desolation, grief, and death to an everlasting serenity which lies beyond them. The tears that Emily sheds in the last canto are not those of undeserved suffering designed to stimulate virtue through pity. They are an expression of profound gratitude to the creature which, by its mere presence, has revealed to her an indispensable, eternal truth. To put the matter into critical terms, they are Emily's thankful recognition of the cogency of the doe's symbolistic logic.[21]

This first experiment of the poet with a new artistic method was not successful. Emily is too indistinctly drawn a woman and too inarticulate to represent powerful human grief; and the doe is not an appropriate symbol for spiritual forces which triumph over time. Yet we can see that his choice of this animal was not arbitrarily inept. When he began to see mutability written in every natural object, he could not confront the world of eye and ear without experiencing deep anguish. Yet he could not close the avenues of these senses nor could he sever his love from the

---

[21] If this analysis of the poem be correct, Miss Sherwood's attractive suggestion that the doe represents "that inner light which is the soul of Emily showing through the form of the beautiful living creature" cannot be accepted (*Undercurrents of Influence in English Romantic Poetry*, p. 157).

hills and dales of Westmorland. He therefore sought a way by which he could make natural objects appeal to deeper levels of his personality than his senses. Their contribution to the esthetic experience which could not be rejected had therefore to be controlled by the transcendent mind. Hence he sought to use their undeniable vividness and immediacy to make concrete conceptions, which he believed necessary for the spiritual liberation of man and for the retention of that serenity which he deemed the essence of any esthetic experience. *The White Doe of Rylstone* thus marks his first employment of a familiar object in nature, not to stimulate a pregnant sense impression but to serve as a symbol of a recondite experience peculiar to that part of the mind which is independent of sensation and other obtrusions of time. The poem is therefore both an exposition of a new philosophy and an example of a new artistic method.

The River Duddon, a Series of Sonnets (1820) is a much finer work, largely because Wordsworth found in the river a symbol better adapted to the purposes of his new philosophy. In his essay, "Upon Epitaphs," he had suggested the propriety of employing a river as a symbol of those spiritual forces which flow forever through time out to an eternal sea:

Never did a child stand by the side of a running stream, pondering within himself what power was the feeder of the perpetual current, from what never-wearied sources the body of water was supplied, but he must have been inevitably propelled to follow this question by another: "Towards what abyss is it in progress? What receptacle can contain the mighty influx?" And the spirit of the answer must have been, though the word might be sea or ocean, accompanied perhaps with an image gathered from a map, or from the real object in nature . . . a receptacle without bounds or dimensions; —nothing less than infinity. We may, then, be justified in asserting that the sense of immortality, if not a co-existent and having birth with Reason, is among the earliest of her off-spring.[22]

Even the simplest, most naïve person thus naturally associates the destiny of a river with thoughts of infinitude.

The River Duddon is a series of thirty-four sonnets which describe the life of the stream from its source to the moment of its disappearance in

[22] *The Prose Works*, Vol. II, p. 29.

the sea. Wordsworth takes pains to inform his readers that his purely sensatory associations with this particular river were unpleasant. The thought of it reminded him of a day of unsuccessful fishing in the rain and of great fatigue, so that his recollections were full of "disappointment and distress." But by the time that he composed the poems the obscure fishing brook had become suffused with the beauty of the auxiliar light of his independent mind. It assumed the form of an archetypal silent stream that flowed through time, unaffected by the decay and desolation which had taken place on its banks. In those regions of change forgotten tragedies had marched to their catastrophes; warriors had lived, fought, and died in the great houses which now lay crumbled in ruins. "Time's unsparing hand" had plucked them down. But the river has been untouched. It still flows serenely toward the ocean in the untroubled course which it has held since the beginning of man's memory. The last lines of the thirty-third sonnet make the obvious application of this symbolism to the poet's own life.

> And may thy Poet, cloud-born stream be free,
> The sweets of earth contentedly resigned,
> And each tumultuous working left behind
> At seemly distance—to advance like Thee
> Prepared, in peace of heart, in calm of mind
> And soul, to mingle with Eternity.

The River Duddon, although it rises nowhere to supreme poetic expression, accomplishes Wordsworth's esthetic purpose more effectively than did *The White Doe of Rylstone.* The river is an intellectually appropriate symbol for the one truth which Wordsworth believed essential for the emancipation of human life from its apparent slavery to time and change. As we follow the course of the stream through the sonnets, we are persuaded that "we are greater than we know." The symbol brings also with this revelation the emotion which Wordsworth had come to regard as the only one which could at once steady and illuminate the mind—a tranquil sense of sublimity.

The *Ecclesiastical Sonnets* (1821-1822) form the third considerable body of poetry written under the influence of the same controlling intellectual forces and with the same devotion to the ideals and methods of his symbolic art. The life of the Church, viewed from the High-Churchman's point of view, he will also regard as a river, a Holy River, which like the River Duddon flows through Time without being defiled by its decay. This is the essential significance of these sonnets. The Church bearing its precious freight of spiritual forces thus flows through all the great moments of English history, muddied and diverted by them now and then, and spreading into manifold ramifications near its mouth, but never swerved from its impulse toward the sea. Thus it suggests serene conquest of the events which it encounters on its passage to infinitude. It is significant that of those sonnets which, to quote Professor Harper, "show the hand of an consummate artist moulding into sensuous form lofty and passionately conceived thoughts"[23] the one written on "Mutability" is by common consent the best. The "unimaginable touch of Time," when viewed from the surface of a river carrying the poet safely beyond the ravages of chance and change, assumes a melancholy grandeur which it never possessed as long as he regarded mutability as an implacable foe from whom there is no escape. It is this serene spirit brooding over the sonnets that evokes the peculiar beauty with which Wordsworth invests all the natural objects and all the materials of history from which the poem is constructed.

These three poems must serve as representatives of Wordsworth's symbolic art. Others of lesser importance represent the same esthetic practice. To be aware of his specific artistic intention when writing these later works is not necessarily to discover in them hitherto unsuspected beauties. But a critic who persists in regarding the poems as Wordsworth's futile attempts to keep burning a dying poetic fire approaches them with unjust preconceptions. If he expects direct reports of vivid sensation, he will find them at their best muted and at the worst faint and forlorn. But if he realizes that Wordsworth in these later works was

[23] *op. cit.*, Vol. II, p. 326.

employing sense impressions and natural objects as characters of some great mental apocalypse, as

The types and symbols of Eternity

he will seek and often find in them that nobility and transparency that suggest sublimity and transcendence.

It should be clear by now that fundamental differences existed between the ideas of the function and methods of poetry which Wordsworth held at two important stages of his artistic career. Yet his conception of the esthetic experience which he believed both of these modes of expression should produce changed but slightly. Both of the resultant subjective states involved the highest faculties of the mind. Even when Words-worth regarded sensations as of prime importance in the experience, they were deeply involved with metaphysical affirmations, the influence of which was wide enough to establish an ordered array of most of the essential human relationships. Later, when sensation became important only for its power of symbolic suggestion, a metaphysical affirmation was again the unifying principle of the experience. The essential emotion generated was in one case ecstasy, in the other, serenity. Both were culminations of the human being's joyful acceptance of his position in the scheme of things which the poetry revealed.

Briefly stated, Wordsworth continued to believe that the esthetic experience made man intensely aware of his appointed place in a universe bound together by an infinite number of relationships. His early poetry established man's oneness with Nature and the identification of his spirit with that of his fellow men. His later work revealed man's personality as possessed of aspirations and powers which emancipated him from the world of eye and ear, and also from his ties with his fellow men. Wordsworth's political and social conservatism was thus a natural result of his deeply felt independence of all the manifestations of mutability.

But the end of poetry he persisted in believing was to stimulate the participation of man's creative soul in the adventure of Being. All his methods were designed to awake within man a subjective state that would arouse his imaginative will to such a consummation of his psychological vitality. To transform the mental event from philosophical belief into esthetic experience, Wordsworth realized that his poetry must awaken some dominant emotion that would flood sensation, metaphysical affirmation, and spiritual aspiration with radiance. At the moment when the chosen feeling thus illuminates one's entire being, then poetry performs its essential function.

THE TRAGIC FLAW IN WORDSWORTH'S PHILOSOPHY

NEWTON P. STALLKNECHT

.
.

> . . . That was the curse prepared
> For me: I would not listen to my voices.
>   E. A. ROBINSON

I

MUCH of the noble enthusiasm which inspires *The Prelude* is of a social and political origin, and no one can say that Wordsworth's earlier writings are not to a large degree strengthened by his political interests. The ideal of liberty is taken up and absorbed into the development of Wordsworth's early philosophy, becoming inseparably united with the bold romantic individualism of *The Prelude*.

The mind of man, the locus of liberty, is the glory of the world, an awe-inspiring subject for contemplation.[1] Man is worthy of himself only when he realizes the dignity and power of which his mind is capable, owing to his essentially human endowment.[2] This power, the proper energy of mind,[3] is manifest in the creations of the imagination and the syntheses of the enquiring intelligence. It is, indeed, what Coleridge called the *esemplastic* power. Unlike the association of ideas or the unconscious forming of habits, this power is not borne in upon the mind from without: it is the fundamental assertion of the mind itself, genuine liberty, the full exercise of which is at once moral freedom and happiness. The philosophy of *The Prelude* centers upon this concept. The

---

[1] *The Recluse*, 788 *ff.*; *The Prelude*, A, iii, 178-94.
[2] *The Recluse*, 811 *ff.*
[3] *The Prelude*, A, xi, 270 *ff.*; ii, 381, and elsewhere.

theories of education,[4] of art,[5] and of democratic politics[6] are founded upon it.

> . . . We added dearest themes,
> Man and his noble nature, as it is
> The gift of God and lies in his own power,
> His blind desires and steady faculties
> Capable of clear truth, the one to break
> Bondage, the other to build Liberty
> On firm foundations, making social life,
> Through knowledge spreading and imperishable,
> As just in regulation, and as pure
> As individual in the wise and good.[7]

This inner nobility of man as man is the very first principle of a democratic philosophy which must ignore

> The differences, the outward marks by which
> Society has parted man from man,
> Neglectful of the universal heart.[8]

This principle of mental power is not to be nourished solely upon learning or the amassing of knowledge. It is imagination[9] and it can be aroused only by art and nature. But give the human mind the opportunity of an awakening, allow nature quietly to stimulate the imagination and education humbly to further this development—in short let the essential power of mind be released—then moral excellence, happiness and a profound wisdom will follow of themselves. For the "inner frame is good and graciously composed" and wants only the enlightenment of its own imagination.

Of course, the dominion of imagination cannot be established by the exercise of an abstract intelligence such as Godwin had advocated. Imagination flowers in the insight of the poet and the artist, orderly and

---

4 *The Prelude,* Book V, especially, A, 449.
5 A, ii, 381; xi, 269 *ff.,* and elsewhere.
6 A, xii, 185-286, especially 249-77.
7 A, ix, 360 *ff.*
8 A, xii, 217 *ff.*
9 A, xiii, 84-210.

comprehensive yet rich in concrete detail. It is often awakened by natural beauty, but it may also be inspired by human affairs, by the heroic or pathetic fact of human life itself. And this was indeed the case with Wordsworth during his first residence in London. We must understand people, not sheerly by classification and analysis, but by characterizing them as a disinterested novelist might attempt to do, marking and evaluating their manners, interests, and ideals against the full and enduring background of their common life.[10] Once we have taken this attitude, we have solved the greatest of our practical problems. We find that we can follow our impulses and treat our fellow men literally as we want to treat them; and that we need never regret our actions, if only we can preface our desires by clear imaginative vision of our fellows and of their lives

> Hence sovereignty within and peace at will
> Emotion which best foresight need not fear
> Most worthy then of trust when most intense.
> Hence cheerfulness in every act of life
> Hence truth in moral judgments and delight
> That fails not in the external universe.
>
> Oh! who is he that hath his whole life long
> Preserved, enlarged, this freedom in himself?
> For this alone is genuine Liberty. . . .[11]

Such liberty and power are, like Aristotle's "unimpeded workings" of the mind, in themselves delightful, the foundation of happiness as well as of moral decisions. They also awaken the mystical awareness of a living universe and of man's union with it which contributes so clearly a religious atmosphere to Wordsworth's romantic philosophy.[12]

Surely then the human "frame is good and graciously composed"; human beings are worthy of self-government and, once truly awakened, quite capable of it. Such is the noble humanism of *The Prelude,* a philosophy of self-confidence and of enlightened self-assertion, which distin-

[10] A, xii, 15-44.

[11] A, xiii, 114 *ff*.

[12] A, xiii, 180 *ff*. See the author's "Wordsworth and Philosophy," *PMLA,* December 1929.

guishes its doctrine from the somewhat too conventional admonitions of
The Excursion and later poems. But despite the energy with which the
teaching of *The Prelude* was presented, its doctrine could not have had
so profound a seat in Wordsworth's mind as we often suppose. As we
all know, the ink was hardly dry upon the first draft of *The Prelude*
when Wordsworth in no equivocal fashion repudiated its philosophy,
for *Elegiac Stanzas* and parts of the *Ode to Duty* amount to a recanta-
tion. Furthermore, a careful survey of the last books of *The Prelude*
itself indicates at least two or three passages where traces of a latent
skepticism and dissatisfaction may be found. In Book XII, good men
are recognized as the genuine "wealth of nations," but Wordsworth
mentions his anxious meditations upon equalitarianism

> . . . I could not but inquire,
> Not with less interest than heretofore,
> But greater, though in spirit more subdued,
> Why is this glorious Creature to be found
> One only in ten thousand? . . .[13]

Again we must remember that the virtues of the full imaginative life
are in the last book of *The Prelude* attributed only to "higher minds,"[14]
although no mention is here made of any possible conflict between this
doctrine and the democratic tenets of earlier passages.[15] We should not,
however, emphasize this point too heavily as we are not told what the
essential criterion of a higher mind really is. The distinction may not be
founded upon innate capacity but upon happy environment and opportunity. In *Elegiac Stanzas,* however, there is no difficulty of interpretation. A wholly new attitude appears.

> Farewell, farewell the heart that lives alone,
> Housed in a dream, at distance from the Kind!
> Such happiness, wherever it be known,
> Is to be pitied; for 'tis surely blind.

[13] *The Prelude,* A, xii, 87 *ff.*
[14] A, xiii, 90.
[15] For instance, with *The Recluse,* 811 *ff.*

Here Wordsworth is repudiating the philosophy of *The Prelude*, which has come to appear as selfish and socially unobservant. Again in the *Ode to Duty* occurs a similar repudiation.

> I, loving freedom, and untried;
> No sport of every random gust,
> Yet being to myself a guide,
> Too blindly have reposed my trust:
> And oft, when in my heart was heard
> Thy timely mandate, I deferred
> The task, in smoother walks to stray;
> But thee I now would serve more strictly, if I may.

The doctrine of *The Prelude* is spoken of with tolerance but is none the less found to be wanting. It seems to the Wordsworth of 1805-1806 to be pitifully subject to self-deceit and the weakness of rationalization. Man requires a standard of morality so firmly defined and rigorously stated that he can in no way alter its dicta or tamper with its integrity by a rationalizing interpretation. We shall presently question the validity of this criticism which Wordsworth directs against his own thought.

But now let us consider Wordsworth's first bit of self-criticism, the notion that in *The Prelude* he had entertained a philosophy "housed in a dream, at distance from the Kind." Certainly a perusal of the magnificent conclusion of *The Prelude* suggests to the reader no strain of selfishness and, if we understand its doctrine, we can hardly feel that it is based upon a sheltered ignorance of human life. Surely Wordsworth does not deny the existence of evil or of suffering. He insists only that we enrich our understanding of life through concrete insight and so widen our sympathies before judging our fellow men or attempting to influence their lives. Where then lies the flaw in his thinking? I, for one, believe that there is in the conclusion of *The Prelude* no serious or fundamental flaw. The weakness of Wordsworth's philosophy is manifest not here but in the great ethical poems which follow, in *Elegiac Stanzas*, the *Ode to Duty*, *The Excursion*, and in *Laodamia*.

There are, most broadly speaking, two attitudes of the intellectual towards democracy: one in which he would raise all men, who, he recognizes, are equal in fundamental capacity, toward a life of responsible self-government; the other in which he recognizes in many if not all of the humble and untutored a strength and wisdom which he may not himself possess, an ability to face the real world, born of stress and its complementary fortitude.

The first of these appears clearly in *The Recluse* and the second occasionally in *The Prelude*[16] and in such poems as *Resolution and Independence* and *Elegiac Stanzas*. These two points of view are not necessarily contradictory. They can exist side by side as they do in Wordsworth's earlier thought. After all, men of intellectual and of moral virtue have much to learn of one another. But there is possible a confusion of these elements and this we may call the *democratic fallacy*, a sadly perverted form of equalitarian doctrine. This appears when the gifted man hesitates to make full use of his gifts, is even suspicious of them, because they are not universal. This line of thought becomes even more dangerous if the man of genius has at one time overestimated the power of his less endowed fellows. He may finally come to suspect even his own strength. This I believe to have been the case with Wordsworth.

As we know, Wordsworth had drawn from Godwin, if only for a brief period, a certainty that man must free himself from convention and sentiment and solve his problems, individual and social, solely by the aid of analytic intelligence. This philosophy he shortly repudiated, having recognized, not without bitter disappointment, that reason by itself, working as it does with abstract terms, offers but meager motivation for man's emotions and engenders but little strength of will.[17] He then supplemented his Godwinism with his own doctrine of the ethical imagination above described. In this doctrine Wordsworth retained something, however little, of Godwinism. The individual remains his own arbiter of right and wrong and man's mind, albeit his imagination rather than his reason, remains its own court of highest appeal. What I really want to do when I have envisaged my situation and the people involved in the full clarity of concrete imagery—that is the right thing to do. There is no other way, rational or traditional, of determining right or

---

[16] *The Prelude*, Book XII; A, ix, 387 ff.
[17] 1850, xi, 309 ff.

wrong. I must face the world, "being to myself a guide." And so must all men who are capable of moral life.

While working upon *The Prelude,* Wordsworth had, as we have seen, pondered the problem: how many men are capable of such responsibility? All, of course, possess the capacity, for all men possess the nucleus of imagination or they would be incapable of the simplest acts of knowing, of the most rudimentary awareness of unity in variety. This fact was at one time enough for Wordsworth. In time, under democratic ideals and wholesome education guided by sound romantic teaching, genuine moral liberty would be the possession of all. Furthermore, men would learn to appreciate the natural religion which must accompany the dominion of imagination. This hope for the future was enough. Until this happy consummation, the "higher minds," the few romantic intellectuals and the rarely gifted children of nature, untutored but happily inspired, must preserve this substantial wisdom.

The unenlightened must be brought slowly to the position of the elect, such is the faith of 1800. This belief is tempered somewhat by doubts and qualifications expressed in *The Prelude*. Some men are perhaps incapable of enlightenment and many fortunate souls need very little enlightening. But the faith remains throughout unretracted: Virtue is the child of imagination and the only path to virtue and wisdom lies through expansion of the individual's imaginative powers. The poet, the true romantic poet, the imaginative man *par excellence,* is the proper teacher of the human race. Thus Wordsworth writes of himself in the last lines of *The Recluse* fragment

> . . . may my life
> Express the image of a better time. . . .

Suddenly, at least in appearance, this faith is retracted: the poets must discipline their wayward genius and assume the patient fortitude and sturdy endurance of the humble. They have withdrawn themselves and housed their ideals in a dream, and their ideals are selfish and futile. They must go to school to the very people that they had once considered their rightful pupils. They must assume the "unfeeling armor of old time," so admired in the *Elegiac Stanzas.*

Even so, the time may come when a romantic individualism, the ethics of imagination, may become feasible.

> Serene will be our days and bright,
> And happy will our nature be,
> When love is an unerring light,
> And joy its own security.[18]

But this Utopian state can apparently arise only as the result of long years of self-discipline on the part of mankind in general. And in Europe of the Napoleonic era, even "higher minds" are incapable of such free self-assertion. They must subject themselves to the authority of a law of duty. Essentially, this doctrine is repeated in *The Excursion,* Book IV, where the Wanderer rebukes a presumptuous generation for having expected to accomplish too much.[19]

To account for this *volte-face,* we find available three or four possible explanations which have been offered at one time or another by Wordsworth's biographers. (1) In the first place, we may attribute it to the temporary failure of French democracy and its passage under Napoleon into imperial dictatorship. The philosophers seemed to have betrayed the people or, at least, advised them so badly that the people became willy-nilly the victims of an archadventurer. Certainly at this time the humble virtues might easily appear to advantage in contrast with the ideals of revolutionary individualism which seemed to have been treacherously perverted to such foul ends.

(2) Again it may be true that, brooding over his unfortunate relations with Annette Vallon and considering the suffering and unhappiness which impulse had produced, Wordsworth may have come to believe that human nature is fundamentally incapable of "being to itself a guide." However, this unfortunate affair lay well in the past, dating from a time when even the philosophy of *The Prelude* was unformulated. Hence had remorse for the desertion of Annette exercised any effect upon this philosophy, it would have checked the first development of such thinking rather than have caused its decline. Furthermore, impul-

---

[18] It is interesting to remember that Wordsworth once wrote "would" for "will" in the first line of this quotation.

[19] 260-331.

sive weakness may easily enough be explained according to the psychology of *The Prelude*. We often act impulsively when our impulses are unenlightened by full comprehension, expressed in concrete imagery, of their present significance and possible consequences.

(3) Perhaps most important of all the reasons advanced is that expressed in *Elegiac Stanzas*:

A deep distress hath humanized my soul.

Under the emotional strain of a cruel bereavement, the loss of his brother John, Wordsworth came to value more highly the virtues of endurance and resignation. This, to be sure, is a natural and quite comprehensible development of his personality. It is only when such insight leads to repudiation of the efficacy of a philosophy of self-enlightenment that we must put it down as a counsel of despair. After all, Wordsworth's bereavement really widened his imaginative sympathies, as the *Elegiac Stanzas* eloquently tell, and included within the sphere of his understanding attitudes never before so clearly envisaged.

(4) It is also important to remember in the above connection that at this time, as the *Intimations Ode* suggests, Wordsworth recognized a certain decline in his own gifts of intense esthetic sensibility and of mystical exaltation. The resultant loss of self-confidence might well be reflected in his emphasis upon the humble virtues and the philosophy of duty. Duty may then appear as the one sure foundation of human dignity, without which man is a poor creature, weak and insignificant.

> Possessions vanish, and opinions change,
> And passions hold a fluctuating seat:
> But, by the storms of circumstance unshaken,
> And subject neither to eclipse nor wane,
> Duty exists. . . .[20]

We might call this a philosophy of self-defense as opposed to the philosophy of self-confidence, so clearly expressed in *The Prelude*.[21]

[20] *The Excursion*, iv, 69 *ff.*

[21] If the reader will turn to Professor Gilbert Murray's famous essay on Stoicism, he will find a masterful account of the psychology underlying acceptance of a philosophy of self-defense. Professor Murray's phrase "loss of nerve" is especially significant and, I think,

These reasons, frequently offered as explanations of Wordsworth's change of heart, are most assuredly not to be dismissed. Certainly the first, third and fourth seem to bear upon our problem. But it seems clear that no one of these influences could have determined Wordsworth's thinking profoundly had it not been for his unhappy readiness to entertain what we have called the democratic fallacy. Had these circumstances arisen before a thinker quite free of any merely sentimental interest in praising his fellow men or of any desire to be as like them as possible, the outcome must have been very different. And, be it said in defense of *The Prelude*, the benevolence which it teaches does not necessarily involve such a sentimentalism.

II

Much can be said, despite the above, in defense of the *Ode to Duty*, even by a Wordsworth enthusiast whose center of gravity lies deep in *The Prelude*, especially if he reads the *Ode* in the version published in 1807, which, alone of all the editions of the poem, contains as its sixth stanza the following lines:

> Yet none the less would I throughout
> Still act according to the voice
> Of my own wish; and feel past doubt
> That my submissiveness was choice:
> Not seeking in the school of pride
> For "precepts over dignified,"
> Denial and restraint I prize
> No farther than they breed a second Will more wise.

applies to Wordsworth. I cannot refrain, in passing, from offering an adverse criticism of all philosophies of duty which try, so to speak, to make of some rational principle or formula a rock upon which human nature may rest secure. The theory is simply that by surrendering ourselves to the dictates of an absolute principle of duty, we transcend ourselves and escape the weaknesses of an unaided human nature. But these principles, modern categorical imperatives or more ancient formulae, must, of course, be interpreted to meet concrete situations. In this very interpretation there lies the danger of rationalization, certainly as great as that attendant upon determining what we really want to do, according to the philosophy of *The Prelude*. If the reader doubts this, he has only to consult the textbook criticisms of Kant's categorical imperative. In a word, practical ethics cannot be reduced to a discipline, however much the weary and the timid may desire to have it so simplified.

Here duty and enlightened inclination seem capable of reconciliation in the life of the morally successful man. The rigor of a categorical imperative and the "confidence of reason" which such a formula is said to supply are seen as preliminary or probationary supports of the comparatively immature moral agent. At least the above stanza suggests such doctrine. Thus Wordsworth seems to have hesitated between a philosophy of complete stoicism and a reformed version of the humanism of *The Prelude*.[22] As late as 1809, the date of the pamphlet on the convention of Cintra, there remains some trace of the earlier philosophy. The people are in many cases, we are told, greater than their leaders who, being immersed in political competition, quite fail to understand and often betray them. Wordsworth speaks enthusiastically of the foundations of popular virtue, "the instincts of natural and social man, the deeper emotions, the simpler feelings, *the spacious range of the disinterested imagination,* the pride in country for country's sake, when to serve has not been a formal profession. . . ." (Italics mine)

But, we may comment, if leaders are not to be trusted, the people in their homely wisdom, ought not to follow them. The moral is clear. Since the people cannot lead themselves, there should be no change in social and political life. And Wordsworth was soon to recognize this conclusion, implicit in the development of his thought. The Cintra pamphlet presents a truncated form of the philosophy of *The Prelude*. Popular virtue is recognized and similarly explained in both writings; but in the later work there is obvious a suspicion concerning the very possibility of great, radical leadership. This is symptomatic of Wordsworth's development, as he passes from *The Prelude* to *The Excursion,* where reactionary politics are clearly manifest. This retreat is inevitable; for unless some individuals are recognized as possessing the right and the strength to consider themselves as prophetic reformers, distinct from the multitude, no philosophy of revolution or even of progress is possible.

The triumph of the democratic fallacy, with its pernicious levelling of great minds and small, leads to an inevitable and ironic conclusion. It

[22] See the author's article in *PMLA*, "Wordsworth's Ode to Duty and the Schöne Seele," for a more complete account of how this vacillation influenced Wordsworth's conception of duty (*PMLA*, March 1937).

finally destroys faith in democracy. If we are to identify ourselves with "the Kind" and accept the virtues of endurance, we will come to accept the traditional supports of the humble and gather stoically beneath the orthodox and conservative strongholds of church and state. With these great fortresses of security we shall not care to tamper. In fact there seems something indecent in any attempt to recast the scheme of things. Of such development in Wordsworth's thinking we are all only too well aware. The extreme illiberalism which resulted in his political thought is too well known to require much comment. His opposition to reform and the timid querulousness of its expression is almost identical with the attitude of an aristocratic arch-conservative, although the fear of change which is its usual aspect has an ultimate origin quite distinct from any aristocratic sentiment. This fear of change led Wordsworth to oppose universal education and the freedom of the press, and this latter as early as 1814, within ten years of the completion of the first draft of *The Prelude*. But Wordsworth's intellectual progress from *Elegiac Stanzas* was an inevitable one. Once doubt the value of the intellectual and spiritual independence of the individual, and the rest follows.

We have described the vacillations of Wordsworth's thought while he passes from *The Prelude* to *The Excursion* as a wavering between the philosophies of "I *want*" and of "I *must*," between the ideal of self-realization and the ideal of self-transcending duty. In this his thought is clearly less balanced than that of Dante or even of Goethe, if we consider the latter's thought as expressed in such a poem as his *Vermächtniss*. It is this vacillation that reveals the tragic flaw in Wordsworth's philosophy. The moral insight so brilliantly presented in *The Prelude* is very shortly marred and finally, in the later poems, wholly obscured by Wordsworth's failure to perceive that these two approaches to morality can be rendered mutually consistent. Wordsworth faces a fatal disjunction either we are to develop ourselves, our insights and our sympathies and proceed according to a romantic version of Augustine's formula, *Ama et fac quod vis*, or we are to submit ourselves wholly to the discipline of an established principle of duty. There can be no alternative or middle course. This becomes clear when we consider Wordsworth's final deletion of the important sixth stanza of the 1807 *Ode to Duty*.

We have only to compare the moral tone of *Laodamia* with that of the *Ode to Duty* to recognize how significant a turning-point the repudiation of this stanza marks. After all, in the *Ode* duty is presented, as also in the letter to *Mathetes*, as an attractive and beautiful ideal in harmony still with Wordsworth's natural religion. The ideal of *Laodamia* is heroic but forbidding, almost dour; the gods frown more readily than the powers laugh.

In the 1807 *Ode*, respect for temporarily unpleasant duty may through our appreciation of its full significance be transmuted into a "second will" free from the earlier tensions. This is in no very important respect inconsistent with the doctrine of *The Prelude*, where Wordsworth admits that in ethical development we must "complete the man . . . made imperfect in himself."[23]

Had Wordsworth proceeded in this way and expanded the important ideas involved, the philosophy of *The Prelude* might well have been richly supplemented. But here Wordsworth failed. Imagination and spontaneous enjoyment are discounted in favor of stoic endurance such as appears in the *White Doe*. And I very much fear that this evaluation is founded largely upon the feeling that in accepting dutiful endurance as the prime virtue, we are identifying ourselves with "the Kind." Thus the democratic fallacy seems to triumph.

Wordsworth's failure to integrate the philosophy of *The Prelude* with a theory of duty constitutes a real loss to our modern culture. It is one of our fundamental weaknesses that we habitually see life as divided between play and real enjoyment on the one hand and important work and duty on the other. What we want to do and what we ought to do stand apart even in theory. This is perhaps inevitable in an irreligious and commercial civilization. But against this error Wordsworth's teaching might well have proven to be a great force had he overcome his own confusion, for he at least faced our problem and in his happier periods held a key to its solution.

But let us here in fairness to Wordsworth admit that the democratic fallacy, as we have described it, confused and perverse as it is, rests upon one sentiment among others, which is clearly an honorable one. This is

23 *The Prelude*, A, xiii, 202.

an intense dislike of making an exception of oneself. It is from th
underlying motive, which in the minds of rationalist philosophers ma
be interpreted as a respect for strict logical consistency in practical life
that the real power of Kant's categorical imperative derives. Conside
Walt Whitman's famous resolve to accept nothing that all men migl
not enjoy on the same terms. This may be a sound foundation for equal
tarian ethical doctrine, but of course it should be read as requiring equa
opportunity rather than any limitation of achievement to the commo
level.

Wordsworth's later attitude toward religion is worth attention. W
may grant that the need of a spiritual security to be drawn from source
external to the self initiates a sound approach to religion. But Words
worth becomes too eager to accomplish his pilgrimage, too dogmaticall
certain of what is to be learned from humility. He will take no chances
so strong is his philosophy of self-defense, in religion any more than i
politics. The "wise passiveness" of his earlier philosophy, the willingnes
to follow where his richly expanding experience might lead him is nov
quite vanished. His religion lacks plasticity and what Professor A. E
Taylor has called the element of surprise.

Compare the fourth *Evening Voluntary* (1834) with any poem whicl
expresses a genuinely active religion, say Blake's *Sunflower* or Herbert's
The Pulley.

> But who is innocent? By grace divine,
> Not otherwise, O Nature! we are thine,
> Through good and evil thine, in just degree
> Of rational and manly sympathy.
> To all that Earth from pensive hearts is stealing,
> And Heaven is now to gladdened eyes revealing,
> Add every charm the Universe can show
> Through every change its aspects undergo—
> Care may be respited, but not repealed;
> No perfect cure grows on that bounded field.
> Vain is the pleasure, a false calm the peace,
> If He, through whom alone our conflicts cease,

> Our virtuous hopes without relapse advance,
> Come not to speed the Soul's deliverance;
> To the distempered Intellect refuse
> His gracious help, or give what we abuse.

What mechanical piety this is! As mechanical as the verse. But we must look for little else. For the Wordsworth of this period faith is no longer seeking understanding. It repudiates the very sources from which understanding once sprang. All is fixed and unquestionable. Doubt and intellectual independence have no real function, not even that of leading us toward profounder insight. Nor does the poet listen with "wise passiveness" for the old Eolian visitations. Neither reason nor inspiration is needed now.

But such considerations only convince us how much the English-speaking world lost by the tragic failure of Wordsworth's philosophy.

WORDSWORTH AND HIS DAUGHTER'S MARRIAGE

ERNEST DE SELINCOURT

•

MONG the stories current of Wordsworth's later life none is, perhaps, more often told, or more often misrepresented, than that of his opposition to the marriage of his daughter, Dora. "His love for his only daughter," wrote Sir Henry Taylor in his *Autobiography,* "was passionately jealous, and the marriage which was indispensable to her peace and happiness was intolerable to his feelings. The emotions, I may say the throes and agonies of emotion, he underwent were such as an old man could not have endured without suffering in health, had he not been a very strong old man. But he was like nobody else, old or young. He would pass the night, or most part of it, in struggles and storms, to the moment of coming down to breakfast, and then, if strangers were present, be as easy and delightful in conversation as if nothing was the matter. But if his own health did not suffer, his daughter's did; and this consequence of his resistance, mainly aided, I believe, by the temperate but persistent pressure exercised by Miss Fenwick, brought him at length, though far too tardily, to consent to the marriage." This statement is undoubtedly true of Wordsworth's affection for his daughter, and his dislike of her marriage, but it is not the whole truth; for it does not suggest that he had any reason, other than "passionate jealousy," for his objection; while the careless copying and dating of three of his letters has given to the phrase "far too tardily" a meaning which is wholly at variance with the facts.

A chatty anonymous article, studded with errors, appeared in *The Cornhill Magazine* of March 1893, under the title "Some Unpublished Letters of William Wordsworth." In one of those letters [A], addressed to "dearest M[ary] and D[ora], undated, but from its reference to the poem *The Triad* clearly written in 1828, occur these sentences:

Say to Mr Monkhouse C. Wilson's behavior shews the good sense of Dr Venables' advice.

Have nothing to do with Quillinan. I am sorry for his disappointment. I hope dear Dora's looks are better, and that she will collect some flesh as Edith [Southey] did.

Then after remarking that Dora's marriage was a severe trial to the poet and his wife, and some inaccurate statements about Quillinan, the article goes on to transcribe two further letters, [B] and [C], again undated.

[B]

Sunday morning, Nine o'clock

My dearest Dora,—I am looking for Mr Quillinan every moment. I hope to revive the conversation of yesterday.

The sum is:—I make no opposition to this marriage. I have no resentment connected with it towards anyone; you know how much friendship I have always felt towards Mr Q. and how much I respect him. I do not doubt the strength of his love and affection towards you: this, as far as I am concerned, is the fair side of the case.

On the other hand, I cannot think of parting with you with that complacency, that satisfaction, that hopefulness which I should wish to feel: there is too much of necessity in the case for my wishes. But I must submit, and do submit, and God Almighty bless you, my dear child, and him who is the object of your long, and long-tried preference and choice.

Ever your affectionate father,

Wm. Wordsworth.

I have said little above of your dear mother, the best of women. O how my heart is yearning towards her, and you, and my poor dear sister.

[C]

Thursday

Your letter to me just received. Thanks: I will write you from Brinsop. W. W.[1]

My dear Daughter,—The letter which you must have received from Wm [i.e. her brother Willy] has placed before you my judgment and feelings:

[1] Error of transcription for M. W. This is a postscript added on the top of the letter by Dora's mother.

how far you are reconciled to them I am unable to divine. I have only to add that I believe Mr. Q to be a most honorable and upright man, and further, that he is most strongly and faithfully attached to you: this I must solemnly declare in justice to you both; and to this I add my blessing upon you and him—more I cannot do, and if this does not content you with what your brother has said, we must all abide by God's decision upon our respective fates. Mr Q. is, I trust, aware how slender my means are; the state of Wm's health will undoubtedly entail upon us considerable expense, and how John[2] is to get on without our aid, I cannot foresee. No more at present, my time is out. I am going to join Miss Fenwick at Miss Pollard's.

    Ever your most tender-hearted and affectionate father,

                        Wm. Wordsworth.

After printing these letters the article goes on: "The allusion to the disappointment in a letter already quoted [i.e. [A]], coupled with the recommendation to his wife and daughter to have 'nothing to do with Quillinan' was probably occasioned by one of Dora's repeated refusals of his suit."

When Professor Knight printed these letters in his *Letters of the Wordsworth Family* he rightly gave 1828 as the date of the first, and he printed the other two immediately after it, as though they were written in the same year, and only a few days later. From similar errors in their texts it is clear that Knight had not seen the manuscripts of any of them, but was printing from the *Cornhill*.

Now Dora was married to Quillinan in 1841; so that her father appears to have opposed her union with him for at least thirteen years. Professor Harper, therefore, in the evidence available to him, was fully justified in his statement that "for many years Wordsworth refused his consent to Dora's marriage." And this view is still commonly accepted. But an examination of the manuscripts of these letters and of the Quillinan-Wordsworth correspondence, shows the whole matter in a somewhat different light.

The manuscript of the letter [A], written in 1828, reads:

Say to Mr Monkhouse, C. Wilson's behavior shews the good sense of Dr. Venables' advice, have nothing to do with Quillinan. I am sorry for his disappointment. I hope that dear Dora's looks are better, etc.

---

[2] John, now Vicar of Brigham, was married and had four children and a very delicate wife. Her father, Mr. Curwen, had just suffered severe financial losses.

Now it is clear from the true punctuation of this passage, that the "have nothing to do with Q." is not an injunction to Dora, but part of Dr. V.'s advice to Monkhouse. What C. Wilson's behavior had been, and why Dr. Venables gave the advice does not immediately concern us; the reference is probably to some business transaction, in which Quillinan would be no safe collaborator.

The other two letters [B] and [C] are printed, both in the *Cornhill Magazine* and by Knight, with comparative accuracy, but the second of them [C] has the postmark April 27, 1839, and the other [B] will be shown to belong to a little later in the same year. Moreover, the Quillinan correspondence[3] proves that though he and Dora had long loved one another, neither of them suspected the other of more than friendship till the late autumn of 1836; that the true state of affairs was not revealed to her parents till January 1838; that her father's active opposition to her engagement only lasted until the following summer: that after the summer of 1839 the only obstacle to the marriage was Quillinan's lack of means to support a wife, and that even if "passionate jealousy" influenced the poet in his dislike of the match he had reasons which, in those days at least, many persons would have regarded as adequate.

Chief among these were the state of Dora's health and Quillinan's financial insecurity.

Dora had always been delicate, and since 1835, when she had a dangerous illness, she had never recovered her strength. She seemed, indeed, to be getting slowly weaker, she ate practically nothing, and though the doctors could not give a name to her disease, it was generally thought that she was in a decline. Clearly she needed all the watchful care and freedom from worry that a comfortable home and assured circumstances could give her. But the man who wished to marry her had not the means to support the healthiest of wives, and he was in imminent danger of losing the little that he had.

[3] Dora tells Q. that she had burnt all his letters *before* she knew of his love for her: she kept the later ones. Q. kept all Dora's earlier letters, as well as many from Mrs. W., W. W., and Sara Hutchinson; but her letters after 1836 do not seem to have survived. But for the purpose of my article this matters little, as Q., in answering her letters, often quotes what she had said in her previous one.

Edward Quillinan, a Roman Catholic of Irish extraction, was born at Oporto in 1791, the son of a wine merchant there. In 1808 he entered the army, and saw some service at Walcheren and in the Spanish campaign of 1814; in 1817 he married the daughter of Sir Egerton Brydges, and accompanied his regiment to Ireland and then to Scotland. In 1822 he left the army, and attracted by his admiration for Wordsworth's poetry settled with his wife and little daughter Jemima at Rydal, where he became intimate with all the Wordsworth family. Mrs. Quillinan and Dora were soon devoted friends, and on the birth of her second child, Rotha, Dora stood godmother. In the following year Mrs. Quillinan died in tragic circumstances, her widower went abroad for a time whilst the Wordsworths looked after his children in his absence, and Dorothy Wordsworth managed for him all the business connected with his vacated house, till it could be disposed of. On his return he went with his children to live with his brother-in-law, Captain Brydges Barrett, first at Lee Priory in Kent and then in London; but his intimacy with the Wordsworths was kept up both by interchange of visits and by frequent correspondence with all members of the household. When Quillinan left the army he seems to have had a comfortable income, but though his financial affairs are shrouded in mystery it is at least clear that a few years later his means were seriously straitened and his future prospects dark. In 1826 he allowed himself to become entangled in the shady business concerns of the Brydges family, and was the participant, through careless confidence, in a fraudulent transaction by which they cleared some fifteen thousand pounds;[4] this resulted, some time later, in a lawsuit which dragged on for years and was not concluded till 1842; in 1828 he writes of "a wicked will that has defrauded him of his just expectations," and the death of Barrett in 1834 involved him still more deeply in "painful and difficult matters of business," so that the education of his daughters became an expense he could hardly meet. Yet though occasionally he did a little business as agent for his brother, who carried on his father's trade in Oporto, he made no serious or consistent effort to earn a living. He disliked business and evidently had little aptitude

---

[4] For an account of this astonishing transaction, see *The Literary Life of Sir Egerton Brydges* by Mary K. Woodworth, 1935.

for it; moreover he was, as he said, "cursed with elegant desires." His delight was in the society of literary men, and in dabbling in literature himself. He was a good Portuguese scholar, he wrote pleasant verses, and had, he thought, a real gift for satire, whilst his letters are proof that he had a facile pen in prose, picturesque and sometimes humorous in description. He was, too, a good talker and a pleasant companion, and there is plenty of evidence that despite an over-sensitiveness of nature, increased, doubtless, by his precarious financial position, which made him quick to take offense and difficult to placate, he was widely popular in the society in which he moved. Not tied down to any occupation, he was often abroad. In 1831 he spent some months in Paris, superintending the education of his elder daughter, while Rotha was left in charge of the Wordsworths; in 1833 he took up his residence at Boulogne with both his daughters, saving expense by undertaking their education himself; from 1834 to 1836 he paid a long visit to his brother in Oporto. During the summer after his return he passed a month or two at Rydal, and declared his intention of settling down with his daughters at Canterbury, but in the following November he had accepted an invitation from his brother to take Jemima to Oporto for the winter, his brother paying all expenses. On his way out, in an unseaworthy ship, they had a narrow escape of drowning, and it was probably after reading his vivid account of their danger that Dora, "by one of those acts of sudden enlightenment," as he puts it, let him into the secret of her heart, which until that moment he had never even suspected. But despite her admission Dora did not entertain the possibility of marriage to him, nor at first does he seem to have proposed it. His first love letter, dated March 1837, urges her to bring out one of her little Hutchinson cousins who had been seriously ill to join him and Jemima at Oporto: Dora replied that she could not come and would not if she could. "It is best as it is," she said, and she recommends him to marry someone with money. To which he replied that he would do so when she set the example, calling her "a nun at large and her own Lady Abbess . . . but I shall be a philosopher in time." Such throughout the year is the strain of their letters. "My love for you," wrote Dora, "is a spiritual Platonism, for your sake I wish you were fairly married to some one else"; but though he admits that he is "not spiritualized enough" for her, and cannot rise to her exalted tone, he seems prepared to accept the situation.

He returned to England in October (1837), but his hopes of seeing Dora at once were frustrated, for by the time he could travel north, Dora had already left for Brinsop, whence she was going, first to London and then to winter with Miss Fenwick at Dover. But he spent a fortnight at Rydal with her parents. One evening, as he was writing to Dora, Mrs. Wordsworth entered the room and seeing Dora's last letter to him spread out on the table asked him the news. On his own confession he was "evasive and ingenuous," and offered to read her a part of the letter, whereupon, seeing his confusion, Mrs. Wordsworth remarked that if she could only hear a part, she would rather not hear any of it. Later in the month, and also in January, the lovers met several times in London, and they travelled together down to Dover; and it was soon evident to Dora that a mere Platonic relationship would satisfy her no better than it satisfied Quillinan. Uneasy at having a secret from her parents, probably conscious, too, that their suspicions might already be aroused, Dora decided to write and break the news to her father. Quillinan warned her of his "presentiment" that her news would not be acceptable, but the warning must have been unnecessary. Fully aware of her father's passionate love for her, she knew the terrible shock he would suffer when he learned that he had a rival in her heart. But quite apart from that wholly natural, if unjustifiable, emotion, we can imagine how Wordsworth would regard the situation. Dora was in a serious state of health, and here was a man, who had long been a trusted family friend, agitating her feelings in a way that could not fail to be injurious to her, by making love to her when he could offer her no prospect of marriage. In his circumstances, Wordsworth must have thought, an honorable man would have avoided her company. On his recent visit to Rydal he had not breathed a word of his intentions, and now he was taking advantage of Dora's absence from her parents to press his suit upon her when they had no opportunity of counteracting his influence. His reply to Dora's letter, written in the heat of the moment, must have expressed all this in no measured terms. Quillinan never saw it, but he judged from Dora's "anguish" on receiving it that it was "cruel." And he was probably right in his conjecture that her father had accused him of being "insidious and base," and trying to "undermine her affection." He wrote to Wordsworth to exculpate himself, but did not elicit an answer; Quillinan was deeply hurt at this, but if Wordsworth had replied, and stated, as he would have done, how he viewed the matter, Quillinan would probably have been hurt still more.

Torn between a father to whom she was devoted, who would have resented any rival, but had, she knew, good reasons for objecting to this one, and a lover who was now pleading with her for a definite engagement, though he admitted in the same breath that he was precluded by his financial straits from urging her to influence her father in his favor, and yet that he would marry no woman without her father's consent, poor Dora was in a desperate position. Nor were the early months of this year any happier for Wordsworth. For he was obsessed with the fear that by his opposition he had forfeited his daughter's love; and it was not for four months that her mother could report to her any alleviation of his despair: "I cannot help writing to you," she writes at the end of April, "though it is idle to plague you with so many letters . . . yet we have been more happy for the last few days than for a very long time. Since the appearance of your being drawing [*sic*] towards us, Father seems quite a different being." Fortunately for all of them they had in Miss Fenwick a wise and faithful friend, devoted alike to Dora and to her parents, able to see the situation from all sides, and to enter with sympathy into the feelings of all of them. Miss Fenwick realized that however unfortunate Dora's attachment might be, her health and happiness were bound up in it, and that somehow or other the financial obstacles must be surmounted, and that her father, whose disapproval was causing so much pain alike to Dora and to himself, must be brought to view the matter with less hostility. She did what she could to soothe and comfort Dora; and when, in the following June, Dora returned to Rydal, Miss Fenwick accompanied her, and took up her abode in a house near by. Then she set to work gently but insistently upon her father, and due to her mediation a compromise was reached, "your father reconciling himself to all objections and willing to consent when there could be any reasonable surety of your being provided for,

and there being no hindrance to your attachment in the meantime."[5]
And then, knowing the affection that Wordsworth and Quillinan really
had for one another, and confident that if they met the old feeling would
revive, Miss Fenwick invited Quillinan to spend a few days with her at
Ambleside. Quillinan was naturally a little nervous about accepting the
invitation, but his mind was set at ease by receiving the following letter:

My dear Mr Quillinan, you are right in supposing that you have not
forfeited my friendship, and as Dora has fully explained to you the state
of my feelings I certainly do not consider it any "intrusion" your accepting
Miss Fenwick's invitation, and shall be pleased to see you at Rydal Mount.
I remain, dear Mr. Quillinan, faithfully and affectionately yours

Wm. Wordsworth.

In February (1839), Quillinan paid his visit. A week or two before
coming he had written to Dora, asking her whether she would "dare" to
take the risk of marrying him without further delay, but she evaded the
question, and while he was at Rydal he never broached it, except on one
occasion to say to her "Dora, you have never answered my question";
nor did Wordsworth ever hint at the attachment, save once when he
expressed to Quillinan a regret that he was a Roman Catholic. On his
departure Wordsworth wrote to Southey: "Q. left this morning on his
way to Ireland. I had no private conversation with him, but through
Dora he understands what my judgments and feelings are, and we all
seemed at ease with one another." His visit had at least eased the situation, even if it had not brought the marriage definitely nearer. "I wish,"
he wrote to Dora on his departure, "I could say what would be quite
satisfactory to Miss Fenwick, for then you and I would be happier than
we are as yet, though my visit has, I trust, removed the ill-omened gloom
that darkened your house to me. How very kind Miss Fenwick has been
to me! God will, I trust, favor an attachment which has excited the
benevolence of a being so excellent."

But naturally enough Quillinan was not satisfied to leave things as
they were; and early in April he wrote again, urging Dora to answer his
question, and making some rather vague statements about his financial

[5] This is Miss Fenwick's statement to Dora in April 1839, recalling the situation that
obtained in the previous year.

position. But the time he had chosen was most unfortunate. Dora's brother Willy had long been ailing, and her parents, together with Miss Fenwick, had just taken him off to Bath to try the effect of the waters on him. Dora sent on a part of Quillinan's letter to her father, with her own comments, among them a plea that the Southey girls had been allowed to marry poor men. To this Mrs. Wordsworth answered, "I wish you had not brought forward the Southeys, as he [i.e. her father] may readily reply that their husbands are young men and have a profession independent of their power (as proved) to increase their income, by which means they can insure their lives. Of course I shall not suggest this." But her father found quite enough to answer in Quillinan's proposals, without touching on the Southeys. For it certainly looked as if Quillinan had been discussing the matter with Dora on his late visit, and then had again chosen the time when her parents were away to work upon her to flout their judgment and break the compact which all parties had accepted. No wonder that he wrote to Quillinan with some asperity:

Bath. 13th April

My dear Mr Quillinan,

By yesterday's post I recd. a letter from Dora, containing a long extract from one of yours to her. Upon the subject of this extract I cannot enter without premising, that calling upon her in so peremptory a manner to act on so important an occasion *during the absence of her parents*, is, to say the least of it, an ill-judged proceeding. And this I must, notwithstanding my present knowledge that the proposal you have made to her, and thro' her to me, was agitated between you when you were at Rydal; and notwithstanding any thing, that appears in your letter, in justification of its being made now.

As sincerity required this declaration from me, I make no apology for it, nor do I, dear Sir, think you will require one.—I will now come to the point at once. Your letter contains these sentences, which are the only ones I shall touch upon.

"If hereafter I shall have an opportunity of making a provision for you, I will certainly do so, and I could not ask you to run the risk if I thought it possible that my death would leave you destitute of resources from my side, I have not any fear as to that. The thing is will you *dare* to run the rough chance?"—Before I enter upon the former sentence, I must direct your attention to the fact, that you must have overlooked the state of health in which Dora has long been, or you cannot have been fully aware of it;

or you could not have called upon her Parents, thro' her, circumstanced as they are, as to age, to give their Daughter up to *"a rough chance."*

But from the former part of what I have copied, I must infer, that "tho' you can settle nothing upon her at present, you are not without hope of being able to do so, etc. etc." Now it is *my duty* to request of you, my dear Sir, to state as specifically as you can, upon what the hopes and expectations implied or expressed in the above Quotation from your Letter, rest. I mean in respect of a provision in case of your death.

There is no call for my saying more till I have received your answer upon this point, which I beg may be, on all our accounts, as definite and explicit as possible.

Wm. is here and in a state of health that causes us much anxiety—the Bath waters do not seem to agree with him, and his stomach and bowels are much deranged. Miss F. owing, we hope, solely to the severity of the weather, is not quite so well as she was at Ambleside. We all unite in affectionate remembrances to yourself and Children, and believe me, my dear Mr Q.,

faithfully yours,

Wm. Wordsworth.

Quillinan was deeply offended by this letter, and he sent at once a heated and ill-judged reply which even his best advocate Miss Fenwick strongly condemned. "I can feel with and for you all," she wrote to Dora, "and for Mr. Q. too, but I do most exceedingly regret the tone of his letter, for it has disturbed feelings which certainly were very kindly disposed towards him, and which in time would have been all that he could have required, and which may still be, tho' not so soon. He ought to have taken the rebuke implied in your father's letter more patiently; had he done so I cannot but think that what he said of his expectations would have made your father feel justified to himself in dispensing with an absolute security—as it is we must look for gentler movements in his mind, and Mr. Q.'s, or some circumstance that will put all into a better train again. . . . Your father will not answer Mr. Q.'s letter, what more must come through you—cannot you prompt a more conciliatory letter from him? I think it is due."

The tone of Quillinan's letter can be further conjectured by the way in which, at the same time, he wrote to Dora, losing, in his own wounded pride, all sense of what she must be suffering. He makes no attempt to answer her father's practical question, but after reviewing what seemed to him his own impeccable conduct throughout the whole affair, goes on to meet the charge of having called on her to act in her parents' absence (which, though perhaps unwittingly, he certainly had done). "This," he says, "means and can mean nothing more or less than that I acted like a ———, no, that 'to say the least of it, it was an ill-judged proceeding'—a cowardly attempt to work upon you and induce you to do wrong when you were deprived of the shield of their presence. No parent friendly to me, or even tolerant, could have put such a construction on any sentence I ever penned. . . . I shall never be able to discuss the subject of a union between you and me with the least chance of success for us. Then why should I submit to have my views, circumstances and pretensions discussed in syllogisms? I have been mortified enough already, and you have suffered the torments of suspense too long; you have had too painful a conflict between your love for your father and your kindness for me, and now that the hopelessness of the case is manifest I believe in my soul and conscience that you will be the less unhappy for having arrived at the conviction of its hopelessness."

Dora had already written to her mother, clearing herself and Quillinan from the charge of "inconsideration" of her parents, and at the same time reproaching her father for making too much of financial matters; but Quillinan's letter can only have added to her despair. The good Miss Fenwick wrote to console her: "I do not see, dear Dora, that you should view the affair as closed by anything that has as yet occurred; a little patience and gentleness will set all right."

For despite Q.'s letter to her father, and Dora's criticism of him which wounded him still more, Wordsworth was already relenting. "Father's visit to London," wrote Mrs. Wordsworth on April 20, "may forward brighter hopes and feelings than are now overshadowing us all. But I must say that neither you nor Mr. Q. do your father's feelings justice by such expressions retorted upon him as 'L.S.D.' and 'the business of the matter.' All the feelings, for your sake, that he has extinguished should not, my dearest, have been met in this spirit by either of you"; and three days later, "We have all been calm and talk of your situation and hope of happiness as a matter decided upon—therefore my beloved daughter, do not agitate the matter further or call upon your tender Father (for he *does* deserve that epithet if ever Man did) for more than this passive countenance, which he is, I feel, ready to give. And may his and your mother's blessing be upon you both. When you write, write as I hope you now feel, with thankfulness and hope, and in this spirit regain, if possible, your lost strength before we meet, as I trust we shall do, with hearts overflowing with love to you . . . what we owe to dear Miss Fenwick is beyond all possible conception."

To ease the situation, Willy, a devoted son and brother, had already written both to Quillinan and Dora soothing and explanatory letters; and on the 27th, on his way to London, the poet sent his daughter the letter already printed [C]. But apparently Quillinan was still nursing his grievances: he did not write the conciliatory letter that Miss Fenwick asked for, nor, through Dora, did he make any attempt to answer the poet's practical questions, so that some ten days later Wordsworth wrote to Dora: "I cannot but wish that you were put at rest by Mr. Q. on this under all circumstances harassing and trying affair—I wait for your report of his answer with anxiety. God bless you, my dear daughter." When Quillinan does reply, on May 12, he goes far to admit the justice of her father's objections: "I do not pretend to think that our prospects are such as will not make many people call our marriage madness," and after dilating on the difficulties which they may have to encounter in their first years of married life he says: "My great dread as to our union has always been lest you should find yourself removed from a comfortable to a comfortless home" . . . (This was, of course, just what her father feared, and was his motive in writing the letter which Quillinan had so deeply resented); then, on June 5, because he has not yet received an answer to a letter written to Willy on May 24, he breaks out "he or some of them must have seen my letter by this time—if they have seen my letter and not thought proper to answer it I shall think them all a parcel of churls and never care two twopences more for any of them." There seemed indeed some doubt as to whether, now Wordsworth was in town, Quillinan would bring himself to meet him. No wonder that his daughter Jemima told him that "she thought I did not seem to be treating Mr. Wordsworth with the respectful attention due to him." But at last he put his injured pride in his pocket, and they met on June 8; this was the first time, it must be remembered, that Quillinan had ever himself stated his own case to Wordsworth. They met again two days later and on the 11th Quillinan wrote to Dora in a very different mood: "How delighted you will be, if you are really my own Dora, at what I have to tell you! Your Father and I are right good real friends. After that weary first interview of which I gave you a doleful and yet half hopeful account, I never was so thoroughly subdued in my life. That expression 'too old to be transplanted'[6] almost killed me. . . . On Sunday Morning I went again to Mr. Marshall's by Mr. W.'s appointment. I was shewn in to all the family at breakfast, he among them, that being his breakfast-breakfast, the one to follow at Kenyon's was to be his talking breakfast. Presently he went with me into the library and there read me that most kind letter which he had written to you [i.e. the letter already quoted as [B]]. From that moment all was right. I dismounted from my high horse, never more to get on its back, by my fault at least, to him. Willy kindly gave me his seat in the Cabriolet and walked to Kenyon's, that I might ride with his father to Harley Street. In the Cab. he spoke to me with all the affection of a friend and a father, and if he holds to that, it must be my delight as well as my duty to shew that that *is the right course.*"

But poor Dora's troubles were not yet over. For some time her father found it difficult to feel consistently towards his future son-in-law as a friend and a father; and it is probably of this time, as well as the previous summer, of which Taylor, whose informant was Miss Fenwick, speaks in the passage quoted at the beginning of this paper. In September Quillinan wrote to Dora that he had not the same pleasure in going to Rydal as in the past, and complained that her father was still trying to exert his influence against him. But that is the last suggestion in his letters that he had anything to complain of in the poet's attitude either to him or to the marriage, and his natural sensitiveness was such that if he had had any grievance to air we can be sure that he would have felt no scruple in airing it. In December it is not of her father but of his

---

[6] Dora was thirty-five years of age.

poverty that he complains. He admits that his affairs do not justify their marriage. "Oh Dora, so I have been to Rydal and come away again as usual leaving you behind me, without any definite time or plan for claiming you. I will not, however, be dolorous. Something *must* turn up in our favor, the cards have been against us so long." A friend, he tells her, has just asked him why he does not marry. "Because we are too poor." "Nonsense," she says, "He without whose notice not a sparrow falls will not allow true love to starve." "It is true she does not know how very poor I am, nor any of the particulars of my circumstances (how I hate the word), but she knows that I have been very unlucky and much bothered." Apparently he seems at last to have realized himself that if you marry an invalid wife it is as well to have the means to support her.

And throughout the next year, though the marriage is still delayed, there is no sign of friction. In the early months when Dora was in London, enjoying the society of Quillinan and her other friends, the correspondence that passed between her father and lover was cordial; and in the summer, which he spent at Rydal, Quillinan wrote to his daughter Rotha in a tone which suggests that his old affection for the poet had returned. And Quillinan did not make it easier for Wordsworth. For not content with having secured an obviously reluctant consent to the marriage he was now insisting that Wordsworth should come to the wedding and give his daughter away. Crabb Robinson justly wrote that he thought this "was too much to ask." But here again Wordsworth gave way, and in the following May the marriage took place. Whether Quillinan's income had improved we do not know, but it seems certain that Wordsworth gave his daughter some financial help, though some years passed before he made her a definite allowance. Indeed, at this time he could hardly have done so; he was past seventy and was on the point of resigning in favor of his son William the post from which he derived £400 a year, more than half his income; and he was not placed on the civil list till eighteen months later. Knowing the strength of his passions there were those who feared that when it came to the point some of his old resentment at the match might burst into a flame. But they were mistaken. On May 8 Miss Fenwick wrote, "Our marriage stands for the 11th, and I do sincerely trust nothing will interfere with its taking place on that day, for all parties concerned are prepared for it. Mr. Wordsworth behaves beautifully."

And so he behaved after the marriage. In the following year when the Brydges lawsuit came to a head, and Quillinan was in danger of losing, not merely his income but his honor, Wordsworth wrote him this generous letter:

My dear Quillinan,

Your letter to Miss Fenwick moved me much on many accounts. But my motive for writing this short letter is merely to assure you of our sympathy in your vexations and distresses, and still more, very much more, to assure you that you need have no anxiety respecting judgment which we are likely to form of your character on these sad proceedings. We have all an entire confidence in your integrity from the first to the last, in your connection with the Brydges family, and the Barrett property, and furthermore are but too well aware of the generous sacrifices which you have made for them who have proved to be so unworthy of them. The confidence you reposed in them, however chargeable it may be with want of discretion, affords itself a strong presumption of your being incapable of joining in any dishonorable transaction. As I have confidence that you will regulate your mind as becomes you, I have nothing to add but the expression of a wish that the business may be speedily brought to a close, with as little injustice as is possible under the untoward circumstances which the wicked arts of the adverse party have produced.

Believe me, my dear Q., affectionately yours

Wm. Wordsworth.

March 1st 1842

The result of the trial can be learned from Crabb Robinson's diary for April 1842. "I was glad to read in *The Times* a declaration from the Vice Chancellor that he believed Mr. Q. was free from all intention to commit any fraud, but he is made liable with some 4 or 5 others to make up the difference between £22,000 and £7,000, besides costs, which will be a sad dead weight lying on him and prevent his doing anything for his wife."

This news can only have strengthened Wordsworth in his conviction that his opposition to the match had been justified; nor indeed was he ever reconciled to it. To Dora, as ever, he remained passionately devoted, and with her husband he kept upon the best of terms, but there can be little doubt that he did not hide his feelings about it from his wife; whilst to Miss Fenwick, the dearest friend of his old age, who had been the stoutest advocate of the marriage, he did not scruple to speak his mind. He liked Quillinan as a man, and was ready to allow him many good qualities; but, like many parents who have lost their daughters to better sons-in-law than his, he did not think him good enough for Dora, quite apart from all financial considerations; and his letters to Miss Fenwick contain several pregnant reflections on the incomprehensibility of woman's choice of a mate. Moreover he thought Quillinan selfish and inconsiderate. After a visit to his daughter in 1844 he wrote: "The knowledge that my presence was useful to Dora recompensed me in no small degree for unpleasantness of a domestic kind which you are not ignorant of. The worst of it is that Mr. Q. seems incapable of regulating his own temper according to the demands which his wife's indisposition too frequently makes upon it, and it is not to be doubted that his way of spending his time is little suited to make the day pass pleasantly for others. He never scarcely *converses* with his wife and daughters; his papers, his books, or a newspaper, engross all his time. This is surely deplorable; and yet, poor Creature, she is very fond of him, and this I suppose must happen mostly if married pairs do not positively dislike each other—indifference can scarcely exist under that connection except in minds altogether barren or trivial."

But what he chiefly resented was Quillinan's reluctance to make any effort to earn a living for himself and his wife, and his apparent complacency in living to a great extent on the bounty of others. This was the poet's reason for declining to grant Dora a regular allowance when Miss Fenwick first urged it upon him. "I will not bind myself," he said, "circumstanced as Dora is, to make her any fixed allowance. I am convinced it would be wrong to do so, as it would only provoke in certain quarters an effect which I should exceedingly deprecate"; and again a little later, after speaking of Quillinan's general kindness and amiability, he goes on: "Neither this, however, nor anything else, reconciles me to his course of life. You say he could not procure employment—I say he does not try.—the fact is he cannot bring himself to stoop in the direction he ought to stoop in. His pride looks and works the wrong way, and I am hopeless of a cure—but I am resolved not to minister to it, because it ought not to exist, circumstanced as he is. His inaction mortifies me the more because his talents are greatly superior to those of most men who earn a handsome livelihood by literature."

But again, by gentle but insistent pressure, Miss Fenwick won her point, and the allowance was granted. Quillinan has been praised for asking, after Dora's death, that the payment should be discontinued; but how could he possibly have accepted it? And if in this his nice sense of honor stood him in good stead, that morbid sensitiveness which was bound up with it could still lead him to crass misconstruction of the motives and feelings of others. For when the poet, in his uncontrollable grief at Dora's death, could not bring himself to cross the bridge that led to her house, Quillinan interpreted it as a deliberate insult aimed at himself.

This last incident serves to emphasize a fact that must be obvious to all who have followed the story, that Dora's father and her lover lived emotionally upon different planes, so that it was difficult for either of them to do full justice to the other. Quillinan, entirely sincere and genuine in his affections, was yet a man of the normal emotional caliber: Wordsworth was a man of intensely passionate feeling. "Few know," remarked Rogers, a shrewd man of the world, not given to overstatement, "*how* Wordsworth loves his friends"; and his passions were nowhere stronger than where his children were concerned. Aubrey de Vere relates how, forty years after the death of Catharine and Thomas, the poet "described the details of their illnesses with an exactness and intensity of troubled excitement such as might have been expected if the bereavement had taken place but a few weeks before"; and no one can read his letters without noting that his anxiety about the health of those dear to him amounted to an obsession. Dora was the darling of his old age, when her marriage was first mooted she was dangerously ill, and firmly convinced of the risk involved in her union to a man who could ill afford to support her, it was inevitable that he should be difficult to convince that an even greater risk might be involved in opposing a match on which her heart was set. To what extent this conviction was strengthened by a selfish desire to keep Dora for himself, no one can determine, for all human motives are mixed; but if at times he thought more of himself than Dora, Quillinan's letters during the crisis prove that his wounded vanity, a less excusable motive, led him to do the same.

And further, Wordsworth differed from Quillinan in his whole attitude to the practical concerns of life. That passion and imagination which are essential constituents in a great poet were in him combined with an intensely realistic turn of mind. To this combination his poetry owes its distinctive character; to this it owed also that weakness which Coleridge aptly described as "matter-of-factness": in the issues of daily life it was manifested in a resolute insistence on facing the facts, and seeing things as they are. He had indeed all the caution and the hard-headedness of the typical north-countryman. He had known poverty in his youth and early manhood, and later the dilatory slackness of his brother Richard in money matters had impressed on him still further the importance of straight dealing and of meeting a situation instead of shirking it. Dora and her lover might reproach him for thinking too much of "£.s.d.," and the unworldly Miss Fenwick might abet their romantic illusions, but he knew from experience, that if we live in this world, and not in some far-off Utopia, to ignore the part played by "£.s.d." in our happiness is simply a dangerous folly; and he could not bring himself to countenance it. But to such mundane considerations Quillinan showed a lofty indifference. The financial difficulties in which his careless generosity had involved him had become for him the excuse for making no effort to earn his own living. His Micawber-like words to Dora "something *must* turn up in our favor" sum up his attitude to life. He never faced the situation or made any effort to retrieve it; but sensitive as he was of his honor, he was yet content to live for the most part upon the hospitality of others, with no real sense of responsibility. How exasperating this must have been to Wordsworth can easily be imagined. That two men so radically different in outlook should have been good friends where no practical issues were at stake between them, is nothing to wonder at: that they should have remained so as father and son-in-law is, in reality, a striking tribute to both of them, and, perhaps still more, to the woman whom they both loved.

AN IMITATION OF WORDSWORTH

LESLIE NATHAN BROUGHTON

•

•

RECENTLY I received an item from my faithful book dealer, Mr. A. E. Dobell, containing what he believed to be an unpublished poem by William Wordsworth. A hasty examination left me at first with the impression that perhaps he was right. The poem, entitled *The Cursed Tree*, appeared in *The Brighton Magazine*, May 1822, No. V, pp. 483-4, preceded by a brief letter signed with the initials "W. W."

The Brighton Magazine, copies of which are now rare,[1] was published in London, and ran from January through August (eight numbers) in 1822. It is not to be confused with *The Brighton Magazine, etc.*, published at Brighton, July-December 1864. The periodical in question is a rather ambitious monthly, highly "loyal" and Tory, containing a mixture cf quite good material and much in the way of unintelligible banter that is poor, or at least difficult for the modern reader to understand.

In Number V, which contains the letter and poem in question, there are four other references to Wordsworth. On the page following the table of Contents, under the heading, "The Bee-Hive—Notices responsive," appear two notes referring to the poet:

Our friend W. Wordsworth—whose *inimitable* style we immediately recognized—will perceive his star beaming in our azure-clothed pages, in all its native lustre. Why do not Southey,[2] Milman, and the other glories of Britain contribute? Wilson, of the Isle of Palms, is, we are informed, alone restrained by the *amor patriæ*, which still renders him a stickler for Blackwood.

---

[1] There are complete files in the British Museum and in the library of Harvard University, and a copy of No. V in the Wordsworth Collection of Cornell University.

[2] In a later number of *The Brighton Magazine* there are some verses which the editor declares to be by Southey, but which are not in his Collected Works.

The second note on the same page is as follows:

We wish our friend "The Recluse," he of the "Mountain Musings," E. C., W. W., T—, and the rest of the "Celestials," would assist at one of our monthly meetings; we should then indeed have the "noctes cœnæque Deum."—Hor.

The third reference, which perhaps has no bearing on the present problem, occurs as a parenthetical illustration in an article entitled *The Pleasures of Winter* (p. 521):

Or (as Mr. Wordsworth would say, has too much of *oneness*.)

The fourth and last reference to Wordsworth in this issue, aside from the letter and poem under discussion, is on page 531 in a nonsensical epistle, entitled "The Manksman's Budget," signed by Quyllyam M'Quyllyam, and directed to the "Right trusty and well-beloved Editor":

Barring a little delicacy, which you know is always the bore of a young poet, when he first puts out his feelers amongst the rugged ways of author-ship, I have a confidence in my mind, that these "morsels of melody" will go down the stream of time, as gaily as the sonnets of that man of tarns and fells, Wm. Wordsworth, or the soul-cheering strains of the sweet minstrel of Wyoming [Thomas Campbell].

The letter signed "W. W." and the accompanying poem follow:

To the EDITOR of the Brighton Magazine.

SIR—I have just received and carefully perused, the four first Numbers of what I may venture to call your University Magazine; and, though it is long since I quitted for ever the walks and cloisters of St. John's, I have still enough of the Cantab about me, most heartily to wish you success. As a small proof of my good will, I send you the following lines, which I trust, will be found not entirely unworthy of a place in your poetical department. I am, Sir, faithfully yours,

W. W.

THE CURSED TREE

'Tis Nature's mantle wraps Creation round,
Each smile she wears pervades the heart of man,
Her noblest offspring; every tear she sheds,
Wrings from his bosom correspondent drops

Of sorrow: thus she leads him on, by change
Of bright and dark, of sunshine and of storm,
Through every stage of feeling, from a boy
To the full stature of the perfect man.

    Yet are there some who never share her smiles;
Nature's step-children (so I call them), born
In evil hour, and from their birth consign'd
To the chance nurture of *unnatural* hands.

    Her scenes delight them not, her stirring gales
That bound from hill to hill, as winning health
From exercise, still fan their pallid cheeks
In vain; her ever-changing pace, that speaks
Of fickle life, and fleeting time, and love,
And heavenly beauty, has no tongue for them.
They pine, ev'n from their birth; they live unlov'd;
And unregretted, ere the hand of Time
Has touch'd their temples, drop into the grave.

    Nor is it man alone, that thus disown'd
Of love maternal pines—yon prostrate ash,
(It fell beneath the last destructive storm
That vex'd our coast) I've known it twenty years,
Ev'n from a seedling shoot, and to my thought,
It still seem'd haunted with an influence
Shot from the sphere of some malignant star.
The dews of heaven in vain were shed on it:
Its bark was hung with moss, and weather-stain'd,
And rough as with an eating leprosy.
Its leaves, ev'n from their budding with dark spots
Were mildew'd o'er, and still its pendent keys
Were few and weak in Autumn, emblem meet
Of the small store of treasur'd sap within.
Its roots—for in a hedge-row, solitary,
As shunn'd by all its fellows, it surviv'd—
Were circled by a pond, grass-green and foul,
Food for the evil-boding frogs alone.

Last year, the lightning undermin'd the bank
Whereon it grew, and thus (as I have said,)
The storm has laid it prostrate on the earth.
And there it lies despis'd.—I have prevail'd
With him who owns it (for indeed its worth
Is small) to leave it to the elements,
That thus, as if in sport, have curs'd its growth,
And wrought its fall, as outcast from the law
By which, with innate energy, they feed
And nourish all things. Thus it lies,—and now
Upon its wither'd bark, a friend who oft
With me had witness'd its decay, has mark'd,
Half serious, half in sport,—"THE CURSED TREE."

A little study of the poem, the accompanying letter, and references to Wordsworth cited above appear to prove beyond a doubt that *The Cursed Tree* is merely the *jeu d'esprit* of a clever imitator. The italicized word "inimitable" in the first reference may be taken as a key to the whole matter. Wordsworth at the time was laboring on the Ecclesiastical Sonnets. Had the great poet actually honored the magazine with a gratuitous contribution, as stated in the letter, he would hardly have been treated with so much levity elsewhere in the same issue. This conclusion is substantiated by a passage even more insulting in tone in the June number. Here under the title, "Sketch-Book of an Oxonian," apparently a regular column in the magazine, we find these lines discrediting the whole matter:

That *humbug* about Wordsworth won't take,—the "Cursed Tree" is too good for him, every body can understand that—but as your correspondent Salopiensis says—all cannot extract the metaphysical morality of Peter Bell; I mean to have some chat with you on that subject.

In this passage the writer is adopting the tactics employed in the well known parody of *Peter Bell* by John Hamilton Reynolds, who makes Wordsworth deny the authorship of one of his best poems, *The White Doe of Rylstone,* and "deduce moral thunder from buttercups, daisies, celandines, and 'such small deer.'" *The Cursed Tree,* being a

close and plausible imitation, is not to be classed with the famous paro-
dies (though it may have much the same purpose), directed against
Wordsworth in 1819: *The Dead Asses,* and Reynolds's *Benjamin the
Waggoner,* and *Peter Bell,* all essentially potent in ridiculing the style
and subject-matter of the poet; or with *The Simpliciad* in 1808. The
poem does show, however, that in spite of his already established reputation, Wordsworth was still occasionally the target of this kind of
criticism by the younger men of the time.

Each student of Wordsworth, as he reads the poem, will find his
own interest and amusement in discovering passages or expressions that
Wordsworth might have written, and others that could not have come
from his pen. The letter is far inferior to the poem as imitation. The
first line of the poem, in itself absurd, glides into a mixed metaphor
and muddled construction that Wordsworth would have been ashamed
to own. The expressions "Nature's step-children" and "evil-boding
frogs" are hardly Wordsworthian, for the poet never employed the
former term in his poetry and did not believe that frogs are evil-boding,[3]
though he might have made a rustic say as much. Likewise the whole
conception of a "cursed tree" might have figured as folk-lore in his
poems, but not as his personal thought. "The spot is curst" in *Hart-leap
Well,* and the stunted shrub in *The Thorn* is in much the same condition, as is also Harry Gill. He would have condoned the pathetic
fallacy in lines 2-4[4]. Lines 7-8:

> Through every stage of feeling, from a boy
> To the full stature of the perfect man.

remind us of the thought in *Lines composed a few miles above Tintern
Abbey,* though Wordsworth never mentions a "perfect man" and only
once does a "perfect woman" (a tribute to his wife) appear in his poetry.

[3]
> Yet rather would I instantly decline
> To the traditionary sympathies
> Of a most rustic ignorance, and take
> A fearful apprehension from the owl
> Or death-watch.
> *The Excursion,* iv, 613-17.

[4] cf. *The Excursion,* i, 475-81.

The similarity of this poem to the work of Wordsworth (not his best) is instinctively felt, but it is not easy to analyze. The likeness appears to rest in single words and in very brief combinations of words, not in extended phrases and whole sentences. It may also rest to some extent in sentence structure and the metrical composition. For instance, Wordsworth frequently ends a line with "round," and uses several times the expressions: "hill to hill," "fleeting time," and "ever-changing." The sentence "I've known it twenty years," and the frequent use of parentheses recall Wordsworth. The poem as a whole, though in parts it does not ring true, is an interesting specimen of Wordsworthian criticism through imitation.

HELEN MARIA WILLIAMS AND THE FRENCH REVOLUTION

M. RAY ADAMS

•

•

"THE most sensible women," wrote George Dyer in 1792, "are more uniformly on the side of liberty than the other sex; witness a Macaulay, a Wollstonecraft, a Barbauld, a Jebb, a Williams, and a Smith."[1] The establishment of such a generalization perhaps requires a greater range of observation of the sex than George Dyer could boast, but the list of women radicals who were writing with more or less distinction during the revolutionary era is very striking. We might add to those whom Dyer mentions Mary Hays, Maria Edgeworth, Mrs. Amelia Opie, Mrs. Mary Robinson, and Mrs. Inchbald. Of them all Mary Wollstonecraft was the sturdiest and most original intellect, but no one of them knew as much of the French Revolution first-hand, no one of them had such opportunities to observe the very soul of the machine, and no one of them left so complete a record of what she saw and heard and thought as Helen Maria Williams. No modern appraisal[2] has been made in English of this record in thirteen volumes[3] of

---

[1] *Poems*, p. 36 n.

[2] The only extended notice, so far as I have been able to discover, that has been taken of Miss Williams during the last century, is F. Funck-Brentano's *Hélène Maria Williams*, a biographical sketch prefacing his *Le Règne de Robespierre*, a translation, published in 1909, of the four volumes of her *Letters* which deal with the period between Robespierre's rise to power and the establishment of the Directory. I have found it useful for information about her French associations, exclusive of what she herself gives. Funck-Brentano's book has recently appeared in English in the Sundial Illustrated Historical Series under the title, *Memoirs of the Reign of Robespierre*, London, 1929. The sketch in the *Dictionary of National Biography* is inaccurate, if not prejudiced. J. R. MacGillivray, in an unpublished Harvard thesis, *Wordsworth and His Revolutionary Acquaintances, 1791-1797* (1930), has given the details of the relations between Miss Williams and Wordsworth. See pp. 23-5, 44, 70-1, 89.

[3] They are *Letters written from France in the Summer of 1790*, 1790; *Letters from*

her more than thirty years' residence in France. The present study deals with her experiences only in so far as they affected or reflected the history of her opinions. Its primary concern is not her recital of the great public events which shook France during the revolutionary period but the rôle which she played in interpreting France to England.

No Englishman, with the possible exception of Thomas Paine, knew intimately so many of the men and women who shaped the destinies of the French Revolution. In her apartment in the Rue Helvétius were instituted in the autumn of 1792 those political and literary reunions over the teacups on Sunday afternoons which attracted men of light and leading from various parts of the world, and her hospitality was kept up with comparatively little interruption as late as 1816. She had a decided taste for intellectual society and she indulged it on a very

France, 4 vols., 1792-1796 (the first volume is a reprint of the above; the second bears the title, *Letters from France containing many New Anecdotes relative to the French Revolution and the present State of French Manners*; the third and fourth bear the title, *Letters from France containing a great variety of interesting and original Information concerning the most Important Events that have lately occurred in that Country and particularly respecting the Campaign of 1792*); *Letters from France*, 4 vols., 1795-1796 (the first two were issued under the title, *Letters containing a Sketch of the Politics of France from the Thirty-first of May, 1793 till the 10th of Thermidor, Twenty-eighth of July, 1794*; the third volume bears the title, *Letters containing a Sketch of the Scenes which passed in various Departments of France during the Tyranny of Robespierre and of the Events which took place in Paris on the Tenth of Thermidor*; the fourth volume, taking the account from Robespierre to the Directory, was added to the second edition of the other three in 1796); *Sketches of the State of Manners and Opinions in the French Republic towards the close of the Eighteenth Century*, 2 vols., 1801; *A Narrative of the Events which have taken place in France from the landing of Napoleon Bonaparte on the 1st of March 1815 to the Restoration of Louis XVIII*, 1815; *Letters on the Events which have passed in France since the Restoration in 1815*, 1819; *Souvenirs de la Revolution française*, a translation by C. A. Coquerel of unpublished manuscripts. The list is exclusive of her observations in her *A Tour of Switzerland, or a View of the present State of the Governments and Manners of those Cantons, with comparative Sketches of the present State of Paris*, 1798, and in her edition of *The Political and Confidential Correspondence of Louis XVI*, 1803. For convenience I refer to the first four volumes as *Letters from France*, first series, and to the second four volumes as *Letters from France*, second series. Other titles are abbreviated also.

In *Four New Letters of Mary Wollstonecraft and Helen Maria Williams*, edited by Benjamin P. Kurtz and Carrie C. Autrey, Berkeley, Calif., 1937, appears for the first time an important letter of Miss Williams to Mrs. Joel Barlow, conjecturally dated April 6-16, 1794. See the present author's review of this volume in *American Literature*, Vol. IX, pp. 386-8 (November 1937). Four unpublished letters to Mrs. Barlow and one to Joel Barlow, written between 1811 and 1815, are in the possession of Barlow heirs at St. Helena, Calif. Mrs. Sarah S. Van Mater, of St. Helena, has kindly provided me with transcriptions of these letters.

generous scale. Few Englishmen of importance came to Paris in the years after the beginning of the Revolution without calling on Helen Maria Williams. Her home was a sort of political and literary clearing-house for her countrymen on the continent. When Wordsworth went to Orleans in 1791, he was armed with a letter of introduction to her from her friend, Mrs. Charlotte Smith; but he failed to see her, she having just left for Paris. One of her first English guests was Mary Wollstonecraft, who came to Paris in December 1792. Among her visitors in 1802, during the temporary suspension of hostilities between France and England, were Fox, Lord Holland, John Philip Kemble, Benjamin West, John Opie, and Thomas Poole.[4] The Americans, Robert Livingston and Joel Barlow, were entertained. Barlow's letters to his wife tell of twelve visits made to Miss Williams's house between May and September of 1802 alone. At one time he writes of dining there with "the usual great circle of letter folk." At another time he writes: "I was at Helen's last night; I believe she has a party almost every night— 30 or 40 or 50, chiefly English." In an unpublished letter to his wife of August 3, 1802, Barlow has left a vivid picture of the *éclat* received by one of Miss Williams's celebrities, Lady Mountcachell, a British noblewoman of democratic sympathies:

Here is a billet from Helen for this evening, with a promise that I shall have a seat next to Lady M—— and *gratis*—for you must know there is so much of *empressement* to get these seats that I have sometimes raised a little insurrection to vindicate the equality of right in this case. At last I told them (Helen & my Lady) they had better make a speculation of these parties and let the seats next to them *par abonnement*.[5]

---

[4] In a letter to Coleridge, July 20, 1802, Poole writes: "Kemble went with us last night to Miss Williams's house. We there met, first Miss Williams herself, who is a very obliging woman, but a little affected. Lord Holland was there. . . . Carnot, the ex-director, was there. . . . At this party were also Mr. Livingston (the American ambassador), Joel Barlow, Italian Princesses and German Princes, many of the *literati* of Paris, etc., etc." (Mrs. Henry Sandford, *Thomas Poole and his Friends*, London, 1888, Vol. II, pp. 85-6.) In another letter to Coleridge of August 22, he writes that he has been "three times to Miss Helen Maria Williams's *conversations*." (*ibid.*, Vol. II, p. 90.)

[5] The originals of these letters are in the *Barlow Papers*, a collection in the Harvard College Library. Portions of the letters have been published by C. B. Todd, *Life and Letters of Joel Barlow*, New York, 1886, pp. 184, 195, 197, 202. Her intimacy with the Barlows, as four extant unpublished letters of her own to them show, was renewed during the year

Mrs. Amelia Opie and Miss Anne Plumptre[6] visited her in 1805. In 1816 Lady Morgan found at her salon a large and distinguished company of English visitors whom she had welcomed after the restoration. The Miss Hutchisons called upon her in 1817. In 1814 the Clarksons, who had known her in her youth, introduced Henry Crabb Robinson, and he in his turn brought the Wordsworths in 1820.[7]

The list of her close early personal friends in France is almost a roll call of the leaders of the Revolution. She knew well the principal Girondists as well as a number of the Jacobins in the days of their moderation, and she rode in the Bois de Boulogne with Napoleon Bonaparte. Revolutionists, republicans, Bonapartists, monarchists—the whole procession of French political leadership during those shifting and troublous times—she knew, if not in her own drawing room, in theirs. While the Girondists were in power the salons of Miss Williams and of Madame Roland were certainly among the leading places in Paris where responsible opinion was bred. "The deputies of the Gironde and Barère passed most of their evenings at our house,"[8] she wrote in her account of the spring of 1793. Among those leaders of the revolutionary and post-revolutionary periods who are known to have sat at her table are the Rolands, Vergniaud, Grégoire, Barère, Dupin, André and Marie-Joseph

they spent in Paris while Barlow was on his mission to Napoleon as minister plenipotentiary from the United States.

[6] Miss Plumptre, a writer now forgotten, was a novelist of revolutionary sympathies and, according to William Beloe, one of those "female Machievels" who "with the most superficial knowledge presume to pass judgment on the political rights and conditions of nations" and who was deflected from a pious youth by her friendship for Miss Williams. (*The Sexagenarian*, London, 1818, Vol. I, p. 363.) From 1802 to 1805 she resided in France and in 1810 told of her experiences in *A Narrative of Three Years' Residence in France*. She was both a democrat and a worshipper of Napoleon.

[7] On October 25 Miss Williams wrote to Robinson to thank him for introducing the Wordsworths: "I am much flattered that you thought me worthy of them, and am grateful to them for having devoted to me two or three quiet evenings. . . . I left politics, the laws of election, and the charter to take care of themselves, while I was led by Mr. Wordsworth's society to that world of poetical illusion, so full of charms, and from which I have so long been absent. Miss Wordsworth has a desire to see my last little volume [*Letters on Events . . . since the Restoration*], your protégé. Will you obtain a copy for her of the second edition?" (George McLean Harper, *William Wordsworth*, New York, 1923, Vol. II, pp. 319-20.) As late as 1843 Wordsworth spoke in appreciative reminiscence of Miss Williams. See *ibid.*, Vol. I, p. 150.

[8] *Letters from France*, second series, Vol. I, p. 181.

Chénier, Ginguené, Échoucard Lebrun, Paul Rabaut, Rabaut Saint-Étienne, Isnard, L. N. M. Carnot, Champfort, Miranda, François Gérard, La Source, Jean Baptiste Say, and Bernardin de Saint-Pierre. Her house was the rendezvous of distinguished foreigners like Kosciusko, Bitaubé, and Alexander Humboldt. Beyond these, the list of her political and literary friends and acquaintances runs to an amazing length: Brissot, Madame de Villette, Madame Helvétius, Madame de Genlis, the Marquis de Sillery, Gensonné, Dupré, Louvet, Rouget de Lisle, Xavier de Maistre, Pétion, Dorat-Cubières, Servan, Esmenard, Fonfrede, Ducos, Marron, Ducis, Laffon-Ladébat, and Cambacières. Of those who were at one time or another her friends, Madame Roland, Brissot, Vergniaud, Gensonné, Rabaut Saint-Étienne, Sillery, Fonfrede, Ducos, La Source, Dupré, and André de Chénier were victims of the guillotine, and Roland and Pétion committed suicide to escape it. And no Englishman, except Thomas Paine, ran as great a risk of the guillotine as she. Helen Maria Williams was certainly in the center of the wild currents of revolutionary thought and events. Had her table talk been preserved, it would have been a fascinating record from the human point of view and at the same time an invaluable mine of material for the history of literary and political opinion.

That Miss Williams was a political romanticist is obvious enough. Truly for her France "took at once the attraction of a country in romance," as Wordsworth was later to put it. "I sometimes think," she exclaimed in 1792, "that the age of chivalry, instead of being passed forever, is just returned; not indeed in its erroneous notions of loyalty, honor, and gallantry, which are as little 'à l'ordre du jour' as its dwarfs, giants, and imprisoned damsels; but in its noble contempt of sordid cares, its spirit of unsullied generosity, and heroic zeal for the happiness of others."[9] In disposition she seems to have had as much in common with the French as with the English character. She liked the French "mixture of enthusiasm and nonchalance" and was always commending them for their easy mastery of the art of happiness.

But whatever French gayety she might have assimilated was com-

[9] *ibid.*, first series, Vol. II, p. 5. In this series I have used the fifth edition of Vol. I and the second edition of Vols. II, III, and IV.

pounded with a generous infusion of sentimentalism, derived mainly
from Rousseau and Ossian. She was always nursing "that gentle and
tender melancholy which it is luxury to indulge" and many were the
times that she or her tragic characters were "bathed in floods of tears."
The youthful Wordsworth is supposed by some of his editors to have
been moved by such an exhibition of her feelings to compose a sonnet
entitled *On Seeing Miss Helen Maria Williams Weep at a Tale of
Distress.*[10] She wandered pensively about the haunts of Rousseau at
Vevey, and one thing that attracted her to Bonaparte was his "sympathy for the elevated sentiments and pathetic sublimity of Ossian."[11]
In fact, she may even be called a political sentimentalist. With her it
was not so much a matter of intellectual conviction as of emotional
contagion. "My political creed," she wrote in the summer of 1790, "is
entirely an affair of the heart."[12] And she followed the instincts of her
heart unerringly:

When a proposition is addressed to my heart, I have some quickness of
perception. I can then decide in one moment points upon which philosophers
and legislators have differed in all ages.[13]

She probably wore her heart on her sleeve too much; and so she has
frequently been charged with "affectation of sentiment and sensibility." Mary Wollstonecraft spoke of her as affected but goodhearted.[14]
Her melancholy, however, had its roots too deep in tragic experience to
be always merely sentimental.

Of course seeing life about her steadily and seeing it whole was almost
precluded by her disposition, and was made impossible by her experi-

[10] See George McLean Harper, *op. cit.,* Vol. I, pp. 148-9.

[11] *A Tour of Switzerland,* Vol. II, p. 57. But she wrote later: "I did not then know that
Bonaparte valued Ossian for his descriptions of battles, like the surgeon who praised Homer
only for his skill in anatomy." (*Sketches . . . of Manners and Opinions,* Vol. I, p. 6.)
Esmenard once gave her a humorous account of how being forced to carry out a commission to revise certain offensive passages against tyranny in the tragic poets, he was several
times closeted with Napoleon while committing this species of literary murder.

[12] *Letters from France,* first series, Vol. I, p. 66.

[13] *ibid.,* Vol. I, p. 196.

[14] "Her manners are affected, yet the simple goodness of her heart continually breaks
through the varnish, so that one would be more inclined to love than admire her. Author-
ship is a heavy weight for female shoulders, especially in the sunshine of prosperity."
(Letter from Paris, December 24, 1792, to Everina Wollstonecraft, C. Kegan Paul, *William
Godwin, His Friends and Contemporaries,* London, 1876, Vol. I, pp. 208-9.)

ences, which, as she writes, "with all the detail of domestic sorrow, with the feelings of private sympathy, with the tears of mourning friendship . . . rise in sad succession like the ghosts of Banquo's line and pass along my shuddering recollection."[15] We may as well, then, not labor the point of her reliability as a historian. J. K. Laughton wrote that her impressions were "frequently formed on very imperfect, one-sided, and garbled information, travestied by the enthusiasm of a clever, badly educated woman and uttered with the cocksureness of ignorance."[16] It is vain to claim that she was impartial. She was not. She once referred with contempt to "the faction of the impartial." A passionate interest in what is considered a struggle between good and evil hardly admits of rigorous exactness. Moreover, as Funck-Brentano remarks, she was "une femme et une femme passionnée."[17] But Laughton's charge of ignorance is too broadly drawn. She herself witnessed many of the scenes which she has described and knew personally most of the principal actors. It is true that, not being satisfied with merely describing what she saw, she allowed herself often—and sometimes tediously—to be drawn into moral dissertations on matters which were beyond her immediate knowledge. She laid no claim to philosophical depth, but she was undoubtedly a woman of cultivated tastes. Her historical unreliability, however, does not reflect upon her integrity; it is inherent in the very changeableness of the times and in the immediacy of the events about which she wrote. She wrote with honesty, though her "facts" came from interested parties. She was of course too near events to look at them with any perspective. After all, her books on the revolutionary period are probably as correct as any contemporary record by an actor in his own story can be.

Her sentimentalism was deeply rooted in a religious nature, and her sceptical political philosophy was blended with a comparatively positive theology. Her inherent piety revolted against both the spiritual irresponsibility and the scepticism of the French philosophers. She disapproved of "the ribaldry and licentiousness" of Voltaire, Rousseau, and

[15] *Letters from France,* second series, Vol. I, p. 7.
[16] Sketch in the *Dictionary of National Biography.*
[17] *Hélène Maria Williams,* p. 32.

Diderot in their attacks on "inherent prejudices," and she pointed out to her English readers the more respectable manners of Milton, Locke, and Sidney in overthrowing political and ecclesiastical despotism. What recommended Louis XVI to her perhaps more than anything else was the fact that "amid the seduction of philosophical scepticism on the one hand and the licentiousness of a dissolute court on the other, he appears to have retained a deep sense of the importance of religion and was in his own person an example of unaffected piety."[18] Napoleon's indifference to religion was, on the other hand, an article in her final condemnation of him. She found a narrowness in free-thinking as well as in priest-ridden religion. While she accepted Brissot's nobility of purpose and his radical political ideas without question, she considered "his sceptical errors in religion" typical of the French men of letters, "whose ignorance in matters of religion is only equalled by their arrogance in rejecting what they have not examined."[19]

Her attack upon the ecclesiastical system was from the Protestant rather than from the philosophical point of view. She had a horror for what she often referred to as "the spirit of the priesthood,"[20] though she paid her homage to the devout. In Christianity she found support for a modified equalitarianism:

Christianity . . . promotes that spirit of equality which suffers us to call no man master; not that leveling system, which under pretense of destroying distinctions degrades genius and debases virtue.[21]

Her Protestantism was inherited from ancestors who had fought under the flag of the Covenant. But she was a Calvinist in politics only. She renounced the Genevese democracy for shutting the doors against Catholics and wondered that Calvin "should have riveted the chains of religious despotism, while he became by his political institutions the father of civil liberty in Europe."[22] She herself reared two nephews in

18 *Political and Confidential Correspondence of Louis XVI*, Vol. II, p. 40.

19 *Letters from France*, second series, Vol. III, p. 62. See also *ibid.*, first series, Vol. IV, p. 32; second series, Vol. I, p. 47; Vol. II, pp. 88, 107; *Sketches . . . of Manners and Opinions*, Vol. II, p. 202.

20 For her fanatical hostility to monasticism, see *Sketches . . . of Manners and Opinions*, Vol. I, p. 43, and *A Tour of Switzerland*, Vol. I, p. 22.

21 *Sketches . . . of Manners and Opinions*, Vol. II, p. 122.

22 *A Tour in Switzerland*, Vol. II, p. 175.

the freer Protestant tradition.[23] She frequently attended the spacious Protestant church of Monsieur Marron in Paris "with a mind touched and elevated by devotion" and rejoiced in the exercise under full toleration of the rite of the sacrament. Her connection with free-thinkers was habitual; yet she was in friendship with persons who, without renouncing philosophy, believed religion to be a better moral guide and who found in it a solid basis of future hope. Her reason helpless, she attained hope through that "almost intuitive sentiment by which the feelings of the heart overpower the sophistries of the head."[24]

We turn from generalizations to pertinent facts of Miss Williams's career and a more specific review of those of her writings which are relevant to our purpose.

As a whole, her early efforts at verse[25] are now mainly of interest because they show that her poetic bark, though frail, is launched upon the gradually swelling stream of romanticism. *To Sensibility* is dedicated to the benignant power the spirit of which she was never to violate:

> No cold exemption from her pains
> I ever wished to know;
> Cheered with her transport, I sustain
> Without complaint her woe.

Perhaps Bowles should share with Miss Williams some of the credit for the revival of the sonnet. Before the publication of his *Fourteen Sonnets* in 1789, she had employed both the Shakespearean and the Italian forms. Two of the five sonnets of the collected volumes of 1786 are tributes to Burns and Chatterton. Wordsworth commended the *Sonnet*

---

[23] In 1798, her sister, Cecilia, wife of Athanase Coquerel, died, leaving two small sons, Athanase Laurent Charles and Charles Augustin. She became a second mother to the children and reared them in the traditions of the Protestant religion and the liberal ideas which she had espoused. Both became prominent French Protestant leaders. Athanase Coquerel *fils*, well known for his liberal views and his eloquence, published numerous works in Protestant theology and in 1848 became a member of the Assembly. C. A. Coquerel won an important place as the historian of French Protestantism. He wrote an appreciation of his aunt as the introduction to the *Souvenirs de la Révolution française*.

[24] *Sketches . . . of Manners and Opinions*, Vol. II, p. 213. See also in this connection her account of her visit to Lavater, German poet and mystic, *A Tour of Switzerland*, Vol. I, p. 72.

[25] *Edwin and Eltruda* (1782), *An Ode on the Peace* (1783), *Peru* (1784), *Poems*, 2 vols. (1786).

to Twilight and the *Sonnet to the Moon*.[26] In the latter especially and in the *Sonnet to Hope* she achieves concentration, dignity, and grace of utterance. *An Epistle to Dr. Moore* is done with a happiness of expression that suggests the intimacy and the sincerity of her attachment to one who had ministered to both her physical and her intellectual health. Dr. John Moore's travels, which she here recalls her delight in reading, probably had much to do in the arousing of her interest in Europe. The earliest outright expression of her revolutionary sympathies is *The Bastille, A Vision,* a rather turgid poetic interlude in the novel *Julia* (1790), where also first appeared *Sonnet to the Moon*. But her passion for liberty had already found vent in 1788 in the poem, *The Slave Trade.* In a letter to her of August 1789 Burns, who often expressed his pleasure in her work, praised the poem very highly and criticized it in detail. He compared the portion describing a tempest to Thomson's *Winter* and declared that "the most beautiful passage in the poem . . . would do honor to the greatest names that ever graced our profession."[27] But the modern reader will conclude that she might have better attained in prose the heights of indignant feeling which she failed to scale in her poetry. We must look to the prose of the years of her residence in France for the full flavor of her revolutionary writing.

Even before going to Paris the Williamses (Helen Maria resided with her mother and her sisters, Cecilia and Persis) were known for their literary entertainments in London. "They used to give very agreeable evening parties," wrote the ubiquitous Samuel Rogers, "at which I have met many of the Scotch literati, Lord Monboddo, etc."[28] Dr.

---

[26] See letter of May 10, 1830, to Alexander Dyce, *Letters of the Wordsworth Family,* edited by William Knight, Boston, 1907, Vol. II, p. 428. But whatever knowledge Wordsworth had of her work was not reciprocated until rather late. It is surprising to learn that, when in 1814 Crabb Robinson repeated some of Wordsworth's sonnets to her, she did not remember having heard of the poet before. See George McLean Harper, *op. cit.,* Vol. I, p. 149.

[27] *Letters of Robert Burns,* edited by J. De Lancey Ferguson, Oxford, 1931, Vol. I, p. 355. See also *ibid.,* Vol. I, pp. 76-7, 116.

[28] *Recollections of the Table Talk of Samuel Rogers,* edited by Alexander Dyce, New York, 1856, p. 50. A full reproduction of an evening's talk at her house April 21, 1791, was left by Rogers in his diary. On this particular occasion Henry Mackenzie, Joanna Baillie, Jerningham, Merry, Dr. John Moore, and Dr. Kippis were among her guests. See P. W. Clayden, *Early Life of Samuel Rogers,* London, 1887, pp. 145-52.

Andrew Kippis, the non-conformist divine, who was Miss Williams's early literary sponsor and who often took the youthful Rogers with him to literary parties, had introduced him into her home in 1787, and Rogers became very intimate with her. During 1789 Godwin, according to Kegan Paul, was "a very constant visitor at the house of Miss Helen Maria Williams, where many literary people congregated almost every night at tea-time."[29]

There is, however, in Miss Williams's writings no mention of either Godwin or his wife by name. While she undoubtedly accepted most of the conclusions of Godwin's political philosophy, especially his faith in the progress of reason toward political justice, his abstractions were not romantic enough to appeal to her. She seems to have accepted in practice her friend Mary Wollstonecraft's ideas about the rights of women, but she rarely argued about them. She entered a brief against the refusal of educational opportunities to women:

> She has no professor but her music-master, no academy but that of dancing. . . . She who exerts over man an empire which, being founded in nature, is as immutable as her laws and beyond the reach of his imperious institutions, is treated as a being merely passive in the important interests of the state.[30]

She thought that the French republic had been just as remiss in awarding women their political as in awarding them their educational rights.

Miss Williams's one ambitious attempt at fiction was *Julia,* a novel in two volumes published in 1790. *Julia* belongs to the school of sensibility with which her friend Charlotte Smith and other pre-romantic novelists were associated at the time.[31] Though in one place[32] she satirizes the

---

[29] *William Godwin,* London, 1876, Vol. I, p. 63. An entry in Godwin's diary for November 17, 1789, reads: "Tea with Holcroft at Miss Williams'." (*ibid.,* Vol. I, p. 64.)

[30] *Sketches . . . of Manners and Opinions,* Vol. II, p. 54.

[31] See James R. Foster, "Charlotte Smith, Pre-Romantic Novelist," *Publications of the Modern Language Association of America,* Vol. XLIII, pp. 463-76. Like Mrs. Smith's landscapes, Miss Williams's are poetic; but, unlike hers, they are not exotic. They are done in water colors. But most of them are not organically parts of the scene; they are used for figurative purposes only. Some of her similes are exquisite. She often knits up the action or the impression into a long simile at the end which leaves a flashing wake in the path of the narrative. *Julia* has nothing of the paraphernalia of terror which most novels of sensibility had.

[32] Vol. II, p. 48.

addiction of the public to novels of sensibility, its pangs afflict her on many a page. There is little or no hint of the revolutionary ferment in it. The emptiness of fashionable life is shown, but there is no protest against the economic *status quo*. She preaches no economic or social gospel. And yet she has been called a "political novelist."[33] The only possible hint of her association with Godwin the year before its publication is the insistence upon passion's being reined by reason;[34] but reason with Miss Williams is a merely prudential concept rather than a broadly philosophical one.

It was not long before her destiny was shaped for France. In 1785 when she was seeking a French tutor for a young lady, a French woman was recommended to her. This lady, who lived under her maiden name, Mlle. Monique Coquerel, was the young wife of a Norman gentleman, son of a Baron du Fossé, but she herself was of humble parentage. The son had married against the wish of his despotic father, who had him confined for two years at Rouen through a *lettre de cachet*. Meantime the young wife with a child had taken refuge in England. Miss Williams at once became intensely interested in her fate as a victim of social tyranny and frequently befriended her. Undoubtedly much of her initial love for the French Revolution was excited by this instance of parental despotism under the sanction of law. After the Baron du Fossé had died in 1787 and after the son had finally succeeded with many difficulties to his chateau and his title in 1789, he invited Miss Williams and her sister Cecilia to come to France, as Funck-Brentano writes, "pour y contempler de près l'aurore de la liberté." Naturally young Monsieur du Fossé (he renounced his title) was an enthusiastic supporter of the Revolution.

In the sketch of Miss Williams's life in the *Dictionary of National Biography* there is a confusion in both the date and the purpose of this first visit to France. "In 1788," we read there, "she went over to France on a visit to her elder sister, Cecilia, who married Athanase Coquerel, a

[33] S. A. Allibone, *Critical Dictionary of English Literature.*
[34] See Vol. I, pp. iii, **178.**

Protestant minister."[35] The date of her arrival in Paris, as she tells us in the first sentence of her *Letters written in France in the Summer of 1790,* was July 13, 1790, the day before the first anniversary of the fall of the Bastille. Moreover, her sister, Cecilia, accompanied her and was not married until after the release of the Williamses from imprisonment in 1793.[36]

Her first visit to France lasted from July to early September 1790. She seems to have lost no time in giving an account of it to her countrymen; for late in 1790 was issued the book above named, the first of those numerous volumes which, with those of her friend, Dr. John Moore,[37] are the most complete first-hand record by Englishmen of revolutionary France. These volumes make up the great bulk of her writings. In them all the author uses the epistolary form. It gives her an opportunity to vary her style in slipping freely from the grave to the gay; from the argumentative, the pathetic, or the sublime to the colloquial. And her content varies as well as her style: detached memoranda, occasional reflections, anecdotes, and luxuriant descriptions are all thrown together. She is often flighty; so embarrassed is she by the multitude of things to be put down that she sometimes cannot follow an exposition through.

Her style lacks simplicity and would be more elegant, if it were less ornamental. She revels in poetic periods. Crowded figures of speech, emotional ecstasies, and barbarous diction often rob her style of the gravity and decorum which the subject demands. In particular, she often shows an exasperating contempt of anglicism. Such words as "epocha," "phasis," "meridional," "centrical," and "epuration" are without excuse. Her use of un-English idioms leads one reviewer to observe that she has almost forgotten her own language. This handicap, which she never overcame, sometimes puts the English reader almost out of

---

[35] The error is probably traceable to the obituary notice in the *Gentleman's Magazine,* Vol. XCVIII, i, p. 373.

[36] See *Letters from France,* second series, Vol. I, p. 212. O. F. Emerson, though correcting the date of the arrival, has left the date of the marriage confused. Moreover, she had not "gone *to reside* in Paris in 1790." (Italics mine.) See his "Notes on Gilbert Imlay," *PMLA,* Vol. XXXIX, p. 420 (June 1924).

[37] *A Journal during a Residence in France from the beginning of August to the middle of December 1792,* 2 vols. (1793-1794); *A View of the Causes and Progress of the French Revolution,* 2 vols. (1795).

sympathy with her enthusiasm and generous sentiment. In general, as Saintsbury has remarked, her prose is "formal but not ungraceful, neither Johnsonian nor in any way slipshod."[38]

Miss Williams immediately immersed herself in the political swirl of Paris. Her first three letters give a rapturous account of the Festival of the Federation on July 14:

> It was the triumph of human kind; it was man asserting the noblest privilege of his nature; and it required but the common feelings of humanity to become in that moment a citizen of the world.[39]

Like most Frenchmen at the time, she believed that the violent part of the Revolution had ended with the taking of the Bastille. She assiduously attended the sessions of the Constituent Assembly and conceived a tremendous enthusiasm for Mirabeau, particularly because he proposed to the Assembly the abolition of the slave trade. She was invited by Pétion, the mayor of Paris, to dine with him at the Hôtel de Ville. Writes Funck-Brentano of this occasion:

> Si grand était l'enthousiasme pour les réformes nouvelles que, à en croire Miss Williams, dans les salons du maire de Paris, les femmes ne cherchaient plus à plaire, ni les hommes à les aimer.[40]

The palace at Versailles she could not much enjoy for fancying she saw "in the background of that magnificent abode of a despot the gloomy dungeons of the Bastille."[41]

With a letter of introduction from Edward Jerningham, Miss Williams called upon Madame de Genlis at St. Leu, where she resided with the family of the Duke of Orleans, superintending the education of his children. This great admirer of the Revolution and pioneer of modern French education, entertained her with arguments against hereditary rank and in favor of democratic manners. These her guest considered well exemplified in the conduct of her educational charge, the young Prince of Chartres, later Louis Philippe, who rejoiced the young Englishwoman by his ready acquiescence in the abolition of primogeniture.

[38] *History of English Literature in the Nineteenth Century*, London, 1896, p. 30.
[39] *Letters from France*, first series, Vol. I, p. 14.
[40] *op. cit.*, p. 15.
[41] *Letters from France*, first series, Vol. I, p. 83.

During the summer she visited Rouen and was fascinated by its antiquities, but she did not go to Caen, the burial place of William the Conqueror, since she would not "travel twelve leagues to see the tomb of a tyrant."[42] From Rouen she went to the chateau of Monsieur du Fossé in Normandy. Here on August 28 she took part in a dramatic piece, *La Féderation, ou La Famille Patriotique*.

In the last scene, I, being the representative of Liberty, appeared . . . guarding the consecrated banners of the nation, which were placed on an altar on which was inscribed in transparent letters: "A la Liberté, 14 Juillet, 1789."[43]

Upon her return to England the political self-complacency of her countrymen made her chafe with impatience, though the first volume of her *Letters* had been very well received.[44] Besides, she was amazed and pained by the persistent reports of French atrocities and by hearing "the charming societies in which I found all the elegant graces of the most polished manners, all the amiable urbanity of liberal and cultivated minds" spoken of as "the most rude, ferocious, and barbarous levellers that ever existed."[45] This was about the time that Burke's *Reflections* had begun to leaven English opinion. She thought that the French aristocrats who had taken refuge in England were mainly responsible for the lack of English sympathy.

Her movements during the next two years have been followed very vaguely by those who have written about them. Funck-Brentano writes:

Pendant cette année 1791, elle fit encore paraître en Angleterre un volume de vers, puis détermina sa mère à revenir avec ses deux sœurs en France, où elle arriva peu de temps avant les événements du 10 août 1792.[46]

He leaves her second visit to France, which is the subject of the second volume of the *Letters*, out of account entirely. Her failure to date her letters makes the chronology rather difficult. The first letter of this volume was written at the chateau of Monsieur du Fossé. Fortunately a letter of July 31, 1791, written by her friend, Mrs. Barbauld, to Samuel

---

[42] *ibid.*, Vol. I, p. 121.
[43] *ibid.*, Vol. I, p. 204.
[44] See *Monthly Review*, Vol. IX, pp. 93-8; *Analytical Review*, Vol. VII, pp. 431-5; *European Magazine*, Vol. XVIII, p. 472.
[45] *Letters from France*, first series, Vol. I, p. 219.
[46] *op. cit.*, p. 16.

Rogers, sets the approximate date of their second departure from England:

> Perhaps you know that Mrs. Williams and Cecilia are set out for France, and that Helen and the rest of the family are soon to follow. They pay a visit to their old friends [the family of Monsieur du Fossé] at Rouen before they settle at Orleans.[47]

Miss Williams was in Rouen, she writes, "the day before the King accepted the Constitution."[48] This undoubtedly refers to the renewal of the King's oath September 14, 1791. Soon afterwards she is writing from Orleans. Inspired by scenes of plenty and happiness about Orleans, she sends a rhyming letter to her friend, Dr. Moore, in which her French patriotism is loosed in a flood against those who

> . . . hope their eloquence with taper ray
> Can dim the blaze of philosophic day;
> Those reasoners who pretend that each abuse,
> Sanctioned by precedent, has some blest use.[49]

She is exasperated by the haughtiness and insolence of the aristocrats of the city, though she notes with pleasure that manners were becoming disburdened of contempt for commerce and of the "obsequious politeness" which the aristocrats had bred in the lower classes.

She left Orleans in December and passed the winter in Paris, doing the theaters with a truly Parisian taste for amusement, seeing the palaces about the city, attending the Legislative Assembly (which she thought inferior in talent to the Constituent Assembly), and visiting the Jacobin Club. She seems not yet to have sensed the extremes towards which some of the members of this famous revolutionary society were tending. Its main enemy then was the aristocratic faction. With the majority of French patriots at the time, she was "convinced that those watchful, vigilant, noisy Jacobins are the best guardians of French liberty."[50] She exulted with them when the names of Milton, Locke, and Hampden rang through their hall.

[47] P. W. Clayden, *Early Life of Samuel Rogers*, p. 179.
[48] *Letters from France*, first series, Vol. II, p. 2.
[49] *ibid.*, Vol. II, p. 12.
[50] *ibid.*, Vol. II, p. 110.

Apparently it was at some time during this winter or spring that Miss Williams met Madame Roland through the Girondist Lanthenas. A group of spokesmen of the lower orders, including Robespierre, Brissot, Pétion, Buzot, and Vergniaud, all of whom were members of the Jacobin Club, were in the habit of meeting at the Roland's hotel four times a week between February and the early autumn of 1791. According to one writer, "probably one of her [Madame Roland's] guests at that time may have been Helen Maria Williams."[51] But this is impossible as Miss Williams did not arrive in Paris until December 1791 and evidently did not become well acquainted with her until afterwards.[52] "Mme. Roland et Miss Williams allaient ensemble applaudir au club des Jacobins Brissot et Vergniaud,"[53] writes Funck-Brentano. This was probably in the days before the appointment of the Girondist ministry on March 23, 1792; for the breach began to widen rapidly between the moderates and Robespierre's faction soon afterwards. It was then, too, probably that Miss Williams became a frequenter of Madame Roland's evening salons, which were revived after the appointment of her husband to the ministry.

As a picture of French society and politics during this second visit, which ended April 20, 1792, the second volume of the *Letters from France* is quite superficial. As the *Analytical Review* put it,

Miss Williams does not venture into the depths of politics; but, sipping at the brink of the stream, she skims lightly over the subject, catching as she flies some of the shades of manners which the varying atmosphere presents.[54]

Miss Williams was too restless with the desire of witnessing further triumphs of the Revolution to be longer satisfied in England. Upon her insistence, her mother and her two sisters accompanied her back to France, arriving just before the "suspension" of the King, August 10. They took up their residence in a hotel in the Rue de Lille. From this

[51] Winifred Stephens, *Women of the French Revolution*, New York, 1922, p. 114.
[52] Miss Williams herself writes indefinitely: "I had been acquainted with her since I first came to France." (*Letters from France*, second series, Vol. I, p. 204.) But this seems doubtful, since the Rolands were not residents of Paris at the time of her visit in 1790.
[53] *op. cit.*, p. 16.
[54] Vol. XIII, p. 386.

point, on August 10, she witnessed the attack on the Tuilleries and suc-
coured a wounded Swiss, who died on her premises. The next day,
while passing through the garden of the Tuilleries, she noticed two men,
apparently sleeping on the grass, whom, to her consternation, she found
to be dead. The account of this experience passed with gross exaggera-
tion into England, and Boswell in his second edition of the *Life of
Johnson* struck the word "amiable" out of his previous description of
her because he had been repelled by the reported hardness of her
nature.[55] But she stood proof against the insistence of her friends in
England that she get out of France. Ann Seward wrote to her "dear
Helen" to "fly that land of carnage" and was aghast that she should
call "the fire which led the French into chaos the rising sun of Liberty."[56]
Thus the current of abuse and misrepresentation was soon set against
her in England, and it had not subsided several decades afterwards.

After the massacres of September, the Williamses took an apartment
in the Rue Helvétius[57] and here she settled down never, so far as is
known, to return to England. Here, as has been said, was started at this
time her famous salon, at which she was hostess every Sunday evening
to the principal Girondists. She soon became well known, too, among
the English in Paris. At the famous banquet of Englishmen in White's
Hotel, Paris, on November 18, given to celebrate the French victories,
a toast was drunk "To the Women of Great Britain, particularly those
who have distinguished themselves by their writings in favor of the
French Revolution, Mrs. Charlotte Smith and Miss H. M. Williams."[58]

[55] "I was sorry to be obliged to strike it out; but I could not in justice suffer it to
remain, after this young lady had not only written in favour of the savage Anarchy with
which France has been visited, but had (as I have been informed by good authority)
walked without horror over the ground at the Tuilleries, when it was strewed with the
naked bodies of the faithful Swiss Guards, who were barbarously massacred for having
bravely defended, against a crew of ruffians, the Monarch whom they had taken an oath
to defend. From Dr. Johnson she could now expect not endearment but repulsion." (*Life
of Johnson*, Oxford edition, Vol. II, p. 542 n.) In their meeting in 1784 she had won the
old man's heart. See *ibid.*, Vol. II, pp. 542-3.

[56] *Letters of Anna Seward*, London, 1811, Vol. III, p. 205.

[57] Ten years later she moved to the Quai Malaquai. See letter of July 4, 1802, from
Joel Barlow to Mrs. Barlow in the *Barlow Papers*.

[58] J. G. Alger, *Paris in 1789-1794*, New York, 1892, p. 326.

The third and fourth volumes of the *Letters from France* were written during the first four months after the execution of the King in January 1793. Of the third volume, however, only the first letter is her own. Six of them are by her friend, John Hurford Stone, and deal with the campaign of 1792. The final letter is by Thomas Christie, Scotch revolutionary enthusiast. The fourth volume contains little of a personal nature and is concerned largely with the defection of Dumouriez and erroneous opinions of the Revolution in England. To the last topic we shall return in another connection. Her portion of the third volume is a spirited indictment of the Paris Commune, who were responsible for the September massacres, as a set of demagogues who "have committed more crimes than despotism would have achieved in ages" and whose errors, she fears, will lead surrounding nations to "sink back into the torpor of slavery." From the beginning, her firm republicanism did not allow her to countenance the excesses of the Jacobins, whose club, now deserted by the republicans, was filled with intriguers. She laments that "great characters who began the Revolution, . . . Brissot, Condorcet, Sièyes, and Buzot," are being reduced to silence or obscurity, while, as the spirit of faction grows, "all arts are absorbed in the single one of speaking or declaiming." And she flays the faction of the Mountain, headed by Robespierre, Danton, and Marat, as the subverters of the Revolution who "endeavor to lead the people to the last degree of moral degradation by teaching that the love of order is the love of despotism, and that the most unequivocal proof of patriotism is to remain in permanent insurrection."

She discusses the trial and execution of Louis XVI in a very judicial frame of mind. History will condemn the King, she thinks; but it will also condemn his judges, who deprived him, not only of his inviolability as King, but of his rights as a citizen. "Perhaps the irrevocable decree of posterity will reverse that of the National Convention."[59] Yet she has respect for those Girondists who, without fear and in bitterness of heart, did what they considered their cruel duty in voting for his death.[60]

[59] *Letters from France*, first series, Vol. IV, p. 10.

[60] Among the Girondists who came at this time to accept Miss Williams's hospitality and to be charmed by her vivacious manners, one young deputy, Bancal des Issarts, fell

Miss Williams's next publication was the account of her experiences during the Terror, issued in three volumes in 1795, which were the next year supplemented by a fourth volume bringing the account down to the establishment of the Directory in the fall of 1795.[61] These volumes, forming the second series of the *Letters from France,* are replete with revealing details of her personal history and show her to have been something more than a mere observer of this tragic period.

Between May 31 and June 2, 1793, the Convention was invested by the Paris Commune and the Jacobins, and Miss Williams from her window overlooking the Tuilleries witnessed in part the accomplishment of the conspiracy of Robespierre. Upon the arrest of their friends, the Girondist deputies, on June 2, the Williamses "became a subject of discussion at the Committee of Public Safety."[62] The next day the notorious Barère came to her house hypocritically deploring the fate of the arrested deputies and execrating the faction of Robespierre whose lacquey he was immediately to become as one of the chiefs of the Committee of Public Safety and "the great inquisitor of the English in Paris." He later called upon the army "to make no English prisoners . . . and to let no one return to the land of Great Britain nor one remain on the free soil of France."[63] Miss Williams had plenty of reason for suspecting Barère of having betrayed the conversations of her drawing room. Knowing too, as he did, that she was the author of letters published in England attacking Robespierre, he had her life in his power. Besides, Barère had been personally offended by her refusal to receive some deputies of the Mountain whom he had wished to introduce. But nothing came at once of these bad omens.

Meanwhile she was faithful to her friends in adversity. General Miranda, while under the displeasure of the government for his alleged connection with the treachery of Dumouriez, enjoyed her hospitality.

deeply in love with her. In the prosecution of his suit he was encouraged by Madame Roland, but Miss Williams did not fully reciprocate his feelings. One happy result of the attachment, however, was that she persuaded him to vote against the death of the King. See *Lettres de Mme. Roland,* edited by C. Perroud, Vol. II, pp. 466-9.

61 The bibliography of her political writings in the *Dictionary of National Biography* is incomplete at this point. Neither the third nor the fourth volume is listed.

62 *Letters from France,* second series, Vol. I, p. 187.

63 *ibid.,* Vol. III, p. 149.

While the Convention on May 31 was drafting the decree of accusation against the famous Commission of Twelve appointed to investigate the conspiracies, Rabaut Saint-Étienne, its president, escaped from the hall and took refuge in Miss Williams's house until midnight. He later sought safety from arrest at the house of a M. and Mme. Payzac, both of whom were eventually guillotined with him for sheltering him. She twice visited Madame Roland in prison. Amid the horrors of Saint-Pélagie she found her indulging her life-long passion for Plutarch and prepared to meet death with an exalted firmness. After Madame Roland was removed to the Conciergerie she sent to Miss Williams manuscripts, which, along with some of Madame de Genlis and her own, Miss Williams was compelled to destroy when she was later threatened with a domiciliary visit. "Had they been found in my possession," she wrote, "they would inevitably have involved me in her fate."[64] While the Girondists were under arrest in their own houses, she visited Fonfrede, Vergniaud, and Ducos in their hotel. The day before his unexpected proscription Fonfrede had accompanied her to Montmorenci, where they wandered together in the midst of the enchanting scenery described by Rousseau.

On October 11, while she was entertaining Bernardin de Saint-Pierre at tea and he was in the midst of a description of a projected idyllic retreat, a friend rushed in to tell her that all the English not resident in France before 1789 were to be arrested by the Convention as hostages for Toulon. At 2 a.m. the family were hurried out of bed to the guardhouse by commissaries and their property was seized by the nation. The next evening, after a day spent in the committee room, they were sent to the Luxembourg.[65] Here the keeper, Benoit, was very kind to them, but the visits of the vulgar Henriot, commandant of the military guard of Paris, were frightful experiences. The two apartments adjoining theirs were occupied by their friends, Sillery and La Source, who had long been in close confinement and who were soon to be dragged to

[64] *ibid.*, Vol. I, p. 207.
[65] The Temple has been mistakenly given as the place of her confinement. See *Gentleman's Magazine*, Vol. XCVIII, i, p. 373; S. A. Allibone, *Critical Dictionary of English Literature*; and Thomas Sadler (editor), *Diary, Reminiscences, and Correspondence of Henry Crabb Robinson*, London, 1872, Vol. I, p. 367 n.

the scaffold. La Source actually eluded the guard to visit the Williamses in their room and upon a second visit was accompanied by Sillery. They all found comfort together in religious devotions and every night the deputies sang in Miss Williams's hearing a dirge which they had composed together. Upon their final parting each gave her a lock of his hair. Because of a scandal the sexes were separated on October 26, forty women being sent to the English Conceptionist Convent. Here they were allowed to exercise in the garden and to talk to their friends.

The Williamses regained their liberty during the last days of November[66] largely through the application of Athanase Coquerel, the nephew of their friend, Madame du Fossé, who was affianced at the time to Cecilia and who did not delay in marrying her after her release. He was aided in his efforts at obtaining their freedom by the poet Dorat-Cubières and Jean de Bry,[67] later a leader in reconstruction after the Terror.

As the Terror continued on its bloody way she does not seem to have sought retirement. On April 5, 1794, she saw Danton, Desmoulins, and thirteen other victims on their way to execution. But on April 16 Robespierre caused a law to be passed ordering all nobility and strangers to leave Paris in ten days under penalty of the law. The Williamses retired to a retreat one half mile from Marly near Versailles, passing on their way the Square of the Revolution, where they saw the guillotine surrounded by a crowd awaiting the execution of a company of victims just entering the place. It was not long, however, before "two benevolent commissaries" of the revolutionary committee

[66] P. W. Clayden incorrectly states that she was "liberated after the fall of Robespierre." Furthermore, he has exaggerated her danger in the statement that "but for an oversight she would have been carried to the guillotine," as has also J. R. MacGillivray in the assertion that she "barely escaped the final rites of the guillotine." (*Early Life of Samuel Rogers*, pp. 68-9; *Wordsworth and His Revolutionary Acquaintances, 1791-1797*, p. 23.) J. De Lancey Ferguson, too, is mistaken in writing that she "was imprisoned from the fall of the Gironde until the fall of Robespierre." (Appendix to *Life and Letters of Robert Burns*, Vol. II, p. 375.)

[67] Her friend, Marie-Joseph Chénier, who had been asked by these men, to help in the liberation of the English, excused himself. "He was always obsessed," writes Miss Williams, "by the idea of the guillotine." The fate of his brother later showed that he was not unwise.

of their section obtained permission for them to return to Paris with a status which was supposed to exclude them from suspicion and proscription. But in June, haunted more than ever by fear of further persecution for her writings against the Jacobins, she fled to Switzerland with her friend John Hurford Stone[68] and took up her residence at Basel.

She seems from the extent of her travels and from the statement that during the winter of 1794 they passed through Franche-Comté on their way to Paris, to have spent about six months in Switzerland. Her observations there were published under the title, *A Tour in Switzerland,* in two volumes in 1798. The book is a hodge-podge of natural description, history, political discussion, and social reflections. She did not have a high opinion of Swiss liberty before the French Revolution had affected the country, as "the original freedom of most of their institutions had degenerated into coteries of family domination and personal interest."[69] And she defended the revolution in Switzerland, asserting that the French had destroyed only the liberty of the sovereign magistrates of the cantons not that of the people. But she did not uphold in general the principle of interference with the independence of a foreign country.

Even through the Terror she remained as staunch a friend as ever to the original principles of the Revolution. She thought that the carelessness of the Parisians as to whether Girondists or Jacobins ran the government, was responsible largely for the tyranny of Robespierre. But, in the end, she absolves the French people as a whole from responsibility for the crimes of the period:

[68] From this point on, Stone played a very important rôle in the life of Miss Williams, though she writes little directly about him. He had been arrested on October 10, 1793, and confined in the Luxembourg at the same time as Miss Williams. He was released after seventeen days, but was arrested again in April 1794 because of his Girondist sympathies and released on condition that he should leave France. Stone and Helen Maria Williams were made to understand each other. Both were generous in their feelings and ardent for liberty. Why they kept the exact nature of their relationship secret, it is hard to say. It has been thought that Bishop Grégoire secretly married them after Stone announced his divorce from Rachel Coope in June 1794.

[69] *Sketches . . . of Manners and Opinions,* Vol. I, p. 22.

I should be equally unjust to present the English as a barbarous nation because a Clive has starved the provinces of Asia or because upon the coasts of Africa the slave merchants traffic in human life.[70]

Upon returning to Paris "when Liberty, bleeding with a thousand wounds, revived once more," she took up her restless pen to write the second series of her *Letters*. In 1795 she brought out her translation of her friend Bernardin de Saint-Pierre's *Paul et Virginie,* a work which she had begun while in prison and the first of a series of translations.[71] In the spring of this year she attended with satisfaction the trial of the notorious Fouquier-Tinville, who was guillotined by the Directory for his part in the Terror. Her life under the Directory and the Consulate is told in a series of letters in two volumes written between 1799 and 1801 and entitled *Sketches of the State of Manners and Opinions in the French Republic towards the Close of the Eighteenth Century*. The theme is of a very rambling nature, part of the volumes dealing with the revolution in Switzerland. Like most Frenchmen, she eventually became disgusted with the inefficiency of the Directory, condemning its persecution of the Catholics, the subjection of the judges to the will and caprice of the people, and the failure to submit cases of property to juries. On the memorable 9th of November, 1799, when she happened to be riding in the Park of St. Cloud, she witnessed in the Orangery the transfer of power from the Directory to the Consulate. Since she saw the best possible could not be soon attained, she contented herself with the best practicable under the new government.

Meantime she tried her powers at short fiction in *Perourou, the Bellows-Mender* (1801). This tale, marred by false taste and sentiment though it is, shows the leaven of the Revolution in its satire of rank and its association of honor and poverty. It was destined to attain a great posthumous fame through Bulwer Lytton's adaptation of it for the stage as *The Lady of Lyons* in 1838.

[70] F. Funck-Brentano, *op. cit.,* p. 151.

[71] She translated eight volumes of Humboldt's travels and Xavier de Maistre's *Lépreux de la Cité d'Aoste*. The *Dictionary of National Biography* incorrectly refers to the latter as "one of the tales of J. de Maistre." In her turn she has been honored by the translation of twelve of her volumes on the revolutionary period into French. J. B. Say translated *A Tour in Switzerland,* and Boufflers and Esmenard, two members of the Academy, translated her poems.

In 1803 she embarked on an ill-starred editorial venture, *The Political and Confidential Correspondence of Louis the Sixteenth, with Observations on each Letter,* in three volumes. The manuscripts of these letters, which were later shown not to have been genuine, were naïvely bought from a bookseller. A special reason for setting her hand to this task was that the French editors of the King's correspondence had praised him in such a way as to detract from the Revolution. The work was met by a storm of abusive criticism from English reviewers.[72] But it was reserved for Bertrand de Moleville, a former minister of state under Louis XVI, to provide a climax for the chorus of disapproval with his *A Refutation of the Libel on the Memory of the late King* (translated by R. C. Dallas, 1804). He heaps scurrility and vulgar abuse on Miss Williams and attacks all her writings with a discourtesy and a demoniac frenzy that won him fewer unprejudiced readers in England than Miss Williams's book itself had won. It appears that she deserved blame only for her credulity. "On ne l'a jamais accusée," writes Breton de la Martinière, "d'avoir en cette publication, joué le rôle de mystificateur."[73] Only war hysteria against France, then threatening invasion of Ireland, can account for such a uniformly hostile reception of the work in England. For, after all, her judgment of the King and royal family accords well with the calm verdict of history.

Her feelings towards Napoleon were consistent with her earlier political sentiments. Of course a woman like her could not escape "that glow of admiration which the rare union of excellent qualities excites." At first he appeared to her a champion of liberty, and he played the rôle well in Italy. Even when he dissolved the Directory, her faith was not shaken. But in spite of her personal liking for him, republican as she was, she could not pardon his self-aggrandizement. She was even to suffer personally for a while his displeasure. An ode, written by her in the early summer of 1802 on the Peace of Amiens, had irritated him by its reference to the "subject waves" of England. She and her whole family were arrested by the police, and she was detained a prisoner for

[72] See *Monthly Review,* Vol. XLIII, pp. 225-35; *Critical Review,* second series, Vol. XXXIX, pp. 36-44; *Annual Review,* Vol. II, pp. 275-9; *Monthly Magazine,* Vol. XVI, p. 616; *Edinburgh Review,* Vol. III, p. 213.

[73] Quoted by F. Funck-Brentano, *op. cit.,* p. 27.

twenty-four hours. From the time that Napoleon made himself consul for life, all her illusion was dispelled. She was soon renewing her intimate relations with the republicans, especially Carnot and Esmenard.

As the course of French empire took its way eastward over Europe, crushing popular liberty as well as crowns, her thoughts withdrew from the political scene, "marked by every turpitude, crime, tyranny, and disgrace that could afflict a country,"[74] into the reserve of her own soul. In explanation of her literary inactivity between 1803 and 1815, she wrote: "The iron hand of despotism has weighed upon my soul and subdued all intellectual energy."[75] In the latter year there appeared *A Narrative of Events which have taken place in France from the Landing of Napoleon Bonaparte on the First of March 1815 till the Restoration of Louis XVIII*. Here for the first time the years seem to be stealing fire from her mind. She is beginning to look with an apologetic air upon her days of high hope for the Revolution when she was "not yet cured of enthusiasm." In this book she is more conscious of the calamities of the Revolution than of its victories. The return from Elba, according to her, was made possible by the remains of the Jacobin party and the military. "The military ravagers of other countries," she declared, "can never become the civic defenders of their own."[76]

The year after Waterloo she reopened her salon and resumed her Sunday afternoon teas. But her means were hardly sufficient to maintain such an establishment long. Her friend Stone, who had been a prosperous printer in Paris, had been ruined in business in 1813. Her last publication, issued in 1819, *Letters on Events which have passed in France since the Restoration in 1815*, was, it appears, hurriedly composed to bolster her income. Almost half the book is taken up by a recital of the persecution of the Protestants in southern France in 1815. The narrative is often completely lost in historical retrospects and moral dissertations. But she did not end, as one writer has said, "an enemy of the Revolution"[77] or "repudiate her revolutionary sympathies,"[78] as an-

---

[74] *A Narrative of Events*, p. 3.
[75] *ibid.*, p. 6.
[76] *ibid.*, p. 32.
[77] Charles Edmonds (Editor), *Poetry of the Anti-Jacobin*, London, 1890, p. 185 n.
[78] J. De Lancey Ferguson, *op. cit.*, Vol. II, p. 375.

other has written. On the first page of this last book she could write:

The interest I once took in the French Revolution is not chilled, and the enthusiasm I once felt for the cause of liberty still warms my bosom.

She did arrive at a very sober realization of the limitations of human nature. Nor was she in any very positive or comprehensive way "a friend of the Bourbons,"[79] as she has been called. The Bourbons whom she really admired were of the more liberal branch—the Duke of Orleans, who was guillotined by the Mountain as a Girondist, and his son, the Duke of Chartres, afterwards Louis Philippe, who was sincerely devoted to the Revolution. She did commend Louis XVIII as the defender of constitutional government against the violent partisans of the oligarchic party. She was, then, a friend of the Bourbons, but not in reaction against the Revolution. She welcomed the accession of Louis XVIII, as she would have welcomed that of almost any other ruler, as a refuge from Napoleonic tyranny. Better a chastened Bourbon than a rampant Napoleon.

Like many of the political romanticists whom France had disappointed, she saw across the Atlantic the promise of the more abundant life which "the American dream" was then offering. In an unpublished letter of June 15, 1815, now preserved in the collection of Barlowana at St. Helena, Calif., she wrote to her friend Mrs. Barlow in America with characteristic sentiment:

If the American government would endow me and my nephews with a cottage on the bank of one of your majestic rivers, thither would I hasten, and pass my days in composing orisons in praise of liberty—but such happiness belongs to the dreams of fancy.

After Stone's death in 1818, her fortune was exhausted, and she and her surviving sister, Persis, were invited to live in Amsterdam with their nephew, A. L. C. Coquerel, pastor of a French Protestant church there. But, removed from her literary circle and personal friends, she was thrown into such depression of spirits by

> The Hollander's phlegmatic ease,
> Too cold to love, too dull to please,

[79] S. A. Allibone, *op. cit.*

that her nephew took her back to Paris and settled an annuity upon her. Here she died December 14, 1827, and was buried beside Stone in Père Lachaise.

Her memory has never been cleared of the obloquy which the enemies of the French Revolution heaped upon her and she still remains almost without honor in her native country. From the time she went to France, not only were her works denounced as fabricated, but her reputation as a woman was attacked. Her sex did not protect her. In that citadel of respectability, the *Gentleman's Magazine,* the reviewer of the second series of the *Letters* wrote:

She has debased her sex, her heart, her feelings, her talents in recording such a tissue of horror and villainy and daring to insult a regular government and a happy people with such details, whose result, we defy her to show has yet been productive of one single good.[80]

And in its obituary notice it referred to her as "preeminent among the violent female devotees of the Revolution." Horace Walpole, with his penchant for the biting phrase, called her "a scribbling trollop." Undoubtedly the irregularity of her connection with Stone was responsible for much of the defamation piled upon her,[81] as well as the fact that he had been under indictment in England for treason in connection with the projected French invasion.[82] The *Anti-Jacobin*[83] impaled Miss Wil-

---

[80] Vol. LXV, ii, p. 1030. It had earlier doubted her story of Monsieur du Fossé. See Vol. LXI, i, p. 63.

[81] Yet their connection was recognized by the abolitionist Clarkson, who in writing to her after a visit in 1818 gave "compliments to Mr. Stone." (J. G. Alger, *op. cit.,* p. 357.) She was referred to as his wife among their friends. See note 82. Although she signed herself "M.S." (Maria Stone) before Stone's divorce in June 1794, it is clear that she planned to marry him, once all obstacles were removed. See *Four New Letters of Mary Wollstonecraft and Helen Maria Williams,* pp. 46-7, 80-2. She is reputed with little authority, in the *Dictionary of National Biography* and elsewhere, to have had a liaison with Gilbert Imlay, first husband of Mary Wollstonecraft.

[82] Stone could not go to England in 1794 for this reason. It appears, however, that she had planned to go there. In an unpublished letter of the *Barlow Papers,* Barlow's friend, Konrad Oelsner, writes to him from Bern on October 19, 1794: "I have had no news of Md. [*sic*] Stone for a long time. I fear that she has met with discomfort upon her arrival in England." See also Miss Williams's letter of April 1794 to Mrs. Barlow, *op. cit.,* p. 46. In this letter it also appears that she had thought for a time of taking refuge with the Barlows in America: "How I shall [should?] like to form a menage with you in America —I think that country would please & suit my Id[e]as exactly. If my affairs are settled as I hope they will be, I will certainly see you there, if nowhere else." At this time it

liams and Madame de Stael together on a bawdy rhyme. In *The Vision of Liberty*, a satirical imitation of Spenser appearing in its successor, the *Anti-Jacobin Review and Magazine*,[84] she is made to represent lechery in a procession of the Seven Deadly Sins. According to it, her works are characterized by "an inveterate hatred of all existing establishments, by an earnest desire to promote their destruction, and by a contempt of truth, decency, and decorum, which constitute the general characteristics of a female mind infected with the poison of democracy." In the broadside attack of the Reverend Richard Polwhele against all women radicals, called *The Unsexed Females* (1798), Miss Williams is given one of the places of dishonor. In this astounding piece of literary barbarity, she is "an intemperate advocate of Gallic licentiousness . . . importing with her a blast more pestilential than Avernus." A sufficient refutation of such calumnies is patent in what has been written above. The piously respectable duly lamented her fall from grace and the fame of her sentimental salad days. We read in the *Ladies' Monthly Museum* for January 1816:

> She had a tenderness and delicacy of soul and was a sincere friend of all order—moral, civil, and religious. But how frail is the best nature when it is powerfully assailed and gradually and habitually corrupted by inhuman and impious and by licentious and profligate examples.

seems that she was uncertain about Stone's success in securing a divorce. It might also be conjectured from this that Stone was expected, if the divorce was arranged, to share her asylum in America.

[83] No. XXVI, May 14, 1798. In a satire, "The New Morality," in No. XXXVI, July 9, 1798, she is represented with Coleridge, Lamb, Lloyd, Southey, Priestley, Wakefield, Thelwall, Paine, Godwin, and Holcroft as a friend of the execrated theophilanthropist Lepaux. The followers of this man, a member of the Directory, called themselves "Friends of God and Man," but were a very miscellaneous group. Feeling that neither materialism nor the worship of reason would fill the void left by the overthrow of religion, they set up as the center of their system the moral government of the world by a Supreme Being and the immortality of the soul. Miss Williams had given a qualified approval, "since the belief in immortality is the most powerful motive to virtue and he who is convinced of the existence of the Supreme Being . . . will be less inclined to sacrifice again at the altar of Moloch and dye his hands in human blood." (*A Tour of Switzerland*, Vol. I, p. 83.)

[84] Vol. I, pp. 146-7. In the index to this volume under "Wollstonecraft" is this reference: "See Helen Maria Williams, Godwin, Prostitution."

William Beloe, writing about her at the very time when she was the cynosure of English eyes in Paris, left this evidence of the asperities of old age:

> She received before she went to France the respect and attention of many of the most considerable persons in this country, both for talent and rank. What is she now? If she lives—and whether she lives or not, few know and nobody cares—she is a wanderer—an exile, unnoticed and unknown.[85]

In short, one cannot escape agreeing with Professor Harper, the only contemporary writer who has suggested a re-evaluation of Miss Williams's career towards a more sympathetic interpretation, when he says:

> The authority of her works has been contemptuously denied, partly because of their bias, but even more, I think, through the partisan prejudice of her critics.[86]

An examination of Miss Williams's writings discloses little or nothing to support the idea that her influence was dangerous to British institutions. Her relations to English political life were not close, and she expressed her ideas on English politics rarely, and generally in an incidental fashion. She charges general misrepresentation of the Revolution, either through ignorance or design, in English newspapers. She defends the originators of the Revolution against the charge of imperialism made by the English. But she does not seem actively interested in revolutionary propaganda in England. In fact, she thought that the genius of the English people would find more moderate means to the same end:

> While France has been obliged to correct *her* government by holding in one hand her philosophic declaration of rights and grasping her unsheathed sword in the other—may England effect the same august purpose with no other arms than those of reason.[87]

She probably hurt the English by her justifiable attack upon Nelson for his treatment of the patriots at Naples in 1799. But in her criticism of Burke there is little of the vehemence with which Paine and others assailed him. She is not of the opinion that kings can do no good; Burke himself, she thinks, delivers "a shocking satire on every humane and just

[85] *op. cit.*, Vol. I, p. 356.
[86] *op. cit.*, Vol. I, p. 148.
[87] *Letters from France*, first series, Vol. II, pp. 115-16.

prince"[88] when he calls the Bastille the King's castle. It appears from a note left by the United Irishman, Wolfe Tone, that she had no sympathy for the invasion of the British Isles by France. In July 1796, when he was in Paris to confer on the French invasion of Ireland, he met Stone walking with her in the garden of the Tuilleries, and dined with them. Stone "was very hearty, but H. M. Williams is Miss Jane Bull completely."[89]

On the whole, it is difficult to see any basis whatever for all this hue and cry against her for attempting to subvert the English government. She simply adopted another country. She does not seem to have been very thoroughly informed about what was going on in England, and what interest she had in a revolution there was very probably only the result of a sympathetic rather than an active enlistment in the schemes of Stone.

Miss Williams did not answer her detractors at all, much less in kind. Such papers as the *Anti-Jacobin* prints, written, as she said for tea-circles in London, did not touch her in Paris with their calumnies; besides "those who have lived amidst the scenes of the French Revolution have learned to parry or despise more formidable weapons."[90] But in England, where the abuse of her grew with no one to scotch it, she was soon consigned to Limbo and she has been there ever since. It is hoped that she has been shown worthy at least of a upper seat in Purgatory.

[88] *ibid.*, Vol. IV, p. 269.
[89] Quoted by J. G. Alger, *Englishmen in the French Revolution*, London, 1889, p. 73.
[90] *Sketches . . . of Manners and Opinions*, p. 6.

ANNA SEWARD AND THE ROMANTIC POETS: A STUDY IN TASTE

SAMUEL H. MONK

•
•

I

THE fame of Anna Seward, slight but persistent, is assured. Her connection with Johnson and Darwin, her personality, her literary vanity, and her soubriquet, "the Swan of Lichfield," have earned for her name a memory that is denied to her works. Perhaps we know her as well as we need. Her letters from the year 1784 she carefully transcribed into notebooks which she left to Constable, who published them at Edinburgh in 1811. Miss Seward wore her heart on her sleeve, and with no reticence at all wrote everything out to her numerous correspondents. The letters, therefore, have provided material for such books as Miss Ashmun's scholarly and exact biography, *The Singing Swan,* and Mr. Lucas's impressionistic portrait, *A Swan and Her Friends.* And they have been useful to literary historians. But no one has examined with care the *obiter dicta* on literature with which the letters abound, or has sought the implications of Miss Seward's ideas about her favorite art: poetry.

"No man," said Dr. Johnson, "is a hypocrite in his pleasures." Now Miss Seward took pleasure in literature; in fact, it may be said that she lived it, that it quite literally "modified her sensibility." She saw the world through a haze of literary allusions; she associated places and emotions with quotations from the poets; she regarded herself as a tenth Muse, whose duty it was to defend all literature, especially that of her own day. And she never doubted her judgment. Hence her frequent and lengthy discussions of poets living and dead; hence her naïvely frank and sometimes self-damaging utterances. She enjoyed and she said so, and in reading her letters one realizes that in these neglected passages the real Anna Seward remains as nowhere else.

Our interest at the moment, however, is not in the woman herself, nor in the worth or the absurdity of her opinions, but in what those opinions represent. Is Miss Seward an instance of the critical dilemma of the closing decades of the eighteenth century? Do her opinions articulate the blunted, limited, and perhaps perverted poetic sensibility of her times? Eighteenth century "romanticism" is distinctly to be seen after about 1750. Is there a difference between this romanticism and the romanticisms of the newer poets whom she read and discussed? Is her taste typical of her generation?

Miss Seward was born in 1742, two years before the death of Pope; she lived to read the early writings of Southey, Coleridge, Wordsworth, and Scott. Her life covered a crucial period of English literature, which is interesting because of its esthetic and critical confusion. The world of the Augustans, homogeneous, orderly, self-assured, slowly disintegrated; and a new world, based on different values, emerged at the close of the century. Except for Blake, perhaps, there were no romantics in those years, and yet in criticism and in literature the new "romanticism" began to appear in works that in many respects typify the older order. Augustan influences survived with vitality while new emotions and new themes were exploited. Sentimentalism, melancholy, humanitarianism, the cult of terror and of original genius, enthusiasm for wild scenery (all except the last observable in Pope, nascent and controlled by his perfect art) were altering a world whose manners bore a marked resemblance to the Age of Anne. The criticism of the period of transition during which this process was carried on was incoherent and perplexed, and Miss Seward's taste illustrates the difficulties of her contemporaries as they sought to try the new and to lay the old aside.

Without understanding the drama that was being enacted before her eyes, Anna Seward watched the literary scene with an absorbing interest. Her sympathies were given to many varied characters, though she lacked any real insight into the parts that they were playing in the plot. Endowed with no remarkable critical perceptions, responsive like an Aeolian harp to every gust that blew from Parnassus, she had distinctly modern tastes, and it is her modernity that enables us to consider her a representative figure.

II

Miss Seward's taste was formed at home, under the supervision of her father, a typical eighteenth century ecclesiastic, who read, considered himself a judge of literature, and wrote verses of sufficient distinction to win a place in Dodsley's *Miscellanies*. Shakespeare and Milton, of course, she knew from childhood. Pope, Addison, Young, Thomson, Prior, Swift: these were the writers who first taught her just standards in the art that she was to practise. Dr. Seward could give her an admiration for the Augustans, but she was a child of a new generation, one that did not strive so much to know as to feel. She was by nature a sentimentalist and an enthusiast, and her enthusiasm set her apart from her father's generation. As an enthusiast she responded to almost every literary event of her times. And although she was willing to go the mile that led to pre-romanticism, she was incapable (dating as she did from the 1740's) of going the twain that led to romanticism.

This perfectly natural limitation is brought out in her remarks on the letters of Lady Mary Wortley Montagu, which she read in 1804. At once her distaste was aroused. She scorned the Augustan for lacking enthusiasm and declared her to have been as "dead as an Egyptian mummy, to all the various genius and learning which sprung up and bloomed in England during the period of her existence." But Lady Mary had committed a grosser error: she had satirized Pope's grotto in her *Court of Dulness*. Miss Seward quoted the offensive lines with indignation:

> Her [Dulness'] palace, plac'd beneath a muddy road;
> And such the influence of the dull abode,
> The carrier's horse above can scarcely drag his load.
> Here chose the goddess her belov'd retreat,
> Which Phoebus tries in vain to penetrate;
> Adorn'd within with shells of small expense,
> Emblems of tinsel rhyme, and trifling sense.
> Perpetual fogs enclose the sacred cave,

The neighbouring sinks their fragrant odours gave;
In contemplation here she pass'd her hours,
Closely attended by subservient powers.

This is not great satire, but it has a certain amount of wit. Lady Mary
was none too subtly repaying Pope in kind. But good or bad, it awoke
the wrath of Anna Seward.

> With what different ideas did I, in my youthful years, medi-
> tate the same scene, when the following sonnet was poured from
> my pen:

ON READING A DESCRIPTION OF POPE'S GARDEN AT TWICKENHAM

> Ah: might I range each hallow'd bower and glade
> Museus cultur'd, many a raptur'd sigh
> Would that dear local consciousness supply
> Beneath this willow, in this grotto's shade,
> Whose roof his hand with ores and shells inlaid:
> How sweet to watch, with reverential eye,
> Through the sparr'd arch, the streams he oft survey'd,
> Thine, blue Thamesis, gently wandering by:
> This is the poet's triumph, and it towers
> O'er life's pale ills, his consciousness of powers
> That lift his memory from oblivion's gloom;
> Secure a train of these recording hours,
> By his idea deck'd with tender bloom,
> For spirits rightly touch'd, through ages yet to come.[1]

This is an instructive moment in Miss Seward's correspondence. Two
well defined ages touch. Lady Mary would have found Lichfield's Swan
ridiculous and incredible; Miss Seward found Lady Mary simply odious.
Lady Mary hated; she surveyed the object of her hatred with a venomous
glance; she seized the tools that Pope had taught her to use: the result
was satire in coarse and brutal couplets. Miss Seward was an enthusiastic worshiper of poets; bardolatry was her forte. She sentimentalized

---

[1] *Letters* (1811), Vol. VI, pp. 145-50.

and emasculated the object of her adoration in a pseudo-Miltonic sonnet that "was poured" from her pen. The age of gush was in full swing.

Miss Seward was not alone in her dislike of satire. The letters of Mrs. Carter and Mrs. Montagu bear witness to the increasing distaste for that most typical of Augustan arts. To sentimentalists satire is merely ill-natured. And the art that Dryden and Pope and Johnson had shaped into beauty became feebler and feebler as the literary terrain sloped down to the romantics, among whom Byron alone was capable of converting hatred into wit and music.

Let no one be deceived into thinking that Miss Seward understood Pope. She professed admiration for him and once wrote (*Gentleman's Magazine*, 1789) a long defense in his behalf, which is remarkable chiefly for its total lack of insight into Pope's art. She genuinely admired his skill in versification, but there is nothing in her correspondence or her works that leads one to believe that she valued him for his great qualities: his wit, his clarity, his economy, his unerring sense for structure and form, his uncanny genius for "the best words in the best order." To her he was "the sweet swan of Twickenham,"[2] a god, whose shrine in the Temple of the Muses was consecrated by time; and on occasion she offered incense, but she knew that there were many gods of equal importance: Hayley, for example. Praise from Miss Seward is not fame, for always she had a Hayley to bracket with any of the numerous objects of her catholic admiration. Thus Jephson rubs elbows with Shakespeare, Whalley with Gray, Crowe with Thomson.

Miss Seward was not at ease among the Augustans. She gave her heart to Shakespeare, Milton, Akenside, Gray, Collins, and to the vast hoard of poetasters who wrote in her own day. She sought the sentimental and the emotional in poetry, and although she gave praise enough to Pope, her praise rings a bit hollow. But she was incapable of entering the world of the romantics. The qualities which she shared with, say, the Wartons made her more at home among the pre-romantics than among the wits of the days of Queen Anne, while her natural

[2] *Letters*, Vol. V, p. 384.

predilection for rhetoric (itself a heritage of the earlier age) as well as her concept of the nature of poetry made her deaf to the virtues of the new manner when, late in her life, it began to be manifest in poetry.

III

Nowhere did Miss Seward formally draw up her critical principles, but one can deduce something from her occasional remarks. As a modernist she enjoyed the thrill of believing that she lived in an age of copious genius, a conviction that led her to praise almost all poetry that came her way. As she herself said:

> The amor patriae is fervid in my bosom. The superiority of English talents, in all the walks of genius, I proudly feel. The sons of the song, the pencil, and the lyre support it more and more every day, and hour, and I burn to assert their claims whenever I see them questioned.[3]

This is the source of much of Anna Seward's weakness as a critic, and it is related to her attitude toward Lady Mary's satire on Pope. An Augustan could write satire because he sought to think and see; Miss Seward almost abandoned thought and objectivity for feeling. Hence she was often absurd (for the Augustans were right: enthusiasm does tend to absurdity). We must recognize then in Miss Seward a personal idiosyncracy that is not representative of her times: poetry that was modern and English stood a fair chance of winning her praise.

More specifically, Miss Seward prescribed the following test for poetry:

> . . . in poetical composition are lovely, or terrible objects brought to the eye?—are the metaphors, similes and allusions ingenious and happy? does the sentiment speak to the heart, or the understanding?—and is every line in itself harmonious?[4]

This formula very neatly reveals the defects in her critical point of view and contributes to the understanding of much poetry that was written in her time—Darwin's, for instance. It is a curious melange of old and new emphases. First of all, we observe a demand that poetry should be pictorial, that it should present lovely or terrible objects to the eye. The old doctrine *ut pictura poesis,* mistakenly derived from Horace

[3] *ibid.,* Vol. V, p. 351.
[4] *ibid.,* Vol. I, p. 239.

and long resident in English critical theories, was in Miss Seward's day strengthened by the new cult of the picturesque, against which Wordsworth, who eventually recognized its heretical implications, struggled. The rhetorical element in eighteenth century poetry is represented in the question about figures of speech; the sentimental is there in the appeal to the heart; finally, verbal and metrical music finds quite properly a prominent place in Miss Seward's formula.

There is never a hint in her writing that she valued a poem for anything beyond its meretricious ornaments or its sentiments. Poetry as a complex structure of language that arranges experience in enduringly true and significant patterns did not occur to her mind. It is inevitable that her view of poetry should have led her to admire Darwin's verses, for they, as well as her own, were the embodiment of her taste. And the popularity of *The Botanic Garden* and of her own verses indicates that the common reader shared her opinions.

She never ceased to defend Darwin against those of her contemporaries who took exception to his style. For her he was the "great bard of imagination, by turns, the Claude, the Salvator, and the Titian of verse."[5] But she knew that there was a greater style than that of her friend.

In writing to Lady Eleanor Butler of the sublimity of Southey's *Joan of Arc* (a poem that caused her to weep and thrill before its author "of miraculous juvenility"), she contrasted Darwin's and Southey's description of a simoon.

> Fierce on blue streams he rides the tainted air,
> Points his keen eye, and waves his whistling hair;
> While, as he turns, the undulating soil
> Rolls its red waves, and billowy deserts boil.

Miss Seward considered the picturesque epithets and the useless personification "highly poetic."

Southey spares us the epithets and the personification, but indulges in pseudo-Miltonic breadth of treatment and rolling periods of blank verse.

[5] *Letters*, Vol. VI, p. 126.

                    Such ominous fear
Seizes the traveller o'er the trodden sands,
Who marks the dread Simoon across the waste,
Sweep its swift pestilence.—To earth he falls,
Nor dares give utterance to the inward prayer,
Deeming the Genius of the desert breathes
The purple blast of Death.

"When circumstances are in themselves sublime," explained Miss
Seward, "and all things horrid are sublime in poetry, it argues a taste
of meretricious luxuriance, rather than of chaste and dignified judgment, to call in the aids of fancy and fable."[6]

"All things horrid are sublime in poetry." Burke had taught his
generation too well. The chief emphasis of *The Sublime and Beautiful*
was upon "objects" that, because of their emotional effect, could be
classified under the one or the other head. As the eighteenth century
drew to its end, poets and painters came to depend primarily on the
objects represented rather than on the expressive value of their words
or lines. Real poets were few in Miss Seward's time, but the poetasters
and criticasters read sublimity into any poetry that contained objects
large or horrid if they were presented vividly to the eye. Poetry thus
became rhetoric, as it had tended to do throughout the century; and
sensibilities grew so blunted that readers like Miss Seward could not
perceive the nuances in Wordsworth's still, small voice.

So little did Miss Seward value organic structure in poetry that she
could declare:

After all, it is a small part of the intrinsic excellence of poetry, that depends
on what Drydenic slovenliness, or the Popeian elegance can give or take
away. A composition is worth little, that does not remain fine poetry after
being taken out of all measure.[7]

This, from a professed admirer of Gray, fulfils the prophecy of that
poet that his *Elegy* would be liked for the wrong reasons.

Such opinions, and they were not peculiar to Miss Seward, represent
the destruction of poetry as an art. Content, not form; objects, not

[6] *ibid.*, Vol. IV, pp. 305, 307.
[7] *ibid.*, Vol. II, p. 239.

plastic language; thought, not imaginative synthesis were valued. The old rules were passing away with the older age, and in their place was established a new body of criteria which robbed poetry of all distinction, and put it within reach of the Hayleys, the Whalleys, and the Sewards, although we should not forget that, in their own ways, Cowper, Crabbe, Burns, and Blake were writing as artists. But of these, only Cowper and Burns, the most traditional of the four, were noticed by Anna Seward.

Her fervor for her age went hand in hand with a scorn for critics. She was forever dramatizing the literary scene by seeing it as a milieu in which geniuses (received with laurel crowns by herself) were destroyed by reviewers who, because of "their false rules and blundering analizations," were incapable of judging poetry.[8] It must be confessed that England had little criticism to be proud of in the last two decades of the century. No figure so eminent as Jeffrey was writing for the periodicals; no man, except Johnson, attempted with success the task of formal criticism. But Miss Seward scorned the restraints of criticism as she scorned satire. She looked to like, and looking liking moved, and then she poured out her praises to her friends. If the anonymous reviewers did not agree with her, they were blind and deaf, or worse— hirelings of "Gothic" dulness, bent on the destruction of the arts. Miss Seward's impatience of critics bespeaks the disregard into which judgment, the keystone of Augustan criticism, had fallen.

This fixed idea is one of her most disagreeable traits. Through it she rationalized her dislike of Johnson, for she regarded the *Lives of the Poets* as a mixture of envy, misinterpretation, and obscurantism, whose influence was spreading the darkness of night over England's Parnassus. Johnson, she said, was "the greatest enemy the poetic science ever had, or ever can have."[9] Impatience of criticism, as Matthew Arnold pointed out, is an English weakness. Miss Seward's sentimental resentment of critics is thoroughly English.

[8] *Letters,* Vol. II, p. 242.
[9] *ibid.,* Vol. II, p. 145.

IV

Miss Seward's letters are full of evidence of her liking for eighteenth century romantic literature. I have elsewhere written of the relation between Burke's esthetics and her love of natural sublimities as they were revealed in rugged mountains, stormy seas, and electrical storms. In literature and in art she was also a devotee of what she termed "the terrible graces." Here is her feeling for nature:

We wander with you ideally over your mountain-walks, and through your forest haunts; fully aware that an imagination like yours, can enjoy alike their summer loveliness and winter sublimity. If my frame had the elastic powers and strength of yours, I, too, should delight to breast the wintry winds, and to hear them booming through a leafy forest—to fancy I listened in their blasts, to the voice of former times, to the Druids of ancient Britain, yet hovering round their oaks, or to the Caledonian heroes, whose spirits are in the storms of the hills. . . . A flooded valley, beneath the cloudy lour of a wintry moon, is one of those terrible graces in scenery, which the survey of danger, and the consciousness of protection, always form to people of strong imagination. I gaze with pleasing awe on the swoln, the extravagant and usurping waters, as they roll over the fields, and, white with turbid foam, beat against the banks.[10]

For a lady of sixty-five, this bespeaks a stout spirit. The presence of Burke, the reference to Ossian, the word *extravagant,* with its echo of *Hamlet* ("the extravagant and erring spirit"), the pleasure taken in terror, the sense of the decorative function of nature, all date this passage as of the late eighteenth century.

Her taste for natural terrors was, perhaps, both a cause and a result of her admiration for Ossian, references to whose poems are so frequent in her letters that it is difficult to choose examples. Although Scott persuaded her that the poems were Macpherson's she remained convinced of their greatness. She told him that, at the age of sixteen, when she first read the Ossianic poems, she "wept for joy." But she could never read them for long at a time. "Our imagination, whatever be its poetic appetite, will not bear the protraction of unrelieved sublimity."[11] For quite other reasons we do not read Ossian today.

---

[10] *ibid.,* Vol. V, pp. 26-7.
[11] *ibid.,* Vol. VI, p. 316.

Other literary terrors delighted Miss Seward: Bürger's *Leonora*, for example, both in Scott's and in Spencer's translations. She read it for the first time in 1796, and found it sublime, "the *ne-plus-ultra* of horrific greatness."[12] There are many moments in Miss Seward's life that one regrets not having been able to share. But if one could choose to visit her, it would not be on that evening when she walked by the stormy sea with Mr. Dewes's servant; or any of the Parnassian evenings with the Ladies of Llangollen; or for those twenty-four hours when Mr Scott paid his respects to an old lady who, for reasons that elude us, had become the most famous poetess in England. It would be on that evening in Buxton in 1796, when, at the house of Mrs. Powys of Berwick, she read *Leonora* to a select circle of aristocrats (all carefully listed in her correspondence) and made their blood run cold with her "Siddonian" powers. Her performance became famous, and she reports that she gave no less than fifty to people of irreproachable gentility, including on one occasion, Mr. Wilberforce.

. . . everything that was everything, and everything that was nothing flocked to Leonora; and here [Lichfield], since my return, the fame of this business having travelled from Buxton hither, the same curiosity has prevailed. Its terrible graces grapple minds and tastes of every complexion. Creatures that love not verses for their beauty, like these verses for their horrors.[13]

This is amusing, but it is also instructive, for it represents the extreme of pre-romanticism. The titillation that Bürger's horrors evoked in the reading public of 1796 passed for a genuine esthetic experience. The crude horrors of this poetic thriller suggest what Wordsworth had in mind when he denounced in the Preface to *Lyrical Ballads*, 1800, "the frantic novels, sickly and stupid German tragedies, and deluges of idle and extravagant stories in verse" that had perverted the taste of the times.

Though professing contempt for modern novels and an unfaltering loyalty to Richardson, Miss Seward took pleasure in the tale of terror. Mrs. Radcliffe's novels, with their combination of mountain scenery

---

[12] *Letters*, Vol. IV, pp. 212-13, 231, 234, 314.
[13] *ibid.*, Vol. IV, pp. 286-7.

and supernatural terror suited her taste,[14] as did Mrs. Reeve's *Old English Baron.* And in *Caleb Williams* she discovered a work "where the terrible graces extend their petrifying wands."[15]

Original geniuses always won her approval. Burns interested her from the start, and she rightly preferred his Scots to his English poems. "They abound with the irregular fires of genius whether they describe rural scenery, or the customs and characters of village life."[16] And she saw that he was superior to the unfortunate Lactilla.

Chatterton she always regarded as one of the ornaments of the age,[17] and Southey was interesting to her partly because of his youth, which reminded her of the boy of Bristol. One reason for her interest in the forger of the Rowley poems was that he filled the rôle of the genius oppressed by critics. The romantic genius, as typified in the lives of Shelley, Byron, Keats, and Landor, already existed completely in Miss Seward's imagination, and Chatterton, scorned by the world, burning in sleepless agony, and at last consigning his fame to a distant posterity, happily illustrated her conception of the Poet.

V

At first glance Miss Seward seems to make the transition from the pre-romantic to the romantic poets with no difficulty at all. Scott, for example, won her ardent praises. We have already seen that she liked his *William and Helen. Glenfilas* seemed to her sublime;[18] the *Lay of the Last Minstrel* charmed her.[19] On one occasion his genius reduced her to ecstatic exclamations:

Your epic ballad, "Cadzow Castle," is all over excellence, nothing but excellence, and every species of excellence, harmonic, picturesque—characteristic. It satisfies to luxury the whole soul of my imagination. . . . You Salvator! you Claude!—what a night scene!—what an animated description of the onset of the morning chase! Your bull!—what a sublime creature![20]

14 *ibid.,* Vol. III, p. 389.
15 *ibid.,* Vol. IV, p. 211.
16 *ibid.,* Vol. I, p. 326.
17 *ibid.,* Vol. I, p. 194.
18 *ibid.,* Vol. V, p. 265.
19 *ibid.,* Vol. VI, pp. 207-8.
20 *ibid.,* Vol. VI, pp. 98-9.

Poor Scott! He was to be embarrassed by Miss Seward's effusive praises when they appeared in print. That she regarded him as an Ossian redivivus is plain from the following:

From my earliest youth, Scotland has been to me classic ground, which I could at no time have trodden without the liveliest enthusiasm. You have extremely increased all that inspires it. Sacred to my love and veneration is the Caledonian scenery, Lowland and Highland. From Ramsay to Walter Scott, the sublime and the tender emanations of genius have consecrated the former, while, as the poet Gray observed, imagination, in all her pomp, resided many centuries ago on the bleak and barren mountains of the Hebrides. If *then* by the harp of Ossian, *now* by the lyre of Scott, resounding to us from the brink of the sullen Moneira.[21]

It might be argued from such sentiments that Miss Seward was an admirer of romantic poetry. But was she? Although Scott has been labelled a romantic, there was really nothing new in his poetry. His medievalizing may have been a bit more authentic than that of his eighteenth century forebears, but it is difficult to see how he differs from them in kind. He wrote more poetry than did they based on ballad material; but he modernized and sentimentalized, and he used the outworn, theatrical clichés of character and situation just as they had done. If he added anything to the Gothic tradition of the eighteenth century it was a more authentically imagined *mise-en-scène,* a somewhat more characteristic forthrightness and simplicity. But he did not, like Coleridge in *Christabel* succeed (if he indeed tried) in devising a poetic method adequate to the expression of new and subtler moods. Miss Seward not unfairly recognized in Scott a continuer of a kind of poetry to which she had long before given her approbation. And it is significant that when, in the *Minstrelsy of the Scottish Border,* he brought her face to face with genuine folk poetry, she confessed that she had no taste for it. She found the language and meter too colloquial and crude, though she was able to discover the Terrible Graces in an occasional stanza.[22]

Nor does her commendation of Southey prove her capable of romantic taste. She wept over *Joan of Arc* and said that its author was "an arch-

[21] *Letters,* Vol. VI, pp. 276-7.
[22] *ibid.,* Vol. VI, pp. 13-21.

chymist as to sublimity; he not only creates it at will, but he extracts it from all he reads."[23] The "stripling Southey" was superior to Wordsworth, and in *Madoc* had written a work that was "amongst the first poetry the world had produced."[24] But Southey, more than any of the new poets, continued the eighteenth century manner and method. The pseudo-Miltonic epics that Miss Seward admired might have been written (except for certain political opinions expressed in *Joan of Arc*) at almost any time during the last half of the eighteenth century by any one of a number of slightly talented men. Again we detect in Miss Seward's opinions a liking for the old and familiar, not a sympathy for the new.

But when she was confronted with those poems of Wordsworth and Coleridge that really did express the romantic imagination, her enthusiasm waned. *Leonora,* crude and obvious, satisfied her. But the *Ancient Mariner?* In 1798 she wrote:

Supernatural horrors are the taste of the times. Have you seen the *Ancient Mariner?* It is the greatest *quiz* of a composition I ever met with—but it has very fine strokes of genius. The style of absolute simplicity suits the unmeaning wildness of its plan, and of its terrific features.

And she objected to the irregularity of the rhyme and meter.[25]

Wordsworth fared no better. Coleridge's praise of his friend sent her to his poems: presumably *Descriptive Sketches*, since early in 1798 she said that they had been published for some time. "Wordsworth has genius," she wrote, "but his poetry is harsh, turgid, and obscure. He is chiefly a poetic landscape painter—but his pictures want distinctness."[26] Mr. Lucas is shocked at her description of Wordsworth as merely a "poetic landscape painter," but if the poems that she read were, as one must assume, *Descriptive Sketches,* the phrase is surely justified. What is more interesting is that although Wordsworth wrote these poems under the influence of those very poets that Miss Seward admired, there was enough of the new manner in them to puzzle her.

---

[23] *ibid.*, Vol. VI, p. 305.
[24] *ibid.*, Vol. VI, pp. 280, 359.
[25] *ibid.*, Vol. V, p. 184.
[26] *ibid.*, Vol. VI, pp. 60-1.

One of her last utterances on poetry was a condemnation of Wordsworth in a letter to Scott. The poet, she thought was mad; his poems excited by turns her "tenderness and warm admiration" and her "contemptuous astonishment and disgust." Especially did she dislike *The Daffodils,* a poem that represented to her simply an "egotistic manufacture of metaphysical importance upon trivial themes." The *Ode* baffled her. She liked the first five stanzas, but could not fathom "the dark profound of mysticism" in what followed.[27]

The day has passed when one must regard Wordsworth as a touchstone of poetic taste. We can endure to hear his work disparaged and, for reasons of our own, may even agree with Miss Seward. But we may find her opinions interesting because they represent a moment in the history of English literature in which the voice of one era may be heard informally and naïvely expressing its opinion of the work of its successor. Anna Seward's vision was conditioned by the age in which she had passed her maturity. "A fool sees not the same tree that a wise man sees." Miss Seward saw her tree, not Wordsworth's.

VI

It would be easy to make out a case for the theory that the romantics are, to a very large extent, the continuers of the eighteenth century tradition in poetry. Much recent scholarship has stressed the important fact that the ideas of the poets of the early nineteenth century are to be found completely expressed many years before they were incorporated into romantic poetry. Professor Beatty, for example, has emphasized the importance of Hartley and Alison in giving to Wordsworth the psychology that played an important part in his interpretation of the relation between nature and the mind of man; recently Professor Beach has found the sources of Wordsworth's conception of nature in the divines and philosophers of the seventeenth and early eighteenth centuries. It is well for us to know and to remember that the romantic period was no isolated phenomenon, but that it grew organically out of the past, that it existed, as yet scattered and disorganized, during the lifetime of Pope.

[27] *Letters,* Vol. VI, pp. 366-7.

Miss Seward is useful in reminding us that there was, none the less, a romantic movement: i.e. that, despite all we know of the historical development of the ideas that we regard as characteristic of the romantic generation, something new was added, as the human mind underwent one of those alterations of structure that periodically have led it to reinterpret the world and the significance of human life. And such a change in the fundamental structure of human perceptions lies behind all the so-called "schools" that literary historians have pointed out to us.

If we regard the subject-matter of late eighteenth century poetry and the subject-matter of romantic poetry, we are justified in assuming that Miss Seward would approve of the work of the new poets. She has been commended by romantic critics for saying of Coleridge: "It would disgrace a poetic reader not to have him on their shelves."[28] But if one stops to consider that this remark was evoked by the *Ode to the Departing Year*, one of S. T. C.'s most turgid, rhetorical, and pretentious poems (in other words, a poem in the tradition of the great ode popularized by Gray), one need not attach much significance to her praise. More important is the fact that for all her taste for the Terrible Graces, she could not read the *Ancient Mariner* with sympathy; that after a life spent in reading and writing nature poetry and in seeking the sublime in nature, she found Wordsworth's nature poetry puzzling. Romantic poetry, when it came full blown, was beyond her ken.

The reason lies in the fact that romanticism, if the word is permissible at all, is not to be found in subject-matter, but in the manner in which subject-matter is treated. Pre-romantic poetry, which used the same material that the romantics were to use, is ineffective because poets had not yet discovered a poetic method for the material that became fashionable after the mid-century. When this poetry is bad, it is bad largely because Augustan technique, perfect in the hands of Pope, was inadequate to the expression of the material of the new age. The romantics are romantics because they used a new poetic method, not because they loved nature, were interested in the middle ages, or delighted in the supernatural. And that method was primarily the subjective approach,

[28] *ibid.*, Vol. V, p. 55.

which mingled the object with the perceiving mind and in so doing transformed the object. It was a method that resulted in an art in which more was implicit than was explicit, and which employed imagery in a new way, abandoning the rhetorical and decorative function that it had performed in eighteenth century poetry, and using it with imprecision as vague symbols for obscure feelings and states of mind.

Leonora was a straightforward and obviously untrue tale of the supernatural; suspend disbelief, as Miss Seward was willing to do, and all difficulties vanished. As fact the *Ancient Mariner* is equally false, but it possesses a truth, the truth of dreams, a subjective, a psychological truth that is inherent in almost every image and in its irrational structure. The step from objectivity to subjectivity Miss Seward could not take and the poem remained to her a "quiz." The subjectivity of Wordsworth's *Daffodils* seemed to her the "egotistic manufacture of metaphysical importance on trivial themes." There was too much of the poet's mind, too little of objective picturesqueness.

Miss Seward's wide reading in contemporary poetry and her ready enthusiasm for everything that she had read made her a channel through which flowed the taste of her generation. Her letters give to us an unorganized and unphilosophical body of opinions that one is safe in regarding as characteristic pre-romantic taste. Thanks to her zeal for her art and to her long life, those letters reveal to us in considerable detail the confusion of values at the beginning of the romantic period. And the image that they create of an old lady who had known Johnson, praised Hayley, admired Darwin, loved nature, and thrilled to Ossian and Gothic terror, drawing back from the sharp declivity that led to romantic subjectivism expresses vividly enough the critical dilemma of the pre-romantics.

SAMUEL TAYLOR COLERIDGE DISCOVERS THE LAKE COUNTRY

THE REV. GERARD HARTLEY BUCHANAN COLERIDGE

•
•

MY offering to Dr. Harper can be nothing better, and certainly no more appropriate than these jottings by Samuel Taylor Coleridge, on a Tour in the Lake District in 1799, accompanied by Wordsworth; and the even more characteristic journal of a solitary Tour made in the neighborhood of Scafell in 1802. They have never been published and they speak for themselves. About 1885 my father, Ernest Hartley Coleridge, made a transcript of the first Tour from Samuel Taylor Coleridge's notebooks and sent it to the late Mr. Gordon Wordsworth, along with a copy of the journal-letter of 1802. The original of the latter seems to have been lost, but my father used Sara Hutchinson's copy of the letter. Mr. Gordon Wordsworth transcribed both Tours into a notebook, which he bequeathed to me on his death and which I reproduce here almost exactly.

The annotations appear to have been made partly by my father and partly by Mr. Gordon Wordsworth. In the notes the initials E. H. C. stand for Ernest Hartley Coleridge and G. G. W. for Gordon Wordsworth. Some notes are not initialed, but those that are topographical are almost certain to be Mr. Wordsworth's.

All I might add, is that the reader unfamiliar with the Lake District, who may think more exact knowledge is necessary for the full enjoyment of the first Tour, will, if with patience he proceeds to the second, find not only excitement and wonder; but will learn that he, who has been proclaimed a Pioneer in so many adventures in the country of the Mind, may also be claimed as the First Mountaineer.

GERARD HARTLEY BUCHANAN COLERIDGE

Oh Wordsworth! we receive but what we give,
And in our lives alone does Nature live.

S. T. C., April 1802

This breathing house not built with hands,
This body that does me grievous wrong,
O'er airy cliffs and glittering sands,
How lightly then it flashed along;—

Nought cared this body for wind or weather,
When Youth and I lived in't together.   S. T. C., 1822

S. T. Coleridge's Diary of Tour to the Lake District

October-November 1799

Itinerary

Night of Sunday,		October 27—	Pierce Bridge
Monday,	"	28—	*Greta Bridge*
Tuesday,	"	29—	or *Barnard Castle*[1]
Wednesday,	"	30—	Temple Sowerby
Thursday,	"	31—	Bampton
Friday,	November	1—	?
Saturday,	"	2—	Hawkshead
Sunday,	"	3—	Grasmere
to Thursday,	"	7—	
Friday,	"	8—	*Cockermouth*
Saturday,	"	9—	*Keswick* or
Sunday,	"	10—	*Ouse Bridge*
Monday,	"	11—	Buttermere
Tuesday,	"	12—	*Ennerdale*
Wednesday,	"	13—	Wastdale Head
Thursday,	"	14—	Rosthwaite
Friday,	"	15—	Threlkeld
Saturday,	"	16—	Patterdale
Sunday,	"	17—	*Eusemere* (*Pooley Bridge*)

[1] Places italicized are probable, not certain, resting places.

INTRODUCTORY NOTE

Coleridge, whose stay in Germany had been prolonged till July 1799, spent the remainder of the summer in the West of England. In October hearing alarming accounts of Wordsworth's health he started "in a postchaise with Cottle," on the 22nd of October, and reached Sockburn on the 26th. Wordsworth's health had so far improved that they all three set out the following day, Cottle returning South from Greta Bridge.

The notes taken during the two-days' walk from Sockburn to Barnard Castle were revised and retranscribed by Coleridge in 1803, but he stopped short at the pages descriptive of mountain scenery. No doubt he intended to make a consecutive narrative of these memoranda, and publish it as a picturesque tour.

Part of his equipment on this and other tours was a small clasp notebook furnished with a metallic pencil; and he would take notes of the general aspect of the scene, or of any particular object in it.

Notes written in this fashion are necessarily imperfect and fragmentary, and here and there when the sense demanded it the order of the notes has been transposed, or an unfinished jotting made into a connected sentence. But nothing has been added which is not implied in the text or may not be certainly inferred from the immediate context. Much, however, which required the revision of the writer himself, or seemed to the editor to lack interest and distinction, has been omitted.[2] But such as they are, these notes demand no apology. Scenes which in after years Scott was to make famous in song, which awaited Turner's inspired sketches—how did they strike Coleridge who visited them almost by chance, and had never heard that they were noteworthy?

E. H. C.

---

[2] Inasmuch as Miss K. H. Coburn has kindly made available to the general editor of the present volume (Earl Leslie Griggs) her collection of photographs of S. T. Coleridge's notebooks, he has been able to check the text of the first Tour. The account is almost entirely drawn from notebook five and represents Coleridge's jottings at the time of his journey in October-November 1799. The entries for October 22 and 27, and the first part of October 28 are drawn from notebook twenty-one. A collation of Ernest Hartley Coleridge's transcriptions with the original text shows that in general he followed the editorial policy outlined above.—Earl Leslie Griggs.

October 22, 1799. I left Bristol for my most important journey to the North. At Tadcaster I saw a most interesting picture on the road—a flock of sheep, and, perhaps two hundred yards behind, a sick sheep with its head on the ground, a dog looking up at the little boy's face—and the poor little sheep-boy standing close by the sick sheep, anxiously looking forward to the flock—not knowing what to do! I never saw distressful doubt so strongly painted.

* * *

Saturday, October 26 (Sockburn). Few moments in life are so interesting as those of an affectionate reception from those[3] who have heard of you, yet are strangers to your person.

October 27. We started on Sunday afternoon, myself and Wordsworth on foot, Cottle, his legs hugely muffled up, mounted on [Tom Hutchinson's mare,] Lily . . . Neesham . . . the peninsulating Tees . . . Hurworth . . . Croft . . . we discussed the question of Polytheism and Monotheism. That night slept at the George Inn at Pierce Bridge.

October 28. Started early, our path along the high sylvan-cottaged bank of the Tees. At half past nine we reached Gainford, a sweet village with a mirror-smooth green in front of the parsonage, behind which stands the church whose low tower just looks over it. . . . As we enter the Green we find that the village is an irregular circus, and by the opening near the Parsonage we glance at the Tees. Pass into the churchyard and read the epitaphs. . . . At half past four we arrive at the Abbey,[4] a grey ruin on a slope, and the grey church tower and houses of Castle Barnard in the distance. We pass on and come to a bridge[5] built like castle walls with battlements.[6]

October 31. At Maybrough a stone fence—between the stone fence which is circular an irregular arch of Trees—in the centre of this green

---

[3] Thomas, Mary and Sara Hutchinson.

[4] Egglestone Abbey.

[5] Abbey Bridge between Rokeby and Barnard Castle.

[6] From Greta Bridge Cottle went South, and Coleridge and Wordsworth went by mail over Stainmoor "the road interesting with sun and mist" to Temple Sowerby where they slept the night of October 30, and were joined by John Wordsworth from Newbiggin. On the 31st all three set out for Bampton visiting on their way the Rev. Thomas Myers at Barton. (E.H.C.)

circle-plat thus enclosed an upright stone 10 foot high with an ash close by its side, umbrella-ing it—a scene of religion and seclusion—thence to Bampton where we slept.

November 1. About two miles from Bampton our road began to be walled by mountains. The left hand wall which forms a rude semi-circle named Walla Crag, is said to be haunted by the ghost of old "Jimmy Lowther," Lord Lonsdale's father. The constituent lines of the hillside are all in segments of circles, but with what infinite variety! The hills on the right are bare, but for the enclosed fields (intakes) at their feet, which jut out into the lake. The foot of the Walla is divided into distinct toes which run into the lake *in lingulis,* and the enclosures from the opposite mountains form that narrow part of the lake, which, as you first approach, appears to be the termination, but if you mount a hundred yards, you behold a second reach bounded on the right by a bare mountain, bare even of enclosures, the base of which forms a beautiful bay in the shape of a crescent. Still farther to the right and vastly higher, a mountain cleft into hollow ridges and a mountain top peering over in the mist, enfold the scene.

The wall by the roadside roofed with moss running like a serpent in its fine lines. The solemn murmur of the unseen river, far in the distance behind us, and—the silence of the lake!

In the first and second views the only object of life is a flat roofed grey cottage, a little patch of clustered trees running above it, and above this *sylvula* a silvery steep watercourse.[7]

In the third view after the charming interval the arm, the embracement of the enfolding mountain—and another arm rises again as much higher than this, as this was than the first. Gleaming of the white cows streaming behind the trees of the Walla on the marge of the lake. On that steep of the Walla Crag which terminates your sight at the first approach to the lake and in which Sir James is confined, on the top of this when you come opposite to it, a stone wall on the top appears like a pillar or watchman; then comes the steep precipice which

[7] Fordingdale.

renders the wall useless and impassible, but three-quarters down the hill the green recommences and with the stone wall running in a bold line straight down into the lake.

Fourth view; as we face that part of the lake which narrows into a river, the simple and tame beauty of the encircled lower lake contrasts strangely with the wild be-tongued savage mountained upper tarn. Beyond the lake is the pastoral river flowing between mirror-smooth meadows on its right, and a steep mountain, which seems to form a precipitous huge bank on its left.

Fifth view; I climb the hill to the waterfall, and here the upper lake assumes a character of beauty, but of a bold, many-featured original beauty.

The Walla is before me, now divided into three compartments, the first ending with Sir James's precipice, the second forming the bank of the river reach, and the third running slant down into the lake in a soft tongue. Further to the right is a most woody promontory, then a chasm, then a hill steep as a wall, running behind the embracing Giant's arm, with a chasm interposed—and then the high black rampart mist-covered terminating all.[8]

Sunday Morning, November 3. Leave Esthwaite. On the road survey the whole of the lake on my right—straight before me a peep of Wynandermere, and over a gate on my left five huge ragged mountains rising one above the other in wild relations of posture. Our road turns; we pass by Blelham Tarn, and now the five mountains face us.

Amid these awful mountains, Mr. Law has built a white palace,[9] at the head of Wynandermere, with his twenty cropped trees, four stumps standing up upon the trunk of each, all looking like strange Devils with

---

[8] W.W. writes to D.W.: "We proceeded along Haweswater, a noble scene which pleased us much. The mists hung so low we could not go directly over the Ambleside, so we went round by Long Sleddale to Kentmere, Troutbeck, Rayrigg and Bowness— a rainy and raw day—went to the ferry, much disgusted with the new erections about Windermere—thence to Hawkshead; great change among the people since we were last there." (1794) (*Letters of the Wordsworth Family*, Vol. III, p. 368.) They slept on November 2 at Hawkshead and November 1 apparently at Bowness. (E.H.C.)

[9] Brathay Hall, built about 1788. (G.G.W.)

perpendicular horns. Opposite us is Calgarth where [the Bishop of] Llandaff lives.

The damned scoundrel on the right hand, with his house, and a barn built to represent a chapel! His name is Partridge from London, and 'tis his brother's Cow-pen. This *fowl* is a stocking weaver by trade—have mercy on his five wits!

While at Sir [Michael le] Fleming's, a servant, red-eyed, came to us to the room before the waterfall to reprove us for having passed before the front of the House—by our Trespass of Feet with his Trespass on the eye by his damned whitewashing (i.e. weigh the two trespasses in scales, the whitewashing kicks the beam—E. H. C.).[10]

Tuesday, November 5. Flies on the snow mangled by the hailstorm on the top of Helvellyn. We catch sight, first of the lake of Grasmere looking like a sullen tarn, then the black ridge of mountains, then as up high among the other mountains the luminous Curneston [*sic*] Lake and far away in the distance and far to the left the gloomy shadow of Wynandermere with its islands—Pass on—the Tarn and view of the gloomy Ulleswater and mountains behind, óne black, one blue.

Grisedale Halse, Gowdrell Crag, Tarn Crag—that smoother eminence on the right is called Fairfield.

Churn milk Force[11] appears over a copse, the steam from the waterfall rising above the trees. As we come nearer, a rock stands up and intercepts all but the marge and rims of the lower half of the fall, but the trees sometimes yielding and parting in the wind make the waterfall beneath the rock visible. A little way below the waterfall is a one-arched bridge with ferns growing on it, its parapet or ledge of single stones not unmortared, yet cemented more by moss and mould. (This is known

[10] From Rydal they went on to Grasmere where they stayed in the Village (at Robert Newton's) till November 8. On Tuesday the 5th they "accompanied John Wordsworth over the Fork of Helvellyn on a day when light and darkness co-existed in contiguous masses, and the earth and sky were but one. Nature lived for us in all her grandest accidents"—and bade him farewell at Grisedale Tarn. (E.H.C.)

[11] Sour Milk Ghyll. Cf. D.W.'s *Journals,* December 9, 1801. (E.H.C.) Churn Milk Force, appearing over the copse—the steam rising above it—the waterfall—the rock that stands up and intercepts all but the marges and rims of the lower half—the copse whose trees sometimes yielding. (S.T.C.)

as "Willy good Wa-er's" Bridge, that is the Bridge of Willy the good Waller.)[12]

Friday, November 8. We pass over the inverted arch, Saddleback, white and streaked with snow, which for a long time I took for a cloud.

We leave behind us the inverted arch, and before us, in the narrowing and end of the view, that rude, wrinkled, beetling forehead of rock,[13] while all between and on both sides is savage and hopeless, obstinate sans-culottism.

From the window of the Inn[14] at Ouse Bridge we overlook the whole length of Bassenthwaite, a simple majesty of water and mountain, and in the distance the Bank (Skiddaw Dodd) rising like a wedge < , and in the second distance the crags of Derwentwater. What an effect of the shades in the water! On the left the Conical shadow—on the right a square of splendid black, all the intermediate area a mirror reflecting dark and sunny cloud but in the distance the black promontory with a circle of melted silver, and a path of silver running from it like a flat cape in the lake. The snowy Borrowdale in the far distance, and a ridge of nearer mountains, sloping down as it were to the bank of Bassenthwaite.

November 11. Monday. On our left hand from Ambleton to Lorton the smooth hill sinks into an inverted arch, and over the arch appears a fantastic ridge, brown, ironbrown, but spotted all over with snow. Close

12 See *Letters of the Wordsworth Family*, Vol. III, p. 458. (G.G.W.)

13 Raven Crag? or more probably Saddleback at the end of St. John's Vale. (G.G.W.)

14 "Till within a few years past there was, near Ouse Bridge at the foot of Bassenthwaite Lake, a good inn, where those in pursuit of pleasure or improvement might either refresh or take up their abode for the night. The house formerly an inn is a little beyond the bridge, and on the Bassenthwaite (N.E.) side of the river." (Green's *Guide*, 1819.)

Gray dined at it on October 6, 1769, and "sauntered a little by the waterside." Clark in his *Survey of the Lakes* (2nd ed. 1789) says of it, "It is pleasantly situated on the edge of the lake. It is a very good new building, a good dining room and parlour with a bow-window, which has a pretty lookout." (G.G.W.)

On Sunday, November 10, Coleridge wrote to Southey from Keswick. Whether they slept at Cockermouth or Keswick is uncertain. It is possible they slept at Ouse Bridge, a supposition that seems strengthened by the mention of Ambleton (Embleton) next day. (G.G.W.)

by the place where I stood is a square *tumulus*[15] with a deep trench on three sides, a remnant of antiquity. We crossed a small common. The hills before us intermitted on each side, and a plain animated by hillocks formed the interspace, the front view being terminated and ramparted by the snowy tent-shaped mountains. The unseen river, the Cocker, roaring.

Passed through Lorton and just over the bridge (where the brook flings itself over a small chasm of rock) in a field on the right, a Yew,[16] prodigious in size and complexity of numberless branches, flings itself on one side entirely over the river, the branches all verging water-wards over the field it spreads 17 strides. On its branches names numberless are carved, of which some, which are grown up, appear in *alto relievo*.

Beyond Lorton, opposite to Grasmere [i.e. Grasmoor] is Melbreak, a huge, long, single-ridge hill; fronting us snowy ridges. Before we come to Melbreak we catch sight of a single hill covered with wood, and fantastically shaped, called Red How; we pass its gable and precipice woody, with peeping rocks.

Grasmere is a most sublime crag, of a violet colour, patched here and there with islands of the heath-plant, and most picturesquely wrinkled and guttered, whereas the hills on my right though ridgy and precipitous in form are yet smooth and green. We pass the Inn and Scale Hill, leaving it and Lowes Water, which is now in sight, on our right. 'Tis a sweet country which we see before us, Somersetshire Hill, and scattered here and there many a neat house, with its little group of trees, the homesteads of the Estatesmen. Here white rough-cast houses are beautiful, and look at the river and its two-arched bridges! We have curved round the hill,[17] and at my back and before me, O God, what a scene! The foreground a wood sloping down to the river and

[15] The Ordnance Map (1865) shows a "Moat" one mile S.W. of Embleton on the direct road to Lorton. (G.G.W.)

[16] See Wordsworth's "There is a yew-tree, pride of Lorton Vale." In High Lorton there is a Yew Tree of a surprising size spreading its branches on every side to a great distance, covering with its shade above 300 feet in circuit. Hutchinson's *History of Cumberland*. (G.G.W.)

[17] The wooded hill between Scale Hill and Lanthwaite Green. (G.G.W.)

meadow; the serpent river; beyond the river and the wood, meadows terminated by Melbreak, walled by Melbreak, and where the wall ends a peep of Crummock Water. In the same line with Melbreak, but after the break, run on the snowy ridges which seem to curve round, and now a huge gable crag starts up in the middle of the ridge and fronts me. Close by my left hand a rocky woody hill[18] and behind it, half hidden by it, the violet crag of Grasmere.

I climb the woody hill and here we have gained a view of Crummock Water, but lost the violet crag. We pass through the wood, the road ascending, and then I can see nought but woody hill, and a stone wall with trees growing over it on my right. And now the whole violet crag rises and fronts me, and there is a sound of waters. We are near the upper end of Crummock Water. The archipelago of tiniest islands, seven Pleiades, and two near the opposite shore.

November 12.[19] We ascend the hill to Scale Force.[20] The first fall dashes in a thin, broad, white ribbon, from a stupendous height, uninterrupted though not unimpinged by the perpendicular rock, down which, or rather parallel with which, it falls. There is no pool at the bottom but a common shallow brook which flows over small flattish pebbles. But the chasm through which it flows is stupendous, so wildly wooded that the mosses and wet weeds and perilous Tree increase the horror of the rocks which ledge only enough to interrupt not stop

---

18 Lanthwaite Hill. (G.G.W.)

19 They appear to have spent the night of November 11 at Buttermere where there was in 1799 only one inn, at which the famous "Mary of Buttermere," then at the age of twenty-one, and in the full heydey of her remarkable beauty, was in attendance—Green in his *Guide* gives a full account of her. It is, however, possible they returned to Scale Hill for the night. But this was probably the occasion to which Wordsworth refers in *The Prelude*, vii, 296-329. See also de Quincey's *Recollections of S. T. Coleridge.* The estimates of Mary's age given by de Q. do not agree with those of Green, who was more likely to be accurate. They agree fairly well in the description of her person. (G.G.W.)

20 S.T.C. wrote: "On ascending the Hill to Scale Force, we behold the Grand Ness and about half of the concave semi-circle [of Buttermere], the rest is cut off by a Ness running down from my right as I now stand, into the plain that divides Crummock and Buttermere. It is not a plain, but a lovely slope whose highest point is the Town of Buttermere, and hence the lovely river runs half visible by the side of the Hill on the right hand."

your fall! And the Tree, O God! to think of a poor wretch hanging with one arm from it! The lower fall, that is, from the brook is broader, but very low in comparison, and only mark-worthy as combining admirably with the other.[21] Before the great fall there are six falls, each higher than the other, the chasm still gradually deepening till the great fall, the height and depth of which are sudden and out of all comparison. I never saw trees on rock zigzag in their lines more beautifully—trees white in bark, and more than half overpatched with blackish moss—then the green moss upon the rock.

On the island of rock in the lake (Ennerdale) the black-headed Seamews build in May. In sowing-time they follow the ploughman, and pick up the worms. Being quite harmless Mr. Syms[22] will not let them be destroyed. Two years ago a friendly farmer, saw Eagles. One took off a full-fed harvest goose and bore it away, but becoming weary whelped [sic], when a second Eagle came up and relieved it. Another tale was of an old man named Jerome Bowman who slipped and broke his leg on the fells a little beyond Scale Force. He crawled on his hands and knees up and down hill for three miles as far as that cottage in the Sycamores (where we met the dirty old woman with the two teeth) but died soon after from the festering of his wounds. Before this took place his son broke his neck by falling off a crag.[23] He is supposed to have lain down and slept—walked in his sleep, and so came to this crag and fell off. (This was at Proud Knot on the mountain called Pillar up Ennerdale.) His pike staff stuck midway and stayed there till it rotted away.

The Lake is so full of Springs that it scarcely ever freezes. The lower end of Ennerdale forms a circular bay, like the head of a battledore;

---

[21] "The lower fall . . . is wonderfully aided by the upper fall, which, involved in gloom and consequently lowered in tone, is not only a fine apex, but an elegant contrast, to the spreading waters and the sparkling lustre of the lower fall." Green's *Guide*, 1819. (G.G.W.)

[22] Probably a local Statesman. (G.G.W.)

[23] This incident forms the conclusion of Wordsworth's poem of *The Brothers* which was certainly completed by August 1, 1800. (G.G.W.)

and supposing the handle clumsily broad, the remaining part is the handle exactly.

No house! no tree! the unbroken line of the steep Crag is tremendous! But on the left hand of the lake as you ascend up it a Crag[24] with sheep, picturesque as goats, and as perilously feeding. On the very summit stand two large yews or hollies. (In Wastdale) Screes—opposite Middle Fell—Next to the Screes is Scawfell—Great Gavel and Great Yewbarrow face us.[25]

November 14. We left T. Tyson's (Wastdale Head) on Thursday morning for Borrowdale. The brooks in their anger—All the gullies full and white, and the chasms now black now half-hid by the mist, and ever and anon the waterfall within the chasm flashing through the mists. On one hill I counted seven huge gullies, to say nothing of numberless Tapes, white tiny streams, to which in conjunction with the frost-shattered chasms of stone—stone cataracts—the largest stone still at the bottom of the solid stream, the mountains owe much of their colouring.[26]

[Friday, November 15. E. H. C.] We passed (Friday morning) by Grange; saw Lodore—passed through a grove of birches. The lake extends to the marge of the grove—the high crags of Lodore over them in a broad all-comprehending background. A plan was formed for opening the lake at the foot of Derwentwater, and by this means preventing the meadows from being flooded. But Colonel Pocklington (of Barrow) dissented as "it would join his kingdom to England." Commonplace Cascade—old King Pocky's—Whale Jaws—which remind me of the same at Osterode—Battlements at the top of the Cascade. Pocklington shaved off the branches of an oak, whitewashed it, and shaped it into an obelisk—So Art beats Nature.

A mile and a half from Keswick we came to a Druidical Circle. On the right is the road and Saddleback. On the left a fine but unwa-

---

24 Bowness Knotts.

25 The travellers crossed by Floutern Tarn ("We climb the hill and now have entered entirely enclosed by hills a plashy plain. S.T.C.") to Ennerdale and made their way along the lake to Gillerthwaite, and thence by Black Sail to Wastdale Head—whether they slept by the way is uncertain. (E.H.C.)

26 They crossed Sty Head Pass and slept Thursday night at Rosthwaite. (E.H.C.)

tered vale walled by grassy hills and a fine black Crag standing single at the termination as sentry. Before me, that is towards Keswick, the mountains stand one behind the other, in orderly array, as if evoked by and attentive to the assembly of white-vested Wizards.

Friday night we sleep at Threlkeld.

Saturday morning (November 16). We proceed over a barren peat moss to Matterdale. The whole huge tract is tree-less, yet admirably adapted for wood. But under such a tenure who would plant it?

Arrive at Matterdale and we are struck as by a flash, with its similarity to the Devonshire Cleaves. Here too are bare green hills, the Knobs of them black-mossed, so cleft, so sloped, so coombed, so cottaged and the cottages here as there the sole tree-possessors—all as between Manaton and Ashburton. The stream is a Devonshire brawling brook. One cottage we noticed more particularly—it stood two or three hundred yards above a cascade, in a small but sweet curve of the brook, the front to the hills—one gavel with its two wildly-placed windows facing the cascade, and the other gavel over branched by stately trees, and the whole roof greener than the grass field on which it stood.

As we proceed we come to a lovely delve, the Wye in miniature, but the brook brawled and foamed unsteadily. The scene, as we turn, is still Devonshire. One field, a small inclosure of about an acre, stands out from the rest. In the background a hill mellowed in part with stone fence, knobby with bare stones, the interspaces black, yellow, brown, red, yea! all colours with the mosses, and withered. A slender wicker hedge with twenty-nine trees, all slim, but varying in height from six to twenty feet, formed one side of the field, and a stone fence the other. There were three occupants of the field—(1) A stick with a rimless hat on it, looking like a bell. (2) Another stick with the hat sunk down to the bottom, and a bit of the crown remaining on the top. (3) A single ram.

I have come suddenly upon Ulleswater, running straight on the opposite bank, till that noble promontory Place Fell runs into it and gives it the winding of a majestic river. A little below Place Fell a large slice of calm silver, and above this a bright ruffledness or atomic sportiunculi motes in the sun, vortices of flies—how shall I express the banks, waters all fused silver? That house too, its slates rain-wet, silver in the sun—its shadows running down in the water like a column!

The woods on my right shadowy with sunshine, and in front of me the sloping hollow of sun-patched fields,[27] sloping up into hills so playful, the playful hills so going away in snow-streaked savage black mountain. But I have omitted the two island Rocks in the lake, the one scarce visible in the shadow-coloured slip now bordered by the melted silver, the other nearer to me like wine in the glassy shadow, but far removed from the dazzle and quite conspicuous. The sun, it being just past noon, hangs over the lake, clouded so that any but a weak eye might gaze on it; the clouds being in part bright white, and part dusky rain-clouds with islets of blue sky. How the scene changes—what tongues of light shoot out from the banks!

We visited the waterfall (Airey Force). There was too much water, and nowhere ground low enough to view it from. The chasm is very fine—violet-coloured Beeches, and Hawthorns quite trees, red and purple with fruit, as if the berries were flowers. The higher part of the water, where the two streams run athwart each other, is original, but where the wheel-part is broken, it spreads into a muslin apron, and the whole waterfall looks like a long-waisted Lady-Giantess, slipping down on her back. But on the bridge, where you see only the wheel, it is very fine. The waters circumvolve with a complete half-wheel thus (. We gain the road that runs close by the lake—the lake so full as in some parts to be invading the inner rim—curve round over a bridge[28]—fine trees between us and the lake through whose branches we glimpse the bare knotty cliff opposite, and the shadow of it so soft in the water.[29]

Sunday morning, November 17. We left our bad inn and went down the lake by the opposite shore—the hoar-frost on the ground. The lake lay calm and would have been mirror-like, but that it had been *breathed* on by the mist. That shapely white cloud, the day-moon,

27 Sandwick to the life. (G.G.W.)
28 Glencoin. (G.G.W.)
29 Minute descriptions of various points of view with an explanatory diagram are here omitted.
They slept the night at Patterdale. (E.H.C.)

hung over the snowy mountain opposite to us. We passed the first great promontory, and what a scene! Where I stand on the shore is a triangular bay, taking in the whole of the water view. On the opposite shore is a straight deep wall of mist, and behind it one third of the bare mountain stands out, the top of the wall only in the sun—the rest black. And now it is all one deep wall of white vapour, save that black streaks shaped like strange creatures seem to move in and down it, in the opposite direction to the motion of the great body. And over the fork of the cliff behind, in shape so like a cloud, the sun sent cutting it his thousand silky hairs[30] of amber and green light. I step two paces and have lost the glory, but the edge has exactly the soft richness of the silver edge of a cloud behind which the sun is travelling. The fog has now closed over the lake, and we wander in darkness, save that here and there the mist is prettily coloured by the withered fern over which it hovers.

Now as we return the fog begins to clear off from the lake, still however leaving straggling detachments on it, and clings viscously to the hill. All the objects on the opposite coast are hidden, and yet all are reflected in the lake; trees, the Castle, Lyulph's Tower and the huge cliff which dwarfs it—divine!

Lyulph's Tower gleams like a ghost dim and shadowy—and the bright shadow thereof, how beautiful it is, cut across by that tongue of *breezy* water! Now the shadow is suddenly gone, and the Tower itself rises, emerging out of the mist, two-thirds wholly hidden, the minarets quite clear—and in a moment all is snatched away. Realities and shadows!

Monday morning, November 18. Sitting on a tree-stump at the brink of the lake by Mr. Clarkson's (Eusemere) perfect serenity. That round fat backside of a hill with its image in the water made together *one* absolutely undistinguishable form, a kite or a paddle or keel turned towards you. The road appeared a sort of suture. I never saw so sweet an image.[31]

[30] Compare *The Three Graves*, ll. 519-523. (E.H.C.)
[31] There is no record of the return to Sockburn. (G.G.W.)

Tour—August 1802

S. T. C. Slept Sun. Aug. 1 at Ennerdale.
Mon. 2 St. Bees
Tues. 3 Egremont
Wed. 4 Wastdale
Thur. 5 Eskdale
Fri. 6 Ulpha
Sat. 7 Coniston
Sun. 8 Brathay
Mon. 9 Greta Hall.

*A Letter-Journal or Journal-Letter
to S. H., M. H., D. W. and W. W.*

August 1-6, 1802.

Wednesday Afternoon, ½ past 3, August 4, 1802.

Wastdale, a mile and a half below the Foot of the Lake, at an Ale-house[1] without a sign, 20 strides from the Door, under the shade of a huge sycamore tree, without my coat—but that I will now put on, in prudence—yes, here I am, and have been for something more than an hour, and have *enjoyed* a good dish of tea (I carried my tea and sugar with me) under this delightful tree. In the house there are only an old feeble woman and a *"Tallyear"* Lad upon the table—all the rest of the Wastdale world is a hay-making, rejoicing and thanking God for this first downright Summer Day that we have had since the beginning of May. On Sunday August 1,[2] half past 12, I had a shirt, cravat, 2 pairs of stockings, a little paper and half a dozen pins, *a German book* (Voss' Poems), and a little tea and sugar, with my night cap, packed up in my natty green oil skin, neatly squared and put into my *net* knap-sack, and the knapsack on my back, and the Besom stick in my hand, which for want of a better, and in spite of Mrs. C. and Mary, who both raised their volly against it, especially as I left the Besom scattered on the kitchen floor, off I sallied—over the Bridge, through the hopfield,

---

[1] Strands, Nether Wastdale.
[2] The day on which D. and W. Wordsworth reached Calais.

thro' the Prospect Bridge at Portinscale, so on by the tall Birch that grows out of the centre of the huge oak, along into Newlands—Newlands is indeed a lovely place, the houses, each in its little shelter of ashes and sycamores, just under the road, so that in some places you might leap down on the roof, seemingly at least; the exceeding greenness and pastoral beauty of the vale itself, with the savage wildness of the mountains, their coves and long arm-shaped and elbow-shaped ridges—yet this wildness softened down into a congruity with the vale by the semicircular lines of the crags, and of the bason-like concavities. The Cataract between Newlands and Kescadale had but little water in it (of course was of no particular interest). I passed on thro' the green steep smooth bare Kescadale, a sort of unfurnished Passage or antechamber between Newlands and Buttermere, came out at Buttermere and drank tea at the little Inn, and read the greater part of the Revelations—the only part of the New Testament which the Scotch Cobbler read, because why? *Because it was the only part that he understood*. O 'twas a wise Cobbler!

Conceive an enormous round Bason mountain-high, of solid stone (cracked in half and one half gone); exactly in the remaining half of this enormous Bason does Buttermere lie, in this, beautiful and stern embracement of Rock. I left it, passed by Scale Force, the white downfall of which glimmered thro' the trees, that hang before it like bushy hair over a madman's eyes, and climbed till I gained the first level—Here it was "every man his own path-maker," and I went directly cross it—upon soft mossy ground, with many a hop, skip and jump, and many an occasion for observing the truth of the old saying "where rushes grow a man may go." Red Pike, a dolphin shaped peak of a deep red, looked in upon me from over the fell on my left; on my right I had first Melbreak (the mountain on the right of Crummock as you ascend the lake) then a vale running down with a pretty stream in it to Loweswater, then Heck Comb,[3] a fell of the same height and running in the same direction with Melbreak, a vale on the other side too—and at the bottom of both these vales the Loweswater Fells running abreast. Again I reached an ascent, climbed up, and came to a ruined sheep-fold

[3] Hen Comb in all recent maps. (*sic*. S.H.)

—a wild green view all round me, bleating of sheep and noise of waters. I sate there near 20 minutes, the sun setting on the hill behind with a soft watery gleam, and in front of me the upper halves of huge deep furrowed Grasmere[4] (the mountain on the other side of Crummock) and the huge Newland and Buttermere mountains, and, peeping in from behind, the top of Saddleback. Two fields were visible, the highest cultivated ground on the Newland side of Buttermere, and the trees in those fields were the only trees visible in the whole prospect. I left the sheepfold with regret—for of all things a ruined sheep-fold in a desolate place is the dearest to me, and fills me most with dreams and visions of tender thoughts of those I love best. Well! I passed a bulging, roundish-headed, green hill to my left, (and to the left of it was a frightful crag) with a very high round head right before me; this latter is called Ennerdale Dodd, and bisects the ridge between Ennerdale and Buttermere and Crummock. I took it on my right hand, and came to the top of the bulging green hill, on which I found a small tarn called Floutern tarn, about 100 yards in length and not more than 7 or 8 in breadth, but O! what a grand precipice it lay at the foot of! The half of the precipice called Herdhouse nearest to Ennerdale was black with green moss cushions on the ledges; the half nearest to Buttermere a pale pink, and divided from the black part by a great streamy Torrent of crimson Shiver, and screes, or Skilly (as they call it); I never saw a more heart-raising scene. I turned and looked on the scene which I had left behind, a marvellous group of mountains, wonderfully and admirably arranged —not a single minute object to interrupt the oneness of the view, excepting those two green fields in Buttermere—but before me the glorious sea with the high coast and mountains of the Isle of Man, perfectly distinct—and three ships in view. A little further on, the lake of Ennerdale (the lower part of it) came in view, shaped like a clumsy battledore—but it is in reality exactly *fiddle* shaped. The further bank and the higher part, steep, lofty, bare, bulging crags; the nether [hither?] bank green and pastoral, with houses in the shelter of their own dear trees. On the opposite shore in the middle and narrow part

---

[4] Grasmere—Grasmoor.

of the lake there bulges out a huge crag, called Angling Stone, being a famous station for anglers—and the reflection of this crag in the water is admirable—pillars, or rather it looks like the pipes, of some enormous Organ in a rich golden colour. I travelled on to Long Moor, two miles below the foot of the lake, and met a very hearty welcome from John Ponsonby, a friend of Mr. Jackson's. Here I stayed the night, and the greater part of Monday—the old man went to the head of the lake with me. The mountains at the head of this lake and Wastdale are the monsters of the Country, bare bleak heads, evermore doing deeds of darkness, weather-plots and storm conspiracies in the Clouds—their names are Herdhouse, Bowness, Wha Head, Great Gavel, the Steeple, the Pillar and Seat Allan. I left Long Moor after tea, and proceeded to Egremont, 5 miles—thro' a very pleasant country, part of the way by the river Enna with well-wooded banks, and nice green fields, and pretty houses with trees, and two huge sail cloth manufactories—went to Girtskill, a mercer, for whom I had a letter, but he was at Workington, so I walked on to St. Bees, 3 miles from Egremont. When I came there I could not get a bed—at last got an apology for one at a miserable Pot-house, slept or rather dozed in my clothes, breakfasted there, and went to the School and Church ruins—had read in the History of Cumberland that there was an "excellent Library presented to the School by Sir James Lowther" which proved to be some 30 odd volumes of Commentaries on the Scripture utterly worthless, and which with all my passion for ragged old Folios I should certainly make serviceable . . .[5] for fire lighting. Men who write Tours and County Histories I have by woeful experience found out to be *damned Liars,* harsh words, but true! It was a wet woeful oppressive morning; I was sore with my bad night—walked down to the beach, which is a very nice hard sand for more than a mile, but the St. Bees Head, which I had read much of as a noble cliff, might be made a song of on the flats of the Dutch coast—but in England 'twill scarcely bear a looking at—returned to Egremont, a miserable walk, dined there, visited the Castle, the views from which are uncommonly interesting. I looked thro' an old wild

[5] An erasure.

arch—slovenly black houses and gardens as wild as a dream over the hills beyond them, which slip down in one place making a noticeable gap. Had a good bed, slept well, and left Egremont this morning after breakfast, had a pleasant walk to Calder Abbey an elegant but not very interesting ruin, joining to a very handsome gentleman's house built of red freestone, which has the comfortable warm look of brick without its meanness and multitude of puny squares. This place lies just within the line of circumference of a *circle* of woody hills, the area, a pretty plain half a mile perhaps in diameter—and completely cloathed and hid with wood, except one red hollow in these low steep hills, and except behind the Abbey, where the hills are far higher and consist of green fields almost, but not quite, to the top—just opposite to Calder Abbey, and on the line of the circumference rises Ponsonby Hill, the village of Calder Bridge and its interesting mills, all in wood, some hidden, some roofs just on a line with the trees, some higher, but Ponsonby Hall far higher than the rest. I regained the road and came to Bonewood, a single Alehouse on the top of the hill above the village Gosforth—drank a pint of beer (I forgot to tell you that the whole of my expenses at St. Bees, a glass of gin and water, my bed and breakfast, amounted to 11 d). From this Bonewood is a noble view of the Isle of Man on the one side, and on the other side all the bold dread tops of the Ennerdale and Wastdale mountains. Indeed the whole way from Egremont I had beautiful sea views, the low hills to my right dipping down into inverted arches, or angles, and the sea, often with a ship seen thro'; while on my left the steeple and Scawfell, facing each other, far above the other fells, formed in their interspace a great gap in the heaven.

So I went on, turned eastwards up the Irt, the sea behind and Wastdale mountains before—and here I am, and now I must go and see the lake, for immediately at the foot of the lake runs a low ridge so that you can see nothing of the water till you are at its very edge.

Between the lake and the mountains on the left a low ridge of hill runs parallel with the lake for more than half its length; and just at the foot of the lake there is a Bank even and smooth and low like a grassy bank in a Gentleman's Park. Along the hilly ridge I walked thro' a lane of green hazels with hay fields and hay makers on my right beyond the river Irt and, on the other side of the river, Irton Fell with a deep perpendicular ravine, and a curious pitted pillar of clay, crozier shaped, standing up on it. Next to Irton Fells and in the same line are the Screes, and you can look at nothing but the Screes tho' there were 20 quaint Pillars close by you. The lake is wholly hidden till your very feet touch it, as one may say, and to a stranger the burst would be almost overwhelming. The lake itself seen from its foot appears indeed of too regular shape; exactly like the sheet of paper on which I am writing, except it is still narrower in respect of its length. In reality, however, the lake widens as it ascends, and at the head is very considerably broader than at the foot. But yet in spite of this it is a marvellous sight, a sheet of water between 3 and 4 miles in length, the whole (or very nearly the whole) of its right bank formed by the Screes, or facing of bare rock of enormous height, two thirds of its height downwards absolutely perpendicular; and then slanting off in *Screes* or Shiver, consisting of fine red streaks running in broad stripes through a stone colour slanting off from the perpendicular as steep as the meal newly ground from the Miller's spout. So it is at the foot of the lake, but higher up this streaky shiver occupies two thirds of the whole height, like a pointed decanter in shape, or an outspread fan, or a long-waisted old maid with a fine prim apron, or—no, other things that would only fill up the paper. When I first came the lake was a perfect mirror, and what must have been the glory of the reflections in it! This huge facing of rock *said* to be half a mile in perpendicular height with deep ravine, the whole winded[6] and torrent-worn, except where the pink-striped screes come in, as smooth as silk—all this reflected, turned into pillars, dells and a whole new world of Images in the water!

The head of the lake is crowned by three huge pyramidal mountains, Yewbarrow, Scawfell and the Great Gavel; Yewbarrow and Scawfell nearly opposite to each other, yet so that the Ness or Ridgeline, like the line of a fine nose, of Scawfell runs in behind that of Yewbarrow,

[6] The typist could not read the word, nor can I. Perhaps S.H. could not either. Wrinkled? Winded? (E.H.C.)

while the Ness of Great Gavel is still further back between the two others, and of course instead of running athwart the Vale, it directly faces you. The lake and vale run nearly from East to West.

Melfell (lying South of the lake) consists of great mountain steps decreasing in size as they approach the lake.

My road led along under Melfell[7] and by Yewbarrow, and now I came in sight of its other side called Keppel Crag, and then a huge enormous bason-like cove called Green Crag, as I suppose from there being no single patch of green to be seen on any one of its perpendicular sides— so on the Kirk Fell, at the foot of which is Thomas Tyson's house, where W. and I slept November will be 3 years, and there I was welcomed kindly, had a good bed, and left it after breakfast.

Thursday morning, August 5. Went down the vale almost to the Water head and ascended the low reach between Scawfell and the Screes, and soon after I had gained its height came in sight Burnmoor Water, a large Tarn nearly of that shape, its tail towards Scawfell, at its head a gap forming an inverted arch with Black Coomb and a peep of the sea seen through it. It lies directly at the back of the Screes, and the stream that flows from it down through the gap is called the Mite—and runs thro' a vale of its own called Miterdale, parallel with the lower part of the Wastdale, and divided from it by the high ridge called Irton Fells. I ascended Scawfell by the side of a torrent, and climbed and rested, rested and climbed till I gained the very summit of Scawfell—believed by the shepherds here to be higher than either Helvellyn or Skiddaw—Even to Black Coomb before me all the mountains die away, running down westward to the Sea, apparently in eleven ridges and three parallel vales with their three rivers, seen from their very sources to their falling into the sea, where they form (excepting their screw-like flexures) the Trident of the Irish Channel at Ravenglass—O my God! what enormous mountains these are close by me, and yet below the hill I stand on, Great Gavel, Kirk Fell, Green Crag, and, behind, the Pillar, then the Steeple, then the Hay Cock, on the other side and behind me Great End, Esk Carse (Hause) Bow Fell, and

[7] His road was evidently on the north side of the lake under Middlefell and Yewbarrow. By Melfell he may mean Middlefell and South be a slip for North.

close to my back, two huge Pyramids nearly as high as Scawfell itself, and indeed parts of Scawfell known far and near by these names, the hither one of Broad Crag,[8] and the next to it, but divided from it by a low ridge Doe Crag,[8] which is indeed of itself a great mountain of stones from a pound to 20 ton weight embedded in wooly moss. And here I am lounded[9] so fully lounded that tho' the wind is strong and the clouds are hastening hither from the sea—and the whole air seaward has a lurid look—and we shall certainly have thunder, yet here (but that I am hunger'd and provisionless) here I could lie warm, and wait methinks for tomorrow's sun, and on a nice stone table am I now at this moment writing to you, between 2 and 3 o'clock as I guess. Surely the first letter ever written from the top of Scawfell! But O! what a look down just under my feet! The frightfullest cove that might ever be seen, huge perpendicular precipices, and one sheep upon its only ledge, that surely must be crag! Tyson told me of this place, and called it Hollow Stones.[10] Just by it, and joining together, rise two huge pillars of bare lead-coloured stone (I am no measurer) but the height and depth are terrible. I know how unfair it is to judge these things by a comparison of past impressions with present—but I have no shadow of hesitation in saying that the coves and precipices of Helvellyn are nothing to these! From this sweet lounding-place I see directly thro' Borrowdale the Castle Crag, the whole of Derwentwater, and but for the haziness of the air, I could see my own house. I see clear enough where it stands.

Here I will fold up this letter. I have wafers in my Ink-horn and you shall call this letter when it passes before you the Scawfell letter. I must now drop down how I may into Eskdale—that lies under to my right, the upper part of it the wildest and savagest surely of all the Vales that were even seen from the top of an English mountain, and the lower part of the loveliest.

[8] See final note, *ad. fin.*

[9] Lound or lownd, a dialect adjective signifying sheltered. The verbal or participial use of it does not appear to be frequent.

[10] The gap between Scawfell and Scawfell Pike to the N.W. of Mickledore. Of the pillars one retains that name to this day among the climbers.

Eskdale, Friday August 6 at an estate House called Toes.

There is one sort of gambling to which I am much addicted, and that is not of the least criminal kind for a man who has children and a concern. It is this. When I find it convenient to descend from a mountain I am too confident and too indolent to look round about and wind about till I find a track or other symptom of safety; but I wander on, and where it is first *possible* to descend, there I go—relying upon fortune for how far down this possibility will continue. So it was yesterday afternoon. I passed down from Broad Crag, skirted the precipices and found myself cut off from a most sublime crag-summit, that seemed to rival Scawfell man in height, and to outdo it in fierceness. A ridge of hill lay low down, and divided this crag (called Doe Crag) and Broad Crag, even as the hyphen divided the words broad and crag. I determined to go thither; the first place I came to that was not direct rock, I slipped down and went on for a while with tolerable ease—but now I came (it was midway down) to a smooth perpendicular rock about 7 feet high—this was nothing. I put my hands on the ledge and dropped down—in a few yards came just such another. I *dropped* that too; and yet another seemed not higher—I would not stand for a trifle so I dropped that too; but the stretching of the muscles of my hands and arms, and the jolt of the fall on my feet, put my whole limbs in a *tremble,* and I paused, and looking down saw that I had little else to encounter but a succession of these little precipices—it was in truth a path that in a very hard rain is, no doubt, the channel of a most splendid waterfall, so I began to suspect that I ought not to go on, but then unfortunately, though I could with ease drop down a smooth rock 7 feet high, I could not *climb* it; so go on I must, and on I went; the next three drops were not half a foot, at least not a foot, more than my own height, but every drop increased the palsy of my limbs. I shook all over, Heaven knows without the least influence of fear, and now I had only two more to drop down—to return was impossible—but of these two the first was tremendous, it was twice my own height, and the ledge at the bottom was exceedingly narrow, that if I dropped down upon it I must of necessity have fallen backwards and of course killed myself. My limbs were all in a tremble. I lay upon my back to rest myself, and was beginning according to my custom to laugh at myself for a madman, when the sight of crags above me on each side, and the impetuous clouds just over them, posting so luridly and so rapidly northwards, overawed me. I lay in a state of almost prophetic trance and delight, and blessed God aloud for the powers of reason and the will, which remaining, no danger can overpower us. O God, I exclaimed aloud, how calm how blessed am I now I know not how to proceed, how to return, but I am calm and fearless and confident! If this reality were a dream, if I were asleep, what agonies had I suffered! What screams! When the reason and the will are away what remain to us but darkness and dimness and a bewildering shame and pain that is utterly lord over us, fantastic pleasure that draws the soul along swimming through the air in many shapes, even as a flight of starlings in a wind. I arose and looking down saw at the bottom a heap of stones which had fallen abroad and rendered the narrow ledge on which they had been piled doubly dangerous. At the bottom of the third rock that I dropt from I met a dead sheep quite rotten. This heap of stones I guessed (and have since found that I guessed aright) had been piled up by the shepherd to enable him to climb up and free the poor creature whom he had observed to be cragfast—but seeing nothing but rock over rock he had desisted and gone for help, and in the meantime the poor creature had fallen down and killed itself. As I was looking at these I glanced my eye to the left, and observed that the rock was rent from top to bottom. I measured the breadth of the rent, and found that there was no danger of my being wedged in, so I put my knapsack round to my side, and slipped down as between two walls without any danger or difficulty—the next drop brought me down on the ridge called the How—I hunted out my besom stick, which I had flung before me when I first came to the rocks—and wisely gave over all thoughts of ascending Doe Crag—for now the clouds were again coming in most tumultuously—so I began to descend, when I felt an odd sensation across my whole breast, not pain nor itching, and putting my hand on it I found it all bumpy, and on looking saw the whole of my breast from my neck, exactly all that my Kamell-hair breast-shield covers, filled with great red heat bumps, so thick that no hair could lie between them. They still remain but are evidently less, and I have no doubt will wholly disappear in a few days. It was however a startling proof to me of the violent exertion which I had made. I descended this low hill which was all hollow beneath me, and was like the rough green quilt of a bed of waters. At length two streams burst out and took their way down one side a high ground upon this ridge, the other on the other. I took that to my right (having on my left this high ground, and the other stream, and beyond that Doe Crag, on the other side of which is Esk Halse, where the head spring of the Esk rises, and running down the hill and in upon the vale looks, and actually deceived me, as a great Turnpike road, in which as in many other respects the Head of Eskdale much resembles Langdale). And soon the channel sank all at once, at least 40 yards, and formed a magnificent waterfall,[11] and close under this succession of waterfalls, 7 in number, the third of which is nearly as high as the first. When I had almost reached the bottom of the hill I stood so as to command the whole 8 waterfalls, with the great triangle crag looking in above them, and on the one side of them the enormous and more than perpendicular precipice and Bull's Brows of Scawfell! And now the thunder storm was coming on again and again! Just at the bottom of the hill I saw on before me in the vale lying just above the river on the side of a hill, one, two, three, four objects; I could not distinguish whether Peat Hovels or Hovel-shaped stones—I thought in my mind that 3 of them would turn out to be stones, but that the fourth was certainly a hovel. I went towards them, crossing and recrossing the becks and the river, and found that they were all huge stones,[11] the one nearest the beck, which I had determined to be really a hovel, retained its likeness when I was close beside. In size it is nearly equal to the famous Bowder Stone, but in every other respect greatly superior to it—it has a complete roof, and that perfectly *thatched* with weeds and heath and mountain-ash bushes. I now was obliged to ascend again, as the river ran greatly to the left, and the vale was nothing more than the channel of the river, all the rest of the interspace between the mountains was a tossing up and down of hills of all sizes, and the place at which I am now writing is called Te-as, and spelt Toes—as the Toes of Scawfell.

[11] See final note, *ad. fin.*

It is not possible that any name can be more descriptive of the head of Eskdale. I ascended close under the Scawfell and came to a little village of sheep-folds,[12] there were 5 together, and the redding stuff and the shears, and an old pot was in the passage of the first of them. Here I found an imperfect shelter from a thunder shower accompanied by such echoes! O God! what thoughts were mine! Oh how I wished for health and strength that I might wander about for a month together in the stormiest month of the year among these places, so lovely and savage and full of sounds! After the storm I passed on and came to a great peat road, that wound down a hill called Maddock How, and now came out upon the first cultivated land which begins with a bridge that goes over a stream—a waterfall of considerable height and beautifully wooded above you, and a great water-slope under you. The Gill down which it falls is called Scale Gill, and the fall Scale Gill Force (the word Scale or Scales is common in this country and is said by . . . to be derived from the Saxon sceala, the watling of sheep; but judging from the places themselves, Scale Force, and this Scale Gill Force, I think it is probable that it is derived from Scalle which signified a deafening noise). I peeped thro' some pretty fields and came to a large farmhouse where I am now writing. The place is called Toes or Te-as, the master's name, John Vicars Towers. They received me hospitably. I drank tea here and they begged me to pass the night, which I did, and supped off some excellent salmonlings, which Towers had brought from Ravenglass, whither he had been as holding under the Earl of Egremont, and obliged to "ride the Fair," a custom introduced during the times of insecurity and piratical incursion for the protection of Ravenglass Fair. They were a fine family, and a girl, who did not look more than 12 years old but was nearly 15, was very beautiful—with hair like vine tendrils. She had been long ill and was a sickly child. "Oh, poor Bairn!" (said her Mother) "worse luck for her, she looks like a quality bairn, as you may say." This man's ancestors have been time out of mind in the vale, and here I found that the common names, Towers and Tozers are the same, er signifies "upon," as Miterdale, the dale upon the river Mite, Donnerdale, a contraction of Duddonerdale, the dale upon the river

---

[12] See final note, ad. fin.

Duddon, so Towers pronounced in the vale Te-ars, and Tozers are those who live on the Toes, i.e. upon the knobby feet of the mountain. Mr. Tears has mended my pen.

This morning after breakfast I went out with him, and passed up the vale again due East along a higher road over a lengthy upland, crossed the upper part of Scale Gill, came out upon Maddock, now and then ascending, turned directly Northward into the heart of the mountains, on my left the wild crags under which flows the Scale Gill Beck, the most remarkable of them called Cat Crag (a wild cat being killed there) and on my right hand six great crags which appeared in the mist all in a file, and they were all thro' of different sizes, yet the same shape, all triangles—other crags far above them higher up the vale appeared and disappeared as the mists passed and came, one with a waterfall called Spout Crag, and another most tremendous one called Earn [Heron?] Crag. I passed on a little way till I came close under a huge crag, called Buck Crag, and immediately under this is Four-foot stone, having on it the clear marks of four footsteps. The stone is in its whole breadth just 36 inches (I measured it exactly), but the part that contains the marks is raised above the other part, and is just 20½ inches. The length of the stone is 32½ inches. The first footmark is an Ox's foot; nothing can be conceived more exact, this is 5¾ inches wide; the second is a boy's shoe in the snow, 9½ inches in length; this too is the very thing itself, the heel, the bend of the foot, etc. The third is the footstep to the very life of a mastiff dog, and the fourth is *Derwent's very own first little shoe,* 4 inches in length, and O! it is the sweetest baby shoe that ever was seen. The wie foot in Borrowdale is contemptible, but this really does work upon my imagination very powerfully, and I will try to construct a tale upon it. The place too is very very wild. I delighted the Shepherd in my admiration (and the four foot stone is my own christening, and Towers undertakes it shall hereafter go by that name for hitherto it has been nameless), and so I returned and have found a pedlar here of interesting physiognomy, and here I must leave off for dinner is ready.

After the thunderstorm I shouted out all your names in the sheepfold, when echo came upon echo, and then Hartley and Derwent, and then I laughed and shouted Joanna.[13] It leaves all the echoes I ever heard far, far behind, in number, distinctness and *humanness* of voice, and then not to forget an old friend I made them all say Dr. Dodd, etc.[14]

NOTE TO COLERIDGE'S ASCENT OF SCAFELL

As far as I know this is by many years the earliest record of the pleasures of rock-scrambling, or of any ascent of the Scafell group for the mere love of the fells. It was less than thirty-three years since Thomas Gray had written of Seathwaite "all farther access is here barred to prying mortals," and each of the four miles from Seathwaite to Scafell would have presented to him terrors more appalling than its predecessor. His views of the mountains were shared by the numerous writers of contemporary and subsequent guidebooks who never contemplated the possibility of their readers wishing to leave the beaten tracks. Even Wordsworth, as far as we can gather from *The Prelude,* was only tempted to points of peril by the prospect of plundering the raven's nest; and when he introduced Coleridge to the Lake District in 1799 he appears to have led him on no more adventurous an ascent than that of Helvellyn from Grasmere. Coleridge's letters of the next three years give no hint of any clambering upon the more difficult parts of the mountains, till in August 1802 he found himself, more perhaps by accident than by design, among the gullies and precipices of the Scafell which are now by common consent the finest and most popular test of rock-climbing in England. There he showed his love and knowledge of the fells by identifying them under a wholly new aspect and the remarkable accuracy of

[13] See Wordsworth's poem *To Joanna,* and also Lamb's letter of October 9, 1802, to Coleridge chaffing him for teaching the Cambrian Mountains to re-echo with Tod, Tod, meaning the unlucky doctor, and syllable of hardly Godlike sound. This journal or letter in itself shows the appositeness of the thrust.

[14] The journal or notes or letter end as above on Friday, August 6, and were apparently never completed, owing, among other causes, to the excitement caused by the arrival of Charles and Mary Lamb very shortly afterwards. But in a letter to Southey dated Monday, August 9, Coleridge says that he "proceeded on the Friday evening to Devoke Lake and slept at Ulpha Kirk; on Saturday passed through the Dunnerdale Mountains to Broughton Vale, Torver Vale and in upon Coniston. On Sunday I surveyed the lake, etc., of Coniston, and proceeded to Bratha and slept at Lloyd's house; this morning walked from Bratha to Grasmere and from Grasmere to Greta Hall, where I now am . . . and must defer all account of my very interesting tour, saving only that of all earthly things which I have beheld, the view of Scafell and from Scafell (both views from its own summit) is the most heart-exciting."

his account of his descent is shown by comparing it with Baddeley's directions for the descent from Scafell to Eskdale (p. 226, 9th ed., 1902). "A long but very interesting walk. There is no track whatever till the bottom of the valley is reached. From the Scafell side of Mickledore go down the screes on the left, a steep but safe descent. At their foot, work a little to the left round a hillock, from the base of which a cataract called Carn Spout descends from Mickledore. Cross the stream near the foot of this, and keep well up by a faintly marked track, with the boggy land between it and the Esk river on the left. You will pass some big green-clothed boulders. Where the stream flows, farther away to the left, keep straight on, passing two sheepfolds. Half an hour's more walking will bring you to a peat-bog, whence a cart track zigzags down to the bottom of the valley, crossing a bridge, on either side of which are beautiful falls. Hence the route passes the farmstead of Taw (Toes) House."

Coleridge's movements after reaching the summit are not so easy to follow, and depend on what he meant by Broad Crag. The exact names of special points on Scafell were only known to a few shepherds, and Coleridge can only have learnt them by previous instruction from Thomas Tyson of Wastdale Head or subsequent conversation with John Vickers Towers of Toes in Eskdale. It is curious that these two individuals, who were his hosts on the night before and the night after this expedition, should be the only persons mentioned by Green in his *Guidebook* of 1819 as having climbed from the Wastdale side of Mickledore to the summit of Scafell.

Coleridge describes two separate views from Scafell; the first, that from the very summit, is the finer to the south, the west and the northwest, and comprises the sea with the three valleys and rivers falling into it, but excludes Derwentwater and Castle Crag, which are hidden by a rocky elevation 300 yards to the northward, the nearer of the "two huge pyramids known far and wide as Broad Crag." This seems unmistakably to refer to the Crag which forms the highest point of the plateau which crowns the precipices at the northern end of Scafell and overlooks Hollow Stones, and it must not be confused with the eminence of the same name situated between Scafell Pike and Great End, which is wholly concealed by the former from the spectator on Scafell. By the further pyramid, Doe Crag, Coleridge indicates what is now known as Scafell Pike together with the precipitous and pyramidal crag 250 yards on the southern and Eskdale side of it, which is still known as Doe Crag. It must be remembered that the term Scafell Pike was not in existence in 1802; to the shepherds according to Green in 1819 it was the High Man on Scafell, Scafell being the general name for the whole chain from Great End to the peak that now exclusively bears the name.

The second view which Coleridge begins to describe with the words: "And here I am Lounded" is that from the point where the outlet from Deep Gill joins the rock or plateau which he calls Broad Crag. Several flat-topped rocks apparently made to be used as writing tables can be found there; Borrowdale and Derwentwater lie full in view, while shelter and lounding can be found from the wildest of sou'westers. Within a yard or two are two lead-coloured pillars now called Pisgah and the Scafell Pinnacle (formerly the Scafell Pillar).

From this point to reach the hyphen-like dividing "ridge called the How," in other words Mickledore, Coleridge must have descended by one of the two routes known to present-day climbers as the Mickledore or Scafell Chimney, and the Broad Stand. Mr. G. M. Trevelyan who is familiar with the rocks in question describes the former as a "rope climb that would be extremely dangerous to a solitary amateur of no experience," and the latter as "very easy for any competent scrambler in good weather, but not safe to descend or easy to find for a person unfamiliar with rock scrambling." It was probably down the Broad Stand that Coleridge scrambled despite the fact that the Mickledore Chimney is rather the more suggestive of being in wet weather "the channel of a most splendid waterfall." The safe descent of the Chimney would call for a remarkable combination of courage and good fortune on the part of an explorer. It deserves its name of chimney throughout its difficult portion, whereas S.T.C. did not come upon "the rent rock" on his left hand till the end of his descent, a detail which is only true of the Broad Stand route. Moreover, Mr. Herman Prior in his *Guide* (fourth ed., pp. 322-3) speaks of stones being piled up at one point to assist the ascent by the Broad Stand. The same authority describes both routes as "rather difficult even for a qualified climber."

When he had emerged from the cliffs of Scafell upon the Eskdale slope of Mickledore, Coleridge's route was comparatively easy. The eight-stepped waterfall is now known as Cam Spout and is described by Prior (p. 198) as "a fine cataract coming out of the mountain chambers of the Scafell in three or four plunges altogether of about 260 feet." The same writer also alludes to "the group of enormous detached blocks on a flat solitary knoll near the banks of the stream" as well as to "the rather pretty and picturesque waterfall on Scale Gill Beck, 15 minutes from Taw (Toes) House Farm."

G.G.W.

1912-13

COLERIDGE'S "PREFACE" TO *CHRISTABEL*

B. R. McELDERRY, JR.

•
•

IN publishing a "rough draft of a letter written to a man . . . who offered to review W. Scott's poems to his injury,"[1] written by Coleridge in December 1811, Dr. Raysor pointed out an interesting parallel between a portion of the letter and the passage in the "Preface" to *Christabel,* expressing vigorous contempt for "a set of critics, who seem to hold, that every possible thought and image is traditional; who have no notion that there are such things as fountains in this world, small as well as great; and who would therefore charitably derive every rill they behold flowing, from a perforation in some other man's tank."[2]

One of Coleridge's recently published letters to Byron, dated from Calne, October 22, 1815,[3] furnishes several passages equally close to the

[1] *Coleridge's Shakespearean Criticism,* ed. T. M. Raysor, Harvard University Press, 1930, Vol. II, pp. 231-9. The letter has since been reprinted in *Unpublished Letters of Samuel Taylor Coleridge,* ed. E. L. Griggs, Yale University Press, 1933, Vol. II, pp. 61-7.

[2] *The Poetical Works of Samuel Taylor Coleridge,* ed. J. D. Campbell, London, 1893, p. 601. The parallel passage in the letter is to be found in the second paragraph: "There are two Kinds of Heads in the world of Literature. The one I would call, SPRINGS: the other, TANKS. The latter class habituated to receiving only, full or low, according to the skill of it's [*sic*] Feeders, attach no distinct notion to living production as contra-distinguished from mechanical formation. If they find a fine passage in Thomson, they refer it to Milton; if in Milton to Euripides; or Homer; and if in Homer, they take for granted it's pre-existence in the lost works of Linus or Musaeus. It would seem as if it was a part of their Creed, that all thoughts are traditional, and that not only the Alphabet was revealed to Adam but all that was ever written in it that was worth writing." It is interesting to note that in the letter Coleridge is at pains to deny that Scott is guilty of plagiarism, while in the "Preface" he has just given dates for the composition of *Christabel,* in order to ward off from himself the charge of plagiarism *from* Scott and from Byron as well.

[3] Griggs, *op. cit.,* Vol. II, pp. 146-51. Previously published by Mr. Griggs in "Coleridge and Byron," *PMLA* (December 1930), Vol. XLV, pp. 1091-4.

"Preface" of the next spring. In fact, this letter and the one of 1811 constitute virtually a first draft of the "Preface." A comparison is from several points of view illuminating.

The "Preface"—as it appeared in 1816[4]—consists of three paragraphs: the first refers to the dates of composition, to his plan for the poem as a whole, and to his failure to complete it; the second denies that *Christabel* is an imitation of current writers; and the third describes the meter. The letter to Byron, with some digressions and additions, shows a similar sequence of topics.

Apparently in answer to a specific inquiry about *Christabel*,[5] Coleridge begins his letter as follows:

The *Christabel,* which you have mentioned in so obliging a manner, was composed by me in the year 1797—I should say that the plan of the whole poem was formed and the first Book and half of the second were finished—and it was not till after my return from Germany in the year 1800 that I resumed it—and finished the second and a part of the third book. . . . It is not yet a whole: and as it will be 5 books, I meant to publish it by itself: or with another Poem entitled, The Wanderings of Cain.[6]

This, of course, agrees with the opening statement in the "Preface" about the dates of composition; more interesting is the anticipation of the statement in the "Preface":

. . . as, in my very first conception of the tale, I had the whole present to my mind, with the wholeness, no less than with the liveliness of a vision; I trust that I shall be able to embody in verse the three parts yet to come.[7]

Whether the "wholeness" of his vision is to be understood as mere Coleridgean rhetoric is a question in itself, but Coleridge's vigorous assertion in the letter as well as in the "Preface" is of interest however the question is answered.[8] Puzzling, too, is Coleridge's reference in the letter

---

[4] It remained practically unchanged until 1834. See *The Complete Poetical Works of Samuel Taylor Coleridge,* ed. E. H. Coleridge, Oxford, 1912, Vol. I, pp. 213-15.

[5] "Either Byron wrote to Coleridge an unpublished answer [i.e. to Coleridge's previous letter of October 17], or the two men met in person." E. L. Griggs, "Coleridge and Byron," *PMLA* (December 1930), Vol. XLV, p. 1091.

[6] Griggs, *Unpublished Letters,* Vol. II, pp. 146-7.

[7] Campbell, *op. cit.,* p. 601.

[8] On this point see my article, "Coleridge's Plan for Completing *Christabel," Studies in Philology* (July 1936), Vol. XXXIII, pp. 437-55.

to finishing "a part of the third book." Does this refer only to the passage printed as the "Conclusion" to Part II? Or does it bear out Coleridge's mention of "1300 or 1400 lines" of *Christabel*?[9]

Regarding his failure to complete the poem, Coleridge avers in the first paragraph of the "Preface" that since 1800 (the date of composing Part II) his "poetic powers have been, till very lately, in a state of suspended animation."[10] And for his failure to publish at least the fragment at an earlier date and thus to have secured full recognition of its originality, he adds (paragraph two) that "I have only my own indolence to blame."[11] So in the "Preface." But in the first part of the letter Coleridge says,

What occurred after my return from Italy, and what the disgusts were (most certainly not originating in my own opinion or decision) that indisposed me to the completion of the Poem, I will not trouble your Lordship with.[12]

But a page or so later, in spite of his promise to be silent, he bursts out with a full explanation, fully and passionately argued. It is the heart of the letter; and since it is over-long to quote it may be summarized as follows: Coleridge is gratified at Byron's praise of his poems and "the regrets of many concerning 'the want of Inclination and Exertion which prevented me from giving full scope to my mind.'" Coleridge insists that he should be judged comparatively; this report has done him great harm, and he has replied to it in his Autobiography, "as far as delicacy permitted." His works have never been objected to as trivial, and omitting all that is temporary would amount to at least eight considerable octavo volumes. His Logosophia, when published, will testify at least to his industry. No one imposing work has so far been produced because, since 1800, there has not been "a single half-year, nay, any three months, in which I possessed the *means* of devoting myself exclusively to any one

---

[9] *The Letters of Samuel Taylor Coleridge*, ed. E. H. Coleridge, London, 1895, Vol. I, p. 337. In a letter to Sir H. Davy, dated October 9, 1800, Coleridge says that "Christabel was running up to 1300 lines." Five days later, writing to Thomas Poole, he speaks of 1400 lines; Griggs, *Unpublished Letters*, Vol. I, p. 156. The published fragment includes 677 lines.

[10] Campbell, *op. cit.*, p. 601.

[11] *ibid.*

[12] Griggs, *Unpublished Letters*, Vol. II, p. 147.

of many works, that it would have been my Delight and *hourly* pleasure to have executed. So help me God! never one!" He has, on the contrary, been forced to write sermons and pieces for the newspapers. This long protest concludes: "Excuse my apparent warmth, my Lord! but I felt a desire to let you know the whole truth in proportion as your kindness inspired a wish to gain your esteem of me as a man."[13]

Thus behind the "Indolence" of the "Preface" lies, apparently, Coleridge's despair of ever receiving justice from the public; and an equally deep desire for sympathy from an inner circle of those most interested in his work and in himself. Whether—in view of the Wedgwood annuity, De Quincey's anonymous generosity, Southey's contributions to the support of his family, Stuart's offers, the patronage of his lectures, and other miscellaneous favors too numerous to mention—Coleridge's complaint was justifiable is another question. But certain it is that he represents himself in this letter to Byron as more sinned against than sinning.

Regarding the subject of plagiarism or imitation, which the second paragraph of the "Preface" discusses, the letter to Byron states only that:

This [i.e. Parts I and II, and part of a third book] is all that Mr. W. Scott can have seen. Before I went to Malta, I heard from Lady Beaumont, I know not whether more gratified or more surprized, that Mr. Scott had recited the Christabel and experienced no common admiration.[14]

This refers, of course, to Scott's early familiarity with *Christabel* through hearing it recited by Dr. John Stoddart,[15] a friend of Coleridge who had been given a manuscript copy. It was, in turn, Scott's reciting the poem to Byron in June 1815 (four months before the writing of the letter in question) that gave Byron his first knowledge of *Christabel*.[16]

---

[13] *ibid.*, pp. 147-50.
[14] *ibid.*, p. 147.
[15] Campbell, *op. cit.*, p. 603.
[16] I do not know the authority for Campbell's statement, *Coleridge's Poetical Works*, 1893, p. 603, that "Byron meeting Coleridge at Rogers's in 1811 heard *Christabel*." In his letter to Coleridge on October 27, 1815, Byron enclosed a passage from his then unpublished *Siege of Corinth*, which he assures Coleridge, "was written before (not seeing your *Christabelle*, for that you know I never did till this day), but before I heard Mr. S. repeat it, which he did in June last, and this thing was begun in January and more than half written before the Summer." *The Works of Lord Byron, Letters and Journals*, ed. R. E. Prothero, London, 1899, Vol. III, pp. 228-9. Byron's note to the passage in *The Siege of Corinth* is even more explicit; after acknowledging "the close though unintentional re-

In replying to Coleridge, under date of October 27, 1815, Byron said:

On your question with W. Scott, I know not how to speak; he is a friend of mine, and though I cannot contradict your statement, I must look to the most favorable part of it. All I have ever seen of him has been frank, fair, and warm in regard towards you, and when he repeated this very production it was with such mention as it deserves, and *that* could not be faint praise.[17]

Now what is the meaning of the phrase "your question with W. Scott"? Coleridge's letter raises no question; it merely explains Scott's knowledge of *Christabel*.

It is quite possible that Byron's phrase may refer to "the letter written to a man who offered to review W. Scott's poems to his injury." The manuscript bears as part of its endorsement, "To have been copied and sent to Lord B."[18] It cannot be proved that Coleridge did send a copy of the letter to Byron, but it would explain Byron's reference to the "question with W. Scott," for the letter to the unknown correspondent is a detailed examination of the charge that Scott was guilty of plagiarism. And if we assume that instead of restating his position to Byron, Coleridge merely had the old letter copied, we have also a simple explanation of how he came to use in the "Preface" the striking simile about fountains and tanks which he had used so effectively in the letter of 1811. Touching on the question of Scott's imitation, Coleridge bethought him

semblance" of his lines to those in the still unpublished *Christabel* he goes on: "It was not till after these lines were written that I heard that wild and singularly original and beautiful poem recited; and the MS. of that production I never saw till very recently, by the kindness of Mr. Coleridge himself." *The Works of Lord Byron, Poetry*, ed. E. H. Coleridge, London, 1900, Vol. III, p. 471. E. H. Coleridge, in his edition of *Christabel*, London, 1907, gives a detailed history of the poem, and says nothing of Coleridge reciting it at Rogers's in Byron's presence. Campbell himself in the index to *Samuel Taylor Coleridge*, London, 1894, p. 292 (the volume was a revision of the introductory Life included the previous year in his edition of the *Poetical Works*), adds this note: "While this index was being compiled (November 1793), *Familiar Letters of Sir Walter Scott* appeared. In a letter dated November 14, 1824 (Vol. II, p. 221) Scott writes: 'Byron might have remembered, by the way, that it was I who first introduced his Lordship to the fragment *Christabel* with a view to interest him in Coleridge's fate, and in the play *Remorse* he was then bringing forward.' " Perhaps Campbell inadvertently added a marvel to the famous dinner at Rogers's when Byron ate only potatoes and vinegar; this dinner occurred in 1811.

[17] Byron, *op. cit.*, Vol. III, p. 228.
[18] Raysor, *op. cit.*, p. 231; Griggs, *Unpublished Letters*, Vol. II, p. 61.

of the 1811 letter, of which he happened to have a copy. Glancing through it again, his eye fell on the simile of fountains and tanks. The passage became associated in his mind with the statement of the other circumstances surrounding *Christabel,* and several months later when writing the "Preface" the association was still active. Thus it may have happened that these two of his letters, separated by nearly four years, combined to form a basis for the "Preface" of 1816.[19]

The remaining paragraph of the "Preface," dealing with the meter of *Christabel,* was almost completely anticipated in the letter to Byron:

I have not learnt with what motive Wordsworth omitted the original advertisement prefixed to his White Doe, that the peculiar metre and mode of narrative he had imitated from the Christabel. For this is indeed the same metre, as far as the *Law* extends—the metre of the Christabel not being irregular, as Southey's Thalaba or Kehama, or Scott's Poems, but uniformly measured by four Beats in each line. In other words, I count by Beats or accents instead of syllables—in the belief that a metre might be thus produced sufficiently uniform and far more malleable to the Passion and Meaning.[20]

In the "Preface" there was, of course, no reference to Wordsworth, and so far as I know his name has not previously been understood to be included among the "celebrated poets whose writings [Coleridge] might be suspected of having imitated."[21] Nor were Scott or Southey specifically referred to. The "Preface" gives merely a formal and somewhat more explicit statement of the "new principle" of meter.

To Coleridge's letter Byron dispatched a prompt and courteous, though brief, reply (already referred to above). He acknowledged the manuscript copy of *Christabel* which accompanied Coleridge's letter, and added, "surely a little effort will complete the poem." Then after his diplomatic comment on the "question with W. Scott," he details quickly the situation with regard to a passage in his forthcoming *Siege of Corinth.*[22] Enclosing the passage itself, he explained that though similar

---

[19] Coleridge's phenomenal memory would, of course, be sufficient explanation; and Raysor notes his fondness for repeating similes; *op. cit.,* Vol. II, p. 238 n. 2. But the circumstances mentioned above suggest more than chance recollection.

[20] Griggs, *op. cit.,* Vol. II, p. 148.

[21] Coleridge's "Preface," Campbell, *op. cit.,* p. 601.

[22] See above, n. 16.

to one in *Christabel* it had been written before he had either read or heard Coleridge's poem. This Byron offered to explain in a note to his poem, quoting from *Christabel*; or, if Coleridge preferred, he offered to omit the passage entirely.

This conciliatory attitude on the part of Byron, and his report of Scott's admiration for Coleridge, undoubtedly led Coleridge to make the good-natured remark in the "Preface" that

. . . as far as the present poem is concerned, the celebrated poets whose writings I might be suspected of having imitated . . . would be among the first to vindicate me from the charge, and who, on any striking coincidence, would permit me to address them in this doggerel version of two monkish hexameters:

> 'Tis mine and it is likewise your's;
> But an if this will not do,
> Let it be mine, good friend! for I
> Am the poorer of the two.[23]

Coleridge's letter to Byron on October 22, 1815, was thus in a double sense a "Preface" to *Christabel*. For it was on November 4 of the same year that Byron wrote to Murray offering the manuscript to him and urging him to publish it.[24] And when an agreement was reached, it was only natural and appropriate that Coleridge should turn back to this letter to his noble patron for the ideas suitable to introduce the poem to a larger public.

[23] Campbell, *op. cit.*, p. 601.
[24] Byron, *op. cit.*, Vol. III, p. 246.

AN EARLY DEFENSE OF *CHRISTABEL*

EARL LESLIE GRIGGS

•
•

EARLY in 1816 there appeared a small but significant volume, *Christabel, Kubla Khan, a Vision, and the Pains of Sleep* by Samuel Taylor Coleridge. The reputation of these poems today might lead one to assume that the volume met with a favorable reception. Instead, *Christabel* was greeted with a storm of abuse. Although the volume was published by Murray and bore a sentence of praise from Lord Byron, the *Quarterly Review* (published by Murray) remained silent; and the *Edinburgh Review* and Leigh Hunt's *Examiner* reviewed the poems with exceptional bitterness. These two articles, which are almost certainly the work of William Hazlitt, attack *Christabel*, first for downright simplicity, and second for insidious obscenity. The first charge need not be answered; nor of the second need we say more than that Hazlitt in a fit of cantankerous and unjustifiable malignity read into Coleridge's fairy romance the vulgarity of a cheap novel.

The maliciousness of the reviews of *Christabel* is even less understandable in the light of the popularity of the poem in manuscript. Scott, Wordsworth, and Byron all imitated the meter of *Christabel,* and for years prior to its publication the poem was admired by literary men. Even Hazlitt was known privately to have praised the poem, despite his animadversions in print. To those of us who know Coleridge well these reviews are unparalleled examples of determined derogation, written simply in personal spite or through a desire to condemn Coleridge for his weaknesses as a man.

When *Christabel* was published, Coleridge was settled with the Gillmans at Highgate, on a visit that lasted the remaining eighteen years of his life. Grieved as he was by the attacks on *Christabel,* he made no public protest, though he did write to his friends rather bitterly of Hazlitt's malignity and perverted character. Recently, however, a review of *Christabel* turned up among the papers belonging to Mr. A. H. Hallam Murray. As far as can be ascertained this review is unpublished. It is probably in the handwriting of John J. Morgan, who with his wife and sister-in-law, looked after Coleridge during the four or five years immediately prior to the publication of *Christabel,* at a time when the poet became almost a slave to opium. Certain allusions in the article suggest that it arose from Coleridge's conversation. Such a supposition is confirmed by the fact that Coleridge was from 1811 to 1816 an inmate of the Morgan household, when Morgan not only enjoyed the poet's confidence (as is shown by Coleridge's letters) but also served as his amanuensis during the composition of several chapters of the *Biographia Literaria.* It seems reasonable to assume that when *Christabel* was so needlessly attacked by the reviewers, Coleridge requested his friend Morgan to answer them by a defense of the poem. One might go even further. The first part of the review could be written by any intelligent reader of the poem, and the remarks about meter add but little to Coleridge's Preface to *Christabel*; but the choice of illustrative passages and the quotations from *Macbeth* may very well be the outgrowth of discussions with Coleridge. The continual insistence on the "wholeness of conception" suggests indeed Coleridge standing in the background, protesting that the entire poem is present to his mind; and the defense of the poem against the wholly unjust charge of vulgarity is quite within the Coleridgean manner. I am inclined to believe, therefore, that not only do many of the ideas emanate from Coleridge, but that certain portions of the review may have actually been dictated by him. Though undoubtedly composed by Morgan himself, the review is probably the work of Morgan tempered and inspired by Coleridge's own conversations about the poem.[1]

---

[1] Two further reasons for attributing the review to Morgan may be added: the manuscript is among several of Coleridge's letters to the Morgans; and Morgan, at least by Coleridge's own testimony, was mainly responsible for the articles on Maturin's *Bertram* in the *Courier.*

Although the review is stilted and artificial in style, the author shows considerable critical acumen; and the merits of the essay as well as its relation to the early reviews of *Christabel* should make it of interest to the twentieth century reader. The subject matter may be divided into five sections. The first, which occupies half of the essay, is concerned with the narrative. The reviewer is not satisfied with a mere prose version of the story, but discusses the "management and arrangement of it." The second section is devoted to "some illustration of the moral sentiments of the Piece; as well as of the Descriptive and Imaginative power of the Poet." With considerable skill and by full and well chosen quotations, the reviewer comments on the descriptive and imaginative excellence, especially in reference to the moral effectiveness of the poem. Then follows a discussion of the meter, but here the author is merely expanding on the ideas Coleridge expressed in his Preface. Having thus pointed out the greatness of the poem, the writer turns aside to refute Hazlitt's charge of a "disgusting grossness at the bottom of the subject." In an attempt at satire he says that "Purity itself becomes begrimed to the Eye of Filth," finding the "disgusting grossness" within the critics themselves. In concluding, he insists that *Christabel,* fragmentary as it is, has a "wholeness of no less than . . . the liveliness of a vision"; and he finishes with another fling at the blindness of Coleridge's critics. The review follows.

It is amusing, and may prove not uninstructive, to examine and compare the contradictory opinions and principles uttered on the same subject; and all, as from the mouth of wisdom itself, alike pronounced in the same tone of absolute confidence and authority. This can be, in few cases, more fully exemplified than in the different criticisms on the Christabel. But criticisms so opposite neutralize each other; and we hope for belief when we assure our Readers, that we mean to give our examination of the poem in question, impartially. It is not indeed our intention minutely to descry defects, there is eagerness enough in others for that task, but we will endeavour to point out some beauties in the work, which have hitherto remained either quite unnoticed, or noticed only in a slight and imperfect manner. The poem, we understand has been handed round very widely in manuscript, for some years past, but the first *public* intimation of its existence was given by Lord Byron in a note to his Siege of Corinth, wherein he mentions it, as "that wild and singularly original and beautiful Poem." We agree with his Lordship to the full, and as we assign our reasons for so doing, let us rather be accused of Partiality, than condemned for Malignity.

The story, in itself, is simple. Christabel the daughter of an English Baron Sir Leoline, having been distressed by means of some impending danger to "her own betrothed Knight," retires at midnight into the neighbouring forest to pray "for her Lover that's far away." She there finds a Lady in distress "beautiful exceedingly," and richly clad, who declares her name to be Geraldine, describes herself as "of a noble line," and that she had been forcibly taken from her Father's Mansion by ruffians. She entreats protection, and Christabel immediately conducts her to Sir Leoline's Castle. Geraldine soon appears to her Protectress as a supernatural and malignant being, whose power is however of such a nature, as to prevent Christabel from divulging the discovery to any other, and she has it "alone in her power to declare," that she found the distressed Lady in the Forest, and took her home for Love and charity. Under this latter description, Geraldine is introduced next morning to Sir Leoline. Geraldine on enquiry tells him that she is the Daughter of a neighbouring Baron, whom Sir Leoline recollects to have been the intimate friend of his youth, tho' the causes which not unusually interrupt youthful friendships have long since interrupted theirs. He determines to take this opportunity of renewing his ancient intimacy with Sir Roland de Vaux (Geraldine's father) and to send his bard (Bracy) in all courtesy and ceremony to him with an assurance of his daughter's safety. Christabel, conscious of the false appearance of Geraldine, and of her real Malignity, but yet not being able to disclose it, can only entreat Sir Leoline that this woman shall be instantly sent away. This request Sir Leoline supposes to proceed from an unworthy cause, from "more than woman's jealousy"; he therefore turns abruptly and angrily from "his darling child," sends Bracy off on his mission, and "leads forth the Lady Geraldine."

Such is the fragment of the Poem before us. There is nothing in it (as a story) to terrify or astonish. But it is not in magnitude and splendour of events, or in the dexterously interweaving of a Plot, that poetry rests its charm. It is not on the Story itself but on the management and arrangement of it. It is by the Fitness of the Manners, the Depth of the Passions, the Definiteness and Consistency of the characters, the Beauty and Liveliness of the Descriptions, and the Force and Truth of the Moral Sentiments that the true Poet is known. Shakespeare's Lear and Othello were taken from well known ballads of the day, and even the Story of Paradise Lost, would become bald and uninteresting, if stript of these ornaments, we should rather say essentials, of Poetry. By this Criterion therefore, let us judge of Christabel, and first we will examine the management of the Plot, and arrangement of its events.

The Poet begins by defining the exact point of time in which he takes up the tale; it is not only Night, but

> "'Tis the *middle* of the night by the Castle clock,"
> "And the Owls have awakened the crowing cock."

The old Mastiff is represented as making answer to the clock—

> "Fifteen short howls not over loud"
> *"Some say she sees my Lady's shroud."*

The last line prepares the mind of the Reader for the visionary and dreamlike manner which pervades the Poem. It is a tint thrown into the Foreground of the Picture which gives a prevailing colour or Harmony to the whole. It is indicative also that my Lady's spirit is to make a principal interest in the after story. The following lines are, as far as we recollect, an original manner of narration by answering and questioning.

> "The lovely Lady Christabel"
> "Whom her Father loves so well"
> "What makes her in the wood so late,"
> "A furlong from the Castle Gate?"
> "She had dreams all yesternight,"
> "Of her own betrothed Knight;"

As she kneels beside the oak tree—

> "The lady leaps up suddenly,"
> "The lovely Lady Christabel!"
> "It moan'd as near as near could be"
> "But what it is she can not tell.—"
> "On the other side it seems to be"
> "Of the huge, broad-breasted old oak tree."

The making Christabel first *hear* the moaning on the other side of the old oak, before she discovers the person of Geraldine, is most happily conceived. She then sees Geraldine,

> "I guess 'twas frightful there to see'
> "A Lady so richly clad as she—"
> "Beautiful exceedingly."

Here the very beauty of Person, and richness of attire in Geraldine enhance the terror of her appearance. She however obtains the belief of Christabel, and her promise of protection, and

> "So up she rose, and forth they pass'd,"
> "With *hurrying* steps yet *nothing fast*."

They cross the moat, and arrive at the threshold of the gate, and here is given the first indication of Geraldine's supernatural character.

> "The Lady sank, belike thro' pain,"
> "And Christabel with might and main"
> "Lifted her up a weary weight"
> "Over the threshold of the gate:"
> "Then the Lady rose again"
> "And mov'd as she were free from pain."

The sleeping Mastiff makes an "angry moan" as they pass

> "Never before she uttered yell"
> "Beneath the eye of Christabel."

They cross the hall of the castle, and the dying embers on the hearth emit—

> "A tongue of light, a fit of flame,"

and on reaching the chamber, the Sorceress is again overpowered on Christabel's mention of her departed Mother. Geraldine now seems to be contending for Mastery with the spirit of the Mother, the Guardian Saint of Christabel for "with unsettled eye," and "with hollow voice" she exclaims—

> "Off Woman off! this hour is mine—"
> "Though thou her Guardian spirit be,"
> "Off Woman off! 'tis given to me."

The Lady recovers, and Christabel as yet nothing alarmed, and attributing the Lady's conduct merely to her being "wildered" from the fright, of her late adventure with the ruffians unrobes and

> "Lay down in her Loveliness."

Not being able to sleep, she reclines on her elbow "to look at the Lady Geraldine," and now first discovers the supernatural mark of Shame, of Guilt and Malignity on her companion—

> "full in view"
> "Behold her bosom and half her side"—
> "A sight to dream of, not to tell!"
> "And she is to sleep by Christabel!—"

The first book ends, with the dark mysterious frightful charm uttered by the Sorceress

> "With low voice, and doleful look"

imposed on the lovely Maid, and lording over her very utterance. To this first book, there is added a conclusion, in which the tale is very little advanced, but enough is told to give us hopes of the final emancipation of Christabel from her enthralment, and that all will yet be well. For though her charm affects Christabel in a powerful manner, yet

> "one hour alone was Geraldine's" and then Christabel
> "gathers herself from out her trance"—
> . . . .
> "No doubt she hath a vision sweet"
> "What if her Guardian spirit 'twere"
> "What if she knew her mother near?"

> "But this she knows, in joys and woes,"
> "That saints will aid if men will call:"
> *"For the blue sky bends over all!"*

We have hitherto seen the mysterious Geraldine shrouded in night; shown either by the uncertain light of a clouded moon, or by the glimmer of a dim and oscillating lamp;—at a time too when all nature around her was still, and at rest. The poet has now to introduce this supernatural being in the light, and joyousness of day. This difficulty has been overcome with great judgement, if we may not rather say, that, what was a difficulty, has been changed into a beauty. In preparation therefore for this the Baron is first awakened by the Matin bell, and a meditative gloom is thrown over his mind

> "Each matin bell, the Baron saith,"
> "Tolls us back to a world of Death."

The sacristan, between each toll, by custom and law—

> "Five and Forty beads must tell."

But

> "there is no lack of such, I ween,"
> "As well fill up the space between,"

for

> "In Langdale pike, and Witch's lair,"
> "And Dungeon Gill so foully rent,"

the echoes send back the Death-note. With these preparations the Poet ushers in the day; the day which is scarcely like a day, for

> "The air is still thro' mist and cloud."

All these circumstances are finely ominous of the appearance of the mysterious Geraldine and throw an atmosphere of mystery around her. She awakens Christabel, who now only sees the Lady

> "Whom she"
> "Raised up beneath the old oak tree!"

and Christabel greets her

> "With such perplexity of mind"
> "As Dreams too lively leave behind."

They pass into the Wall, and enter the Baron's presence-room. The Baron welcomes Geraldine with dignified courtesy, and hearing the name of Sir Roland de Vaux her father, instantly remembers him as his former friend.

> "Sir Leoline a moment's space,"
> "Stood gazing on the Lady's face;"
> "And the youthful Lord of Tryermaine"
> "Came back upon his heart again."

He embraces Geraldine affectionately, who eagerly prolongs the embrace with joyous look, and at this moment the power of the Sorceress is again strongly renewed upon Christabel,

> "She drew in her breath with a hissing sound"
> "Whereat the Knight turns wildly round."
> "And nothing sees, but his own sweet Maid"
> "With eyes upraised as one that pray'd."

To the Baron's anxious enquiries Christabel has no power to answer aught, but to beg that Geraldine might be speedily dismissed.

The Baron on the contrary calls for his Bard Bracy, and directs him to proceed immediately to the Lady's father; and here we have a most lively picture of the manners of the chivalrous age in the following lines—

> "And take the youth whom thou lov'st best"
> "To bear thy harp and learn thy song,"
> "And clothe you both in solemn vest,"
> "And over the mountains haste along,"
> "Lest wandering folk that are abroad,"
> "Detain you on the valley road."

And again, Sir Leoline bids his former Friend come—

> "With all thy numerous array"
> "And take thy lovely daughter home,"
> "And he (Sir Leoline) will meet thee on thy way,"
> "With all his numerous array"
> "White with their panting palfrey's foam,"

"And by mine honour! I will say,"
"That I repent me of the day,"
"When I spake words of high disdain"
"To Roland de Vaux of Tryermaine!"

Bracy however requests the Baron that his journey to Sir Roland may be delay'd, for he had been warn'd by a "vision in his rest," that an unholy thing lurked in the neighbouring wood. The Bard's vision is very beautifully made emblematic of Christabel's persecution and danger.

"For in my sleep I saw that dove,"
"That gentle bird, whom thou dost love,"
"And *call'st by thine own daughter's name*"—
"Sir Leoline! I saw the same,"
"Fluttering, and uttering fearful moan,"
"Among the green herbs in the Forest alone."

. . .   .

"I stoop'd, methought the Dove to take"
"When lo! I saw a *bright green snake*,"
"Coil'd round it's wings and neck."
"Green as the herbs on which it couch'd,"
"Close by the Dove's it's head it crouch'd,"
"And with the Dove, it heaves and stirs,"
"Swelling its neck as she swelled her's."

The likening of the beautiful yet malignant Geraldine to the bright green snake, and the contrast to the Dovelike appearance and nature of Christabel, is remarkably appropriate, as well as tasteful. The Baron however hears Bracy with an incredulous smile, and turning again to Geraldine salutes her forehead, assuring her—

"Thy sire and I will crush the Snake."

The Sorceress takes this occasion again to exert her supernatural power over Christabel

"She look'd askance at Christabel—"
"Jesu Maria, shield her well!—"

The effect of this look, is instantaneous

      "One moment, and the sight was fled!"
      "But Christabel in dizzy trance,"
      "Stumbling on the unsteady ground"
      "Shudder'd aloud with a hissing sound;—"

      . . . .

      "So deeply had she drunken in"
      "That look, those shrunken serpent eyes,"
      "That all her features were resign'd"
      "To this sole Image in her mind:"
      "And passively did imitate"
      "That look of dull and treacherous hate."
      "And thus she stood in dizzy trance"
      "Still picturing that look askance,"
      "With forc'd unconscious sympathy"
      "Full before her father's view"—
      "As far as such a look could be,"
      "In eyes so innocent and blue."

Her Spell-bound silence as to any explanation still continues, and she can do no more than renew her request, and by her Mother's soul to entreat that this woman may be sent away. The Poet true to Nature, represents the very affection which the Baron bears to his Daughter, the very recollection that his dear Lady died to give her life "as enhancing his rage and pain" at the thought of her present unworthiness, and of her "more than Woman's jealousy."

      "He roll'd his eye with stern regard"
      "Upon the gentle minstrel Bard,"
      "And said in tones, abrupt, austere"—
      "Why Bracy doth thou linger here?"
      "I bade thee hence! The Bard obey'd,"
      "And turning from his own sweet Maid,"
      "The aged Knight Sir Leoline"
      "Led forth the Lady Geraldine."

Thus has the poet contrived to excite a high degree of interest in a story, which is in itself plain, artless and we had almost said unaffecting. Each event is completely in Harmony with the general wildness of the Poem, and is yet consistent and connected with and dependent upon the other. The Characters of the Poem are naturally drawn, well sustained and defined, and admirably contrasted with each other. We have the highly chivalrous and romantic Sir Leoline, opposed to the cautious and superstitious and timid Bracy; and the Lady Geraldine, whose high and commanding beauty and manners have almost the effect of terror, contrasted with the lovely, the soft, and innocent Christabel. With the like skill the Poet has thrown a visionary uncertainty and wildness over the whole, yet the tale is evidently complete in the author's mind, and uniform and in harmony as far as it now goes. Enough is shown to remove the Pain of Uncertainty, and what is hidden still keeps curiosity awake. We are assured that the innocence of Christabel will finally triumph, and the Sorcery be defeated; but by what particular means, and what trials and sufferings she is yet to undergo we are still anxious to learn.

Having thus gone through the economy of the Story, we now proceed to give some illustration of the moral sentiments of the Piece; as well as of the Descriptive and the Imaginative powers of the Poet. The passage which stands most conspicuous is that which follows Sir Leoline's recollection of his former youthful friendship with the Father of Geraldine. Tho' the breaking up of youthful connections is no very uncommon case, yet has the Poet here found occasion for the following beautiful sentiments and subsequent imagery.

"Alas! they had been friends in youth;"
"*But whispering tongues can poison truth;*"
"*And constancy lives in realms above;*"
"*And life is thorny, and youth is vain;*"
"*And to be wroth with one we love,*"
"*Doth work like Madness in the brain.*"
"And thus it chanced as I Divine,"
"With Roland and Sir Leoline."

These deeply impressive sentiments, founded in truth and in nature, must live and be remembered, not only as long as the language wherein it is written is used, but even as long as natural feelings and passions shall sway the heart of man. Here is no lengthening out a single reflection into a dozen lines, but each line, each half line affords new and ample scope for thought and meditation. We can only liken this to the sentiments which abound in Lear, in Macbeth, in Hamlet, in Othello, and (confessing the greater frequency of them in our divinest of Poets), we do Shakespeare himself no injustice in the comparison. The lines which immediately follow have been no less quoted and perhaps still more admired.

> "Each spake words of high disdain"
> "And insult to his heart's best brother;"
> "They parted—ne'er to meet again!"
> "But never either found another"
> "To free the hollow heart from paining"—
> "*They stood aloof, the scars remaining,*"
> "*Like cliffs which had been rent asunder;*"
> "*A dreary sea now flows between,*"
> "*But neither Heat, nor Frost, nor Thunder,*"
> "*Shall wholly do away I wean,*"
> "*The marks of that which once hath been.*"

The beauties of the above, however eminent, in degree are of an inferior kind. They apply themselves to the Imagination, not to the Heart, and many a writer may strike the one with all the vividness of reality, without being able in the slightest degree to touch the other. But it presents a most lively picture: the cliffs are rent asunder, but the "*scars remain.*" What was once solid and united, is now, not only divided, but "*a dreary sea now flows between*"; yet the very War of the Elements which has made the tremendous Rent can not obliterate, "*The marks of that which once hath been.*"

Excellencies of the descriptive kind abound throughout the Poem. The first we meet with, is that of the night when Christabel goes forth to pray alone.

"Is the night chilly and dark?"
"The night is chilly, but not dark."
"The thin gray cloud is spread on high,"
"It covers, but not hides the sky."

. . .   .

"The night is chill, the cloud is gray:"
" 'Tis a month before the Month of May,"
"And the spring comes slowly up this way."

This method of narration, "Is the night chilly etc."—"The night is
chilly" etc—is lively and original. The "thin gray cloud that covers but
not hides the sky," it being "the month before May," and the spring
coming slowly on, give altogether a fine and exact idea of the degree and
kind of light required. Take next the following lines—

"The night is chill; the forest bare;"
"Is it the wind that moaneth bleak?"
"There is not wind enough in the air"
"To move away the ringlet curl"
"From the lovely Lady's cheek—"
"There is not wind enough to twirl"
"The one red leaf the last of its clan"
"That dances as often as dance it can,"
"Hanging so light and hanging so high"
"On the topmost twig that looks up at the sky."

The stillness of the night is admirably expressed, and a lively image of
the Lady is given at the same time, "there is not wind enough to move
her ringlet curl." "The one red leaf dancing as often as dance it can," is
a striking instance of the axiom: that objects of the most common occurrence, become instantly new and remarkable by the touch of Poetry. The
strength, as well as magnitude of the castle gate is well given—

"The Gate that is ironed within and without,"
"Where an army in battle array had marched out."

But our quotations would be endless were we to quote every passage which we deem illustrative of the Poet's descriptive or Imaginative powers. We shall limit our quotations to a very few more, and content ourselves with barely alluding to the principal passages as they occur to us. Thus we have lively pictures of the stealth and silence, the bared feet and "stiffled breath" with which Christabel and Geraldine pass the baron's room; of the ceiling of Christabel's chamber carved with figures "all made out of the carver's brain"; of the silver lamp suspended from the ceiling, from "an angel's feet"; of Christabel trimming the lamp, and leaving it "swinging to and fro." But the recovery of the Lady Geraldine after having been for a time o'ermastered by the guardian Saint of Christabel we must not omit.

> "Again the wild-flower wine she drank:"
> "Her *fair, large eyes can glitter bright,*"
> "And from the floor on which she sank,"
> "The *lofty Lady* stood upright:"
> "She was most beautiful to see,"
> "Like a *Lady of a far Countree*."

Her beauty is superhuman and terrific. The commanding height of the "Lofty Lady," (how admirable here the alliteration!) is most vividly before us in her action of rising from "the floor whereon she sank," and, to finish the Picture, she is one of "a far Countree." We have an awful being here, one in the glitter of whose "large, fair eyes" we read the triumph of malignity and supernatural power. We shall make one other quotation illustrative of the Poet's imaginative power, and then proceed in the last place to examine the metre of the Poem. After having spoken of the slowly tolling Matin Bell, and of its being re-echoed, he says, that in Langdale Pike, and Witches' Lair,

> "And Dungeon Gill so fondly rent,"
> "With ropes of Rock and Bells of air"
> "Three sinful sexton's ghosts are pent,"

> "Who all give back one after t'other"
> "The Death-note of their living Brother;"
> "And oft too, by their knell offended,"
> "Just as their One—Two—Three—is ended,"
> "The Devil mocks the doleful tale"
> "With a merry peal from Borrowdale."

The towering Rocks, and the Gusts of air giving back the doleful toll, are admirably adapted to the description of the Mountainous country in which the scene of the Poem is laid. We know nothing more finely imaginative than the "three sinful sextons souls pent up in the Rents of the mountains"; and the "Devils merry mocking peal" startles one even as the sudden transition of a Dream.

The author in his preface speaks of the Metre as "being founded on a new principle: namely that of counting by accents and not by syllables." We so far agree with him as to believe that this is the first piece which is professedly so written; tho' at the same time we must acknowledge the truth of a certain judicious critic's observation that many of our old writers especially ballad-writers, occasionally used equipollent feet, in their verse, and by no means confined themselves to the measure of syllables. We find in this poem, not uncommonly a line of ten or twelve syllables corresponding in feet (as well as answering in rhyme) to another of only eight syllables.

Thus we have,

> "And the lādy, whose voice was faint and sweet,"
> "Did thus pursue her answer meet:—"

The accent on the first syllable of the word Lādy, reduces the length of the four first syllables in this line, so that any other two syllables of that or the next line, are equal to it, and thus we have ten syllables in one line, only equal in time, to eight in the last line.

But the beauty, as well as the complicated nature of the metre, is in no passage so well exemplified as in the charm of the Sorceress Geraldine upon Christabel.

"In the touch of this bosom there worketh a spell,"
"Which is Lord of thy utterance Christabel!"
"Thou know'st to night, and wilt know to morrow"
"This mark of my shame, this seal of my sorrow;"
　　"But vainly thou warrest,"
　　"For this is alone in"
　　"Thy power to declare,"
　　"That in the dim Forest"
　　"Thou heard'st a low moaning,"
"Thou saw'st a bright Lady surpassingly fair:"
"And did'st bring her home with thee in Love and in Charity"
"To shield her and shelter her from the damp air."

It is not alone in the originality of counting by accents, that the beauty of the above quotation lies. The involution of the sentences and lines one into another, render the metre particularly fitted to express the spell of a malignant, powerful and mysterious being. The Rhyme and the Verse are complete at the end of every line, and demand a suspension of the Reader's voice, but the sense is incomplete, and the Mind is left, in a perplexing and almost fearful uncertainty of what is to be the effect of the next line.

Thus we have in Macbeth—

　　"Toad that under the cold stone,"
　　"Days and Nights hath thirty one."

Here is necessarily a pause, what *hath* passed in these *days and nights thirty one?*

　　"Sweltered venom sleeping got."—
　　"Boil thou first in the charmed pot."

Again in the same scene—

　　"Scale of Dragon; Tooth of Wolf;"
　　"Witches Mummy; Maw and Gulf"—
　　"Of the ravening Salt-sea Shark."

Having thus gone through this poem, and with truth and we hope with Justice, pointed out, its high moral sentiments; its Imaginative

Power; its liveliness in Description; and the consistency of its characters and manners, we can not refrain from reminding our readers of that
which has been more than once brought against it: a charge of "disgusting grossness at the bottom of the subject."

"To the pure all things are pure." With no less truth may it be said,
that Purity itself becomes begrimed to the Eye of Filth. The founders of
such a charge must look for that "disgusting grossness" within themselves alone; their Imaginations must be as dark as their Dispositions
malignant.

The author in his preface tells us that, "in the very first conception of
the tale he had the whole present to his mind, with the *wholeness* of, no
less than with the liveliness of a vision." This *wholeness* we have with
much pleasure perceived, for even in the very beginning; in the very
second stanza we find an allusion to, and a sort of anticipation of events,
which are not only unrelated in the present unfinished state of the poem,
but which (as far as we can judge) can not be produced in order until
the Piece is nearly arrived at its conclusion. Such we mean as the mention of the Mastiff howling at "my Lady's shroud," and particularly the
instance of Christabel's assuring Geraldine, that tho' her mother died
when she was born, yet she had heard

"How on her Death-bed she did say,"
"That she should hear the Castle bell"
"Strike twelve upon my wedding day."

Here is a direct mention of the interference of a person of the drama,
who has not yet appeared, and of an event (Christabel's wedding day)
which it most likely will conclude or nearly conclude the tale. These
circumstances impress us with a confident hope that Mr. Coleridge
(notwithstanding his character for procrastination) will "be able to
embody in verse the three parts yet to come" in the course of a short
time. In conclusion we remark, that as we began our criticism with an
intention of bringing Beauties alone into notice, so shall we not now stop
to detect faults. Such there are doubtless. In the first book we think there
are many careless lines, and in two instances (whether designed or not
we presume not to determine) we find two lines which want their cor-

responding rhymes. To descant upon such, be the work of others. The task of Envy, is an easy task. The microscopick eye of Malice, taking inch by inch, must be necessarily blind to the harmony of colour, the Grace or the Expression of a Raphael, but will discover at once any inequalities on the surface of the canvass, or cracks in the Pannel.

COLERIDGE ON THE SUBLIME

CLARENCE DeWITT THORPE

•

•

NO writer on esthetic problems has more earnestly endeavored to use language with exact meaning than did Coleridge. He held that "to use each word in a sense peculiarly its own, is an indispensable condition of all just thinking, and at once the surest, easiest, and even most entertaining discipline of the mind."[1] He was perpetually discontented with the careless equivocation with which terms relating to art and mental processes were bandied about and misapplied. Among permanent causes of false criticism he mentions

The vague use of terms, and therein the necessity of appropriating them more strictly than in ordinary life . . . ; this is shewn in the word Taste and the terms connected with it—as the sublime, the beautiful, the grand, the majestic, the picturesque, the delightful, the interesting, and the amusing. What strange work if an author were forced to refer to any one principle all the senses which ignorance or even the subtlety of momentary analogies may have used any one of these terms under.[2]

With admirable intellectual integrity, Coleridge sought, in his letters and conversation and in his more formal lectures and essays, in a manner fitted to evoke the scorn of Croce,[3] to establish more precise limitations

---

[1] "Lectures of 1812-13; Syllabus; Lecture I," *Coleridge's Shakespearean Criticism*, ed. Thomas M. Raysor, 2 vols., London, 1930, Vol. II, p. 246.

[2] "Lecture Notes and other Fragments," Raysor, *op. cit.*, Vol. I, p. 248.

[3] Whose disdain for minute distinctions among words in esthetic use is expressed in Chapters XII and XIV of his *Aesthetic*. Speaking of the inadequacy of such definitions, he says: "So we must leave writers and speakers free to define the sublime or the comic, the tragic or the humorous, on every occasion as they please and as may suit the end they have in view. And if an empirical definition of universal validity be demanded, we can but submit this one: The sublime (or comic, tragic, humorous, etc.) is *everything* that is or shall be so *called* by those who have employed or shall employ these *words*" (Benedetto Croce, *Aesthetic as Science of Expression and General Linguistic*, tr. by Douglas Ainslee, London, 1929, p. 90).

for such words as "beauty," "poetry," "imagination," "fancy" and so forth. The result was immeasurably to refine and enrich the vocabulary of esthetics. Coleridge was capable of adding to this vocabulary by invention—witness "esemplastic"—but his greater service was to fix meanings by definite and profound exposition in which attributes and differentiæ were painstakingly—sometimes almost irritatingly—presented and analyzed. Some of the definitions he thus evolved have not been improved upon by the most scrupulous of subsequent thinkers. "Imagination" is an example. I should like in the pages that follow to call attention to another such achievement that has been, quite strangely in view of its value, neglected by critics: namely, his exposition of the term "sublime."[4]

Coleridge wrote no formal treatise on the sublime, yet his remarks on the subject total rather large, and, individually or collectively, they amply reward study. It is not surprising, in view of the extensive discussion of sublimity in eighteenth century criticism, that Coleridge should give the problem due attention, nor that, in considering it, he should use his term in precise application, with care to distinguish it, not only from beauty, but from other words with which it is often confused.

Dorothy Wordsworth tells in her account of the tour in Scotland of how at the Falls of the Clyde Coleridge was delighted when a gentleman who was present called the falls "majestic," but was instantly discomfited when the man added warmly, "Sublime and beautiful."[5] To

---

[4] For instance Mr. Samuel Monk, who gives some space to Wordsworth's ideas of sublimity (*The Sublime in XVIII Century England*, New York, Modern Language Association, 1935, pp. 227-32), does not mention Coleridge's use of the term.

[5] *Journals of Dorothy Wordsworth*, ed. by Wm. Knight, London, 1925, p. 195. Dorothy's account of this incident, probably the most accurate of several extant versions, will bear quoting here:

"A lady and gentleman, more expeditious tourists than ourselves, came to the spot; they left us at the seat, and we found them again at another station above the Falls. Coleridge, who is always good-natured enough to enter into conversation with anybody whom he meets in his way, began to talk with the gentleman, who observed that it was a *majestic* waterfall. Coleridge was delighted with the accuracy of the epithet, particularly as he had been settling in his own mind the precise meaning of the words grand, majestic, sublime, etc., and had discussed the subject with William at some length the day before. 'Yes sir,' says Coleridge, 'it *is* a majestic waterfall.' 'Sublime and beautiful,' replied his friend. Poor Coleridge could make no answer, and, not very

Coleridge "majestic" was the right word; the Falls could not be beautiful and majestic and sublime at the same time. Coleridge's feeling on this matter is revealed in his own versions of the incident, of which there are at least three. According to one of these accounts, the gentleman having elicited Coleridge's admiration for his use of the word majestic, had warmly continued, "Yes, sir, I say it is very majestic: it is sublime, it is beautiful, it is grand, it is picturesque." Whereupon the lady added, "Ay, it is the prettiest thing I ever saw."[6] In a second account, the gentleman—there was no lady mentioned—upon being complimented by Coleridge for his exact term, had responded, "Yes! how very pretty!"[7] The third version sets the story in a boat on the Lake of Keswick, the object of admiration now not the Falls of the Clyde but the Cataract of Lodore (though the initial incident is undoubtedly the same). Here, as Coleridge sat looking at the great cataract, "a lady of no mean rank observed that it was sublimely beautiful."[8] The first of these accounts Coleridge closes with the confession, "I own that I was somewhat disconcerted"; he prefaces the second with the remark that "some folks apply epithets as boys do in making Latin verses"; and in the third he suggests a "deep absurdity" in such inaccurate use of language. In all of them the implication is the same: sublime, majestic, beautiful, pretty, and so forth, are words of unique denotation; they should not be loosely interchanged in describing the same object or impression.

Only the day before the incident at the Clyde, Coleridge, no doubt in one of his moods of linguistic precision, evidently trying to find exact words to describe the scenery about him—as grand, majestic, or sublime—had discussed the subject at length with Wordsworth.[9] We have no record of what passed between the poets in this conversation, but must infer it from what each had to say elsewhere.

It is possible to reconstruct with reasonable accuracy Coleridge's side of the argument from a number of utterances scattered throughout his

desirous to continue the conversation, came to us and related the story, laughing heartily."

[6] "Lectures of 1811-12," Raysor, *op. cit.*, Vol. II, pp. 62-3.

[7] Dated June 24, 1827. "Appendix," Raysor, *op. cit.*, Vol. II, p. 352.

[8] Raysor, Vol. I, p. 182.

[9] Dorothy Wordsworth, *op. cit.*, p. 195.

writings. One of the most interesting of these occurs in Allsop's *Recollections,* in a passage where sublimity is distinguished from beauty, majesty, grandeur, and the picturesque. I quote the extract in its entirety:[10]

> What can be finer in any poet than that beautiful passage in Milton—
> > *Onward he moved*
> > *And thousands of his saints around.*
> This is grandeur, but it is grandeur without completeness: but he adds—
> > *Far off their coming shone;*
> which is the highest sublime. There is *total* completeness.
>
> So I would say that the Saviour praying on the Mountain, the Desert on one hand, the Sea on the other, the City at an immense distance below, was sublime. But I should say of the Saviour looking towards the City, his countenance full of pity, that he was majestic, and of the situation that it was grand.
>
> When the whole and the parts are seen at once, as mutually producing and explaining each other, as unity in multeity, there results shapeliness, *forma formosa.* Where the perfection of *form* is combined with pleasurableness in the sensations, excited by the matters or substances so formed, there results the beautiful.
>
> *Corollary.*—Hence colour is eminently subservient to beauty, because it is susceptible of forms, i.e. outline, and yet is a sensation. But a rich mass of scarlet clouds, seen without any attention to the *form* of the mass or the parts: may be a *delightful* but not a beautiful object or colour.
>
> When there is a deficiency of unity in the line forming the whole (as angularity, for instance), and of number in the plurality or the parts, there arises the formal.
>
> When the parts are numerous, and impressive, and predominate, so as to prevent or greatly lessen the attention to the whole, there results the grand.
>
> Where the impression of the whole, i.e. the sense of unity, predominates so as to abstract the mind from the parts—the majestic.
>
> Where the parts by their harmony produce an effect of a whole, but where there is no seen form of a whole producing or explaining the parts, i.e. when the parts only are seen and distinguished, but the whole is felt—the picturesque.

[10] Thomas Allsop, *Letters, Conversations, and Recollections of S. T. Coleridge,* 2 vols., London, 1836, Vol. I, pp. 197-9. This extract is reprinted in substance in J. Shawcross' edition of the *Biographia Literaria,* Oxford, 1907, Vol. II, p. 309, and verbatim in the Oxford edition of *Table Talk and Omniana,* London, 1917, pp. 442-3.

Where neither whole nor parts [are seen and distinguished] but unity, as boundless or endless *allness*—the Sublime.

This is almost too much—as if Coleridge had permitted his passion for fine distinctions to run away with his good judgment. Yet there is sense in it, profundity even. From the passage as a whole there emerges a basic distinction to which Coleridge quite consistently adheres: that in objects fitted to excite beauty the sensible form is such that it may be taken in by the mind, both in the whole and in the parts, in a single apprehension; but that in objects fitted to excite sublimity, neither the whole nor the parts are at any moment clearly distinguished, although there is felt a vast indefinite unity, or *allness,* which we may assume elevates the mind to the height of the sublime. So the picture of the "Saviour praying on the Mountain, the Desert on one hand, the Sea on the other, the City at an immense distance below," in its greatness and diversity eluding every effort to grasp it in one image-making act, in its unity compelling an attempt to apprehend not only the whole but the parts, is a typical object of sublimity. Similarly, the image of the approach of the Messiah, too far-off for clear distinction of details, too vast for successful comprehension, yet unified in a large, indefinite way, gives the sense of infinitude characteristic of the sublime. In such an experience, if we may venture an interpretation, the mind tends to expand indefinitely, seeking a unity which it feels but cannot perceive, until it is lost in a sort of pleasing bewilderment in intuitions of endless power and greatness.

Coleridge elsewhere insists upon clear distinctions in referring to the sublime. Thus, in his marginal notes to Herder's *Kalligone*[11] he censures Herder for confusing meanings:

Herder mistakes for the *Sublime* sometimes the *Grand,* sometimes the *Majestic,* sometimes the *Intense,* in which last sense we must render [a hiatus of more than a line in manuscript][12] or magnificent, but as a whole (a

11 J. Shawcross, "Coleridge's Marginalia," *Notes and Queries* (10th series), Vol. IV (July-December 1905), pp. 341 *ff.*

12 Shawcross thinks that Coleridge had adduced here a concrete illustration "of an object which may be called intense or magnificent (and perhaps also beautiful), but not sublime" (*ibid.*).

visual whole, I mean) it cannot be sublime. A mountain in a cloudless sky, its summit smit with the sunset, is a beautiful, a magnificent object: the same with its summit hidden by clouds and seemingly blended with the sky, while mists and floating vapours [encompass it, is sublime].[13]

Shawcross offers the following interpretive comment on this passage:

The sun-smitten mountain is beautiful, in virtue of what it actually and directly presents to the senses; the cloud-capped mountain is sublime, in virtue of the idea of infinity which it suggests to the mind.[14]

This interpretation appears to be the right one. To Coleridge as to Kant[15] sublimity is entirely in the mind of the observer. It is true that Coleridge also regarded beauty as in the mind; but in the emotion of beauty the process is different. Here the mind goes out to its object, and, finding a definite form which can be grasped and held in its unity, it rests there and takes its pleasure in the sensible image. In the act of reconciliation between the objective and the subjective[16] the objective seems to achieve dominance, the mind projecting itself into the external form, and contemplating it in sympathetic union. In sublimity, this process is reversed. The mind, baffled by inability to grasp the object, yet conscious of a totality that fascinates while it eludes, recoils upon itself, finding its pleasure in elevated ideas that rival the greatness of the object, but which center in itself rather than in the object.

A paradoxical aspect of this experience appears in the fact that while it is characterized by a flight of mind from the sensuous reality to its own conceptions, the object giving rise to it so compels and enchains the attention that no comparison with other objects is possible. Coleridge makes a good deal of this principle of suspended comparison in sublimity. There is no better statement of it than in a passage in the little essay written from Ratzeburg, 1799, entitled "Christmas out of Doors":

About a month ago, before the thaw came on, there was a storm of wind; and during the whole night, such were the thunders and howlings of the

---

[13] The words enclosed in brackets are suggested by Shawcross as filling a hiatus in the manuscript.

[14] *op. cit.*, p. 342.

[15] "Sublimity, therefore, does not reside in anything in nature, but only in our mind" (*Critique of Judgment*, Vol. I, i, No. 28).

[16] Described in *Biographia Literaria*, Chap. XII, Shawcross, Vol. I, p. 174.

breaking ice, that they have left a conviction on my mind, that there are sounds more sublime than any sight can be, more absolutely suspending the power of comparison, and more utterly absorbing the mind's self-consciousness in its total attention to the object working upon it.[17]

In a note to Herder's quotation from Kant to the effect, "From this fact it follows that the sublime is not in things of Nature, but in our ideas alone. . . . The above explanation may also be expressed thus: That is sublime in comparison with which everything else appears small," Coleridge writes, "*Here* Kant *has* layed himself open to censure." [18] As Shawcross has noted, Coleridge is no doubt censuring Kant for his use of "comparison" applied to the sublime. For with Coleridge a sublime object admits of no comparison. With this principle in mind we understand Coleridge's stricture on Klopstock, who he clearly felt, lacked the true sublime:

As to sublimity, he had, with all Germans, one rule for producing it; it was, to take something very great, and make it very small in comparison with that which you wish to elevate. Thus, for example, Klopstock says, "As the gardener goes forth, and scatters from his basket seed into the garden; so does the Creator scatter worlds with His right hand." Here *worlds,* a large object, are made small in the hands of the Creator; consequently, the Creator is very great. In short, the Germans were not a poetical nation in the very highest sense.[19]

A long note to the *Kalligone* contains a fairly adequate summation of Coleridge's ideas on the sublime that have been thus far considered:

We call an object sublime in relation to which the exercise of comparison is suspended: while on the contrary that object is most beautiful, which in its highest perfection sustains while it satisfies the comparing Power. The subjective result is [of the second kind][20] when a wheel turns so smoothly and swiftly as to present a stationary image to the eye, or as a fountain (such as either of the two in the Colonnade of St. Peter's at Rome, "Fons omni fonti formasior!"). It is impossible that the same object should be sub-

---

[17] *The Complete Works of Samuel Taylor Coleridge,* 7 vols., ed. by W. G. T. Shedd, New York, 1864, Vol. II, p. 337.

[18] Shawcross, "Coleridge's Marginalia," *Notes and Queries,* Vol. IV, p. 342.

[19] *The Table Talk and Omniana of Samuel Taylor Coleridge* (April 20, 1811), London, 1917, p. 315.

[20] The matter in brackets in this passage represents Mr. Shawcross' suggestions for filling in torn places or obliterations in the manuscript.

lime and beautiful at the same moment to the same mind, though a beautiful
object may excite and be made the symbol of an Idea that is truly [sublime.
A] Serpent in a wreath of folds bathing in the sun is beautiful to Aspasia,
whose attention is confined to the visual impression, but excites an emotion
of sublimity in Plato, who contemplates under that symbol the Idea of
Eternity.[21]

In these words, we find reiteration of the theory that in beauty the
mind rests in the object, the idea of which is adequate to its form and
magnitude, whereas in sublimity the mind, unable to find a basis for
comparing the totality suggested with any sensible form pleases itself
with its own ideas suggested by, but not contained in, the exciting
object. We find also repeated the conviction that no object can be called
sublime and beautiful by the same person at the same moment. There
is a new thought, however, and this serves to reemphasize the completely
subjective nature of sublimity: that is, the same object may be beautiful
to one person and sublime to another. So a serpent, merely beautiful
to Aspasia, may be the means of leading Plato's mind into an emo-
tionalized contemplation of ideas of eternity and infinity.

That these are not isolated ideas, but represent confirmed theory, may
be seen from an examination of various passages from Coleridge's letters and other prose works. Apropos the power of mind to find sublimity
in objects not sublime to others, Coleridge writes in a letter to William
Godwin:

At times I dwell on man with such reverence, resolve all his follies and
superstitions into such grand primary laws of intellect, and in such wise so
contemplate them as ever-varying incarnations of the Eternal Life—that the
Llama's dung-pellet, or the cowtail which the dying Brahmin clutches
convulsively become sanctified and sublime by the feelings which cluster
round them.[22]

The first part of this statement is interesting as a prose version of
Wordsworth's exalted expression in *The Recluse* of reverence for the
dignity and greatness and mystery of the mind of man. The last part is,
however, another way of saying that almost any object, however mean,

[21] *op. cit.,* p. 341.
[22] To William Godwin (September 22, 1800), *Unpublished Letters of Samuel Taylor Coleridge,* 2 vols., ed. by E. L. Griggs, London and New Haven, 1932, 1933, Vol. I, p. 154.

provided it may occur in such a circumstance as to become a symbol for that which is great or eternal, may excite the mind to sublimity.

Habitually, however, Coleridge's pronouncements on sublimity are related to objects or ideas of such quality as to compel the mind to elevated ideas of the peculiar sort that distinguish the sublime. This is not to say that mere vastness of size or greatness of thought is sufficient to arouse sublimity. The true principle of the sublime, with Coleridge, seems to reside not in expanse or bulk *per se,* but rather in such supernumerary qualities as variety and complexity of detail, changing patterns of form, light and shade, obscurity, indefiniteness of outline, anything in fact which tends to baffle the imagination and to suggest to the mind infinite forces working in unseen, incomprehensible ways. Similarly in literature sublimity appears to lie not in representations of largeness alone, but in great ideas and in suggestions of undefined, unlimited power. To Coleridge, then, sublimity may be said to consist of impressions of infinite greatness or power.[23]

Accordingly, we find Coleridge describing certain great prospects as "lovely" and "grand" rather than as "sublime." Others, depending on seasonal and atmospheric conditions, he at one time calls beautiful, at another time sublime. His descriptions of Catlenburg and Ratzeburg scenery will illustrate such distinctions. Near Catlenburg Coleridge tells of coming to a "lovely scene" made up of "hillocks and scattered oaks, and Beeches, a sweet tho' very small lake, a green meadow," all completely encircled by the "grandest swell of woods" he had ever seen. Having walked for two hours under a complete bower in this woods, the travellers finally emerged. "I shall never forget that glorious prospect," Coleridge exclaims:

Behind me the Hartz Mountains with the snow-spots shining on them; close around us Woods upon little Hills, little Hills of an hundred Shapes,

---

[23] I am aware that I have used almost the exact words of A. C. Bradley descriptive of the sublime. Bradley says that sublimity has its origin in "an impression of exceeding or overwhelming greatness," but that this greatness may not be of mere extent—it may be an impression of "greatness of power" excited by a very small object, like Wordsworth's six-year-old child or Turgenief's sparrow. ("The Sublime," *Oxford Lectures on Poetry,* London, 1909, pp. 41-5.) Bradley is often near Coleridge in his ideas, yet I do not see evidence that he drew from him on this particular point.

a *dance* of Hills, whose variety of position supplied the *effect* of, and almost imitated, *motion*. . . . And all these hills in all their forms and *bearings,* which it were such a chaos to describe, were yet all in so pure a Harmony![24]

The word sublime is not used in this description, and the last statement no doubt explains its omission. The scene is harmonious. And harmony belongs to the lovely, the magnificent, the beautiful; it is not characteristic of the sublime. Moreover, as we have seen, a sort of intellectual intuition, produced in intensity of mental exertion, enters with feeling into Coleridge's experiences of sublimity. Here Coleridge records no mental tension or exertion; he is only enjoying. His mind does not flee from the sensible imagery but rests in the scene and finds its pleasure in contemplating its varied charm.

On the other hand, in the following passage, so fine as to deserve quotation in its own right, though the word is not mentioned, the conditions for sublimity are all satisfied:

At length we came to the foot of the huge Fir-mount, roaring with woods, and winds, and waters! And now the Sky cleared up, and masses of crimson light fell around us from the fiery West, and from the Clouds over our heads that *reflected* the western fires. We wound along by the feet of the mount, and left it behind us, close before us a high hill, a high hill close on our right, and close on our left a hill—we were in a circular Prison of Hills, and many a mass of Light, moving and stationary, gave life and wildness to the Rocks, and Woods that rose out of them. But now we emerged into a new scene! close by our left hand was a little Hamlet, each House with its orchard of Blossom-Trees, in a very small and very narrow coomb: . . . but on our right hand was a huge Valley with rocks in the distance and a steady Mass of Clouds that afforded no mean substitute for a Sea. . . . And now we arrived at Hartsburg—Hills ever by our sides, in all conceivable variety of forms and garniture—It were idle in me to attempt by words to give their projections and their retirings and how they were now in Cones, now in roundnesses, now in tonguelike Lengths, now pyramidal, now a huge Bow, and all at every step varying the forms of their outlines; or how they now stood abreast, now ran aslant, now rose up behind each other, or now . . . presented almost a Sea of huge motionless waves, too multiform for Painting, too multiform even for the Imagination to remember them—yea, my very sight seems *incapacitated* by the novelty

[24] To Thomas Poole (May 19, 1799), Griggs, *op. cit.,* Vol. I, p. 115.

and Complexity of the Scene. Ye red lights from the Rain Clouds! Ye gave the whole the last Magic Touch![25]

In this near perfect expression of the variety, complexity, and magic supernumerary touches of mountain scenery—"too multiform for Painting, too multiform even for the Imagination to remember"—Coleridge presents a situation entirely favorable to sublimity. Here there can be no repose in the object, only excitation and bafflement in attempts to apprehend, to be followed, we may infer, by release of the mind in elevated emotional contemplation.

Coleridge's descriptions of Ratzeburg scenery are interesting as showing how to him the same general landscape may be beautiful or lovely at one time, but under different conditions may be sublime. Thus, in bright autumn weather the sun rising and setting over the little lake presented most "lovely spectacles." The October sunset, in particular, was "completely beautiful." At this time,

A deep red light spread over all, in complete harmony with the red town, the brown-red woods, and the yellow-red reeds on the skirts of the lake and on the slip of land.[26]

Again harmony, form, rest in the image; but winter changes the effect completely:

. . . when first the ice fell on the lake, and the whole lake was frozen one large piece of thick transparent glass—O my God! what sublime scenery I have beheld.

As we read what follows, we recall the mists and half-lights and disappearing forms described in the illustration of sublimity in the Marginalia to *Kalligone*:

Of a morning I have seen the little lake covered with mist; when the sun peeped over the hills the mist broke in the middle, and at last stood as the waters of the Red Sea are said to have done when the Israelites passed; and between these two walls of mist the sunlight burst upon the ice in a straight road of golden fire, all across the lake, intolerably bright, and the walls of mist partaking of the light in a *multitude* of colours.

[25] To Thomas Poole (May 19, 1799), Griggs, *op. cit.*, Vol. I, pp. 110-11.
[26] To Mrs. Coleridge (January 1799), *Letters of Samuel Taylor Coleridge*, 2 vols., ed. by E. H. Coleridge, London, 1895, Vol. I, p. 275.

Coleridge's description itself partakes somewhat of the scriptural grandeur he so much admires. He goes on to tell how, a month or so before, the wind had broken the ice, and part of it, quite shattered, had been driven to the shore and had frozen anew. This

> was of a deep blue, and represented an agitated sea—the water that ran up between the great islands of ice shone of a yellow-green (it was at sunset), and all the scattered islands of *smooth* ice were *blood*, intensely bright *blood*; on some of the largest islands the fishermen were pulling out their immense nets through the holes made in the ice for this purpose, and the fishermen, the net-poles, and the huge nets made a part of the glory! O my God, how I wished you to be with me![27]

I have quoted from this description at some length because it is one of the best illustrations in Coleridge's writings of the theory of the sublime he adumbrates in his notes to *Kalligone*. In October clearly defined sun effects on a quiet lake, set against a harmonious background of town and mountains, are lovely, or beautiful; they sustain and satisfy the comparing power, and invite the mind to rest. But a mist-hung lake in winter, with the sun breaking through to stand suspended as it sends a broad road of blood-red colors—a multitude of colors—over the frozen, uneven surface, broken, like an agitated sea, with islands of ice blood-red in the sunset, is sublime. The effect, as we may infer it from passages in the "Marginalia," is not rest in the object, but retreat of the mind upon itself in imaginative contemplations of infinity.[28]

An interesting variation of this account of the Ratzeburg lake in its beauty and sublimity is to be found in "Christmas out of Doors." According to this description on Christmas day itself the lake was "one

---

[27] *ibid.*, p. 276.

[28] These ideas may be compared with the following from A. C. Bradley: "But perhaps we may say this. In 'beauty' that which appears in a sensuous form seems to rest in it, to be perfectly embodied in it, and to have no tendency to pass beyond it. In the sublime, even where no such tendency is felt and sublimity is nearest to 'beauty,' we still feel the presence of a power held in reserve, which could with ease exceed its present expression. In *some* forms of sublimity, again, the sensuous embodiment seems threatening to break in its effort to express what appears in it. And in others we definitely feel that the power which for a moment intimates its presence to sense is infinite and utterly uncontainable by any or all vehicles of its manifestation. Here we are furthest (in a way) from sense, and furthest also from 'beauty'" (*Oxford Lectures in Poetry*, London, 1909, p. 58).

mass of thick transparent ice, a spotless mirror of nine miles in extent." The lowness of the hills "precludes the awful sublimity of Alpine landscape," but the beauties of the scene amply compensate for this loss.[29] Then follows a passage describing the lake the preceding day, with a mist above it and the sun breaking through to make a broad road of light across the ice. This at first glance appears to be the scene that had been labelled "sublime" in the letter to Mrs. Coleridge, but now regarded as beautiful. But closer inspection shows that it is not the same: some of the variety and certain of the wild, suggestive phenomena are lacking. The month before, however, there had been a storm, with sounds of "awful sublimity" in the night,[30] and the ice of the lake had been shattered, and again frozen:

On the evening of the next day, at sunset, the shattered ice thus frozen, appeared of a deep blue, and in shape like an agitated sea; beyond this, the water that ran up between the great islands of ice which had preserved their masses entire and smooth, shone of a yellow green; but all these scattered ice-islands, themselves, were of an intensely bright blood color,—they seemed blood and light in union. On some of the largest of these islands, the fishermen stood pulling out their immense nets through the holes made in the ice for this purpose, and the men, their net poles, and their huge nets, were a part of the glory; say rather, it appeared as if the rich crimson light had shaped itself into these forms, figures, and attitudes, to make a glorious vision in mockery of earthly things.[31]

This more closely parallels the scene of sublimity described in the letter, and, though the word now used is "glory," it is no doubt the glory of the sublime. For after a paragraph of digression on the pleasures of skating, Coleridge writes,

Here I stop, having in truth transcribed the preceding in great measure, in order to present the lovers of poetry with a descriptive passage, extracted with the author's permission, from an unpublished poem on the growth and revolutions of an individual mind.[32]

[29] *The Complete Works of Samuel Taylor Coleridge,* 7 vols., ed. by W. G. T. Shedd, New York, 1853, 1884, Vol. II, p. 336.
[30] See page 203 of this essay.
[31] Shedd, Vol. II, p. 337.
[32] *ibid.,* pp. 337-8.

He then transcribes a considerable passage from Wordsworth's *Prelude,* parts of which have direct bearing on the subject of sublimity. I quote the first few lines:

> Wisdom and spirit of the universe!
> Thou soul, that art the eternity of thought!
> And giv'st to forms and images a breath
> And everlasting motion! not in vain,
> By day or star-light, thus from my first dawn
> Of childhood didst thou intertwine for me
> The passions that build up our human soul,
> Not with the mean and vulgar works of man,
> But with high objects, with enduring things,
> With life and nature: purifying thus
> The elements of feeling and of thought,
> And sanctifying by such discipline
> Both pain and fear, until we recognize
> A grandeur in the beatings of the heart.[33]

If these lines reflect the workings of Coleridge's mind as he watched the Ratzeburg lake in winter, we know that his experience of sublimity was on occasion similar to that of Wordsworth's—an arousal, under the stimulus of great objects, to a consciousness of eternal, universal being, moving in all things, both in nature and in the mind of man, with a consequent new awareness of the power and grandeur of the human soul.[34] This bears a certain likeness to the transcendental sublime

[33] See *The Prelude,* i, 401-63. These lines were published under the title of *Influence of Natural Objects* in the 1815 edition of Wordsworth's poems. The "Christmas out of Doors" in which they were quoted by Coleridge, appeared in *The Friend,* December 28, 1809.

[34] Coleridge is also agreeing with Wordsworth on the ennobling influence on the spirit of man of lofty objects in nature. Related conceptions are expressed in two extracts from letters to William Godwin. In the first (May 21, 1800), he writes—half humourously, yet we may believe, remembering the date, with an undercurrent of conviction: "I left Wordsworth on the 4th of this month. If I cannot procure a suitable house at Stowey I return to Cumberland and settle at Keswick, in a house of such a prospect, that if according to you and Hume, impressions and ideas *constitute* our being, I shall have a tendency to become a god, so sublime and beautiful will be the series of my visual existence" (Griggs, Vol. I, p. 138). In the second (September 22, 1800), he remarks to Godwin: "I look at my doted-on Hartley—he moves, he lives, he finds impulses from

of Kant, but it is perhaps nearer to the English tradition of the religious sublime, exemplified in Dennis and James Usher, and to a less extent in Addison.

Sublimity merged with mystical religious experience to a degree even beyond what was acceptable to Wordsworth is expressed, according to Coleridge's own interpretation, in "The Hymn before Sunrise in the Vale of Chamouni." In this poem, it will be recalled, the poet gazes on the "dread and silent" Mount Blanc and the vale below until the image, though still present to the bodily sense, vanishes from his thought and with "dilating soul, enrapt, transfused," he worships "the Invisible alone." The scene—mountain and valley before sunrise, the silent peak rising in solitary and awful might out of a silent sea of pines and deep, dark air, its details somewhat obscured in the lingering night-time shadows—is fitted to create an instant effect of religious sublimity, which passes, as the poet's mind works upon its impressions, to a definitely pronounced mood of devotional rapture. Coleridge's remarks on the poem furnish the best commentary on his experience:

In a copy of verses entitled "A Hymn before Sunrise in the Vale of Chamouny" I described myself under the influence of strong devotional feelings gazing on the Mountain till as if it had been a Shape emanating from and sensibly representing her own essence my soul had become diffused thro' "the mighty Vision," and there

As in her natural Form, swelled vast to Heaven.

Mr. Wordsworth, I remember, censured the passage as strained and unnatural, and condemned the Hymn in toto . . . as a specimen of the Mock Sublime. It may be so for others; but it is impossible that I should find it myself unnatural, being conscious that it was the image and utterance of Thoughts and Emotions in which there was no Mockery.[35]

Although the lines in the *Hymn* about the dilated soul swelling vast to heaven, to which Wordsworth particularly objected, no doubt best describe sublimity as Coleridge conceived it, he seems to be defending

within and from without, he is the darling of the sun and of the breeze. Nature seems to bless him as a thing of her own. He looks at the clouds, the mountains, the living beings of the earth, and vaults and jubilates! Solemn looks and solemn words have been hitherto connected in his mind with great and magnificent objects only: with lightning, with thunder, with the waterfall blazing in the sunset" (*ibid.*, p. 155).

[35] *To an Unknown Correspondent* (1820), Griggs, *op. cit.*, Vol. II, pp. 261-2.

the whole poem as an exemplification of the true sublime. In either case, we must conclude that, with whatever care he set apart sublimity from beauty, majesty, and so forth, he was not at all so clear in distinguishing it from intense religious experience. Coleridge's description of his response to Gothic architecture corroborates this view:

When I enter a Greek church, my eye is charmed, and my mind elated; I feel exalted, and proud that I am a man. But the Gothic art is sublime. On entering a cathedral, I am filled with devotion and with awe; I am lost to the actualities that surround me, and my whole being expands into the infinite; earth and air, nature and art, all swell up into eternity, and the only sensible impression left is, "that I am nothing!"[36]

With Wordsworth, too, it may be noted, the sublime often merges with the religious; but his stricture on Coleridge's *Hymn* may be in part understood if we recall a rather fundamental difference between Coleridge's poem and the lines on Simplon Pass (*The Prelude*, vi, 592 *ff.*), which in some respects it resembles. To Coleridge the first emotional state in which the expanded soul rapturously rises to mingle with "the mighty vision," changes to a more intellectual, objective phase wherein the mind is occupied with ideas of God, the author of all this splendor, and with the praise that is God's due. To Wordsworth the sublime scene of the Simplon Pass is, likewise, the occasion for an illuminating vision of infinitude, but it is a vision in which the human soul is throughout identified. The intuition of Coleridge is of an elevation of mind commensurate with power to recognize the glory of God; Wordsworth's intuition is of imaginative awareness of the grandeur of man's spirit as a portion of the all-spirit of the universe.[37]

[36] *Coleridge's Miscellaneous Criticism*, ed. by T. M. Raysor, Cambridge, 1936, pp. 11-12.

[37] Wordsworth's ideas on the sublime are worthy of more extended study than they have yet received. The following passage shows him in agreement with Coleridge on the necessity for differentiating sublimity from beauty, grandeur, and so forth, but in disagreement on sublimity in Greek literature. The reference to Longinus is worth noting in view of the fact that writers on sublimity have so far failed to notice it and that one scholar (Elizabeth Nitchie, *The Classical Weekly*, March 5, 1931) has recently stated that Wordsworth did not know Longinus:

"You have been successful in clearing up my doubts as to your meaning upon the picturesque. It would occupy more paper than I have before me, and require more exertion than this languid *summer's day* in April . . . would allow, to establish my position that 'the sublime and beautiful cannot be felt in the same instant of

Religion elsewhere figures in Coleridge's conception of sublimity. The Christian and Hebrew religion seemed to him to furnish more material for sublime poetry than does Greek mythology. Indeed, his distinct preference for the Biblical type of sublimity led Coleridge to undervalue the Greek sublime. "Could you ever," he once inquired, "discover anything sublime, in our sense of the term, in the classic Greek literature? I never could. Sublimity is Hebrew by birth."[38] At another time he remarked, "Think of the sublimity, I should rather say the profundity, of that passage in Ezekiel, 'Son of man, can these bones live? And I answered, O Lord God, thou knowest.' I know nothing like it."[39] In a letter to Thelwall, he amplifies and illustrates his predilection for the Hebrew-Christian sublime. Having finished telling his correspondent that when he thinks he feels and that when he feels he thinks,[40] Coleridge proceeds to defend the Christian religion and the Scriptures against Thelwall's charge of meanness:

You say the Christian is a *mean* religion. Now the religion which Christ taught is simply, first, that there is an omnipresent Father of infinite power, wisdom, and goodness, in whom we all of us move and have our being; and, secondly, that when we appear to men to die we do not utterly perish, but after this life shall continue to enjoy or suffer the consequences and natural effects of the habits we have formed here, whether good or evil. This is that Christian *religion,* and all of the Christian *religion.* That there is

time'; attaching such meaning to the words as I think they ought to bear. One is surprised that it should have been supposed for a moment, that *Longinus* writes upon the sublime, even in our vague and popular sense of the word. What is there in Sappho's ode that has any affinity with the sublimity of Ezekiel or Isaiah, or even of Homer or Aeschylus? Longinus treats of animated, empassioned, energetic, or, if you will, elevated writing. Of these, abundant instances are to be found in Aeschylus and Homer; but nothing would be easier than to show, both by positive and negative proof, that his ὕψους when translated "sublimity" deceives the English reader, by substituting an etymology for a translation. Much of what I observe you call sublime, *I* should denominate grand or dignified. But, as I wrote before, we shall never see clearly into this subject, unless we turn from objects to laws. I am far from thinking that I am able to write satisfactorily upon matters so subtile, yet I hope to make a trial and must request your patience till that time" (Letters to J. Fletcher, April 6, 1825, *Letters of the Wordsworth Family,* ed. by Wm. Knight, London and Boston, 1907, Vol. II, p. 250).

38 *Table Talk and Omniana* (July 25, 1832), p. 191.

39 *ibid.* (May 9, 1830), p. 91.

40 To John Thelwall (December 1796), *Letters of Samuel Taylor Coleridge,* 2 vols., ed. by E. H. Coleridge, London, 1895, Vol. I, p. 197.

no *fancy* in it I readily grant, but that it is mean and deficient in *mind* and *energy* it were impossible for me to admit, unless I admitted that there *could be* no dignity, intellect, or force in anything but *atheism*. But though it appeal not itself to the fancy, the truths which it teaches admit the highest exercise of it.[41]

The proof of this last statement resides in the literature inspired by this religion, which, Coleridge feels, excels in imaginative scope and power anything produced by the Greeks:

Are the "innumerable multitude of angels and archangels" less splendid beings than the countless gods and goddesses of Rome and Greece? And can you seriously think that Mercury from Jove equals in poetic sublimity "the mighty angel that came down from heaven, whose face was as it were the sun and his feet as pillars of fire: who set his right foot on the sea, and his left foot on the earth. And he sent forth a loud voice; and when he had sent it forth, seven thunders uttered their voices: and when the seven thunders had uttered their voices, the mighty Angel lifted up his hand to heaven, and sware by Him that liveth for ever and ever that *Time* was no more"?[42]

Here, we may believe, is Coleridge's conception of the highest sublime: ideas and imagery, elevated, grand, infinite in scope and in suggestive energy, that send the mind soaring into the realms of the eternal. As for Milton, he continues, he is a sublimer poet than Homer or Virgil, his personages more sublimely clothed; yet there is scarcely a page in *Paradise Lost* in which he has not borrowed his imagery from the Scriptures, and, great as he is, he has not attained to anything like their sublimity. "After reading Isaiah, or St. Paul's 'Epistle to the Hebrews,' Homer and Virgil are disgustingly tame to me," Coleridge asserts; indeed, Milton himself seems barely tolerable.[43]

Coleridge's convictions are so strong on the superior quality of Biblical sublimity that he can only infer a fundamental difference in psychological organization and taste in one who disagrees with him:

You and I are very differently organized if you think that the following (putting serious belief out of the question) is a mean flight of impassioned eloquence in which the Apostle marks the difference between the Mosaic

[41] *ibid.*, p. 199.
[42] *ibid.* Coleridge is citing Revelations x. 1-6.
[43] *ibid.*, p. 200.

and Christian Dispensation: "For ye are not come unto the mount that might be touched" (that is, a material and earthly place) "and that burned with fire, nor unto blackness, and tempest, and the sound of a trumpet, and the voice of words; which voice they that heard entreated that the word should not be spoken to them any more. But ye are come unto Mount Sion, and unto the city of the living God, to an innumerable company of angels, to God the Judge of all, and to the spirits of just men made perfect." *You* may prefer to all this the quarrels of Jupiter and Juno, the whimpering of wounded Venus, and the jokes of the celestials on the lameness of Vulcan. Be it so (the difference in our tastes it would not be difficult to account for from the different feelings which we have associated with these ideas); I shall continue with Milton to say that

> "Zion Hill
> Delights me more, and Siloa's brook that flow'd
> Fast by the oracle of God!"[44]

The bias Coleridge has here expressed may lie in the fact that he felt that Biblical conceptions gave more room for the imagination than did the Greek and Roman. There is evidence for this in a letter to Wedgwood, in which he compares the Christian and pagan religions. Having remarked on the possibilities for writing on "how far a Passion for Statues, etc., may smuggle a sort of Idolatry into the Feelings although it *may be* too late in the World to introduce it into the understanding," he goes on to say:

The more I think, the more I am convinced that the greatest of differences is produced when in the one case the feelings are worked upon thro' the Imagination and the Imagination thro' definite Forms (i.e. the Religion of Greece and Rome); and in the other cases where the Feelings are worked upon by Hopes and Fears purely individual, and the Imagination is kept barren in definite Forms and only in cooperation with the Understanding labours after an obscure and indefinite Vastness—this is Christianity.[45]

As we have seen, Coleridge regarded "obscure and indefinite vastness" as one of the chief sources of sublimity. The hopes and fears, the aspirations for infinite perfection, the strivings for comprehension of a God whose voice is the winds and the thunder and whose abode is the heavens, which are characteristic of Christianity, are peculiarly con-

[44] E. H. Coleridge, *op. cit.*, p. 200. Coleridge is quoting, somewhat freely, Hebrews xii. 18-22.

[45] To Josiah Wedgwood (1799), Griggs, Vol. I, p. 117.

genial to this view. The anthropomorphic conceptions of the Greeks and Romans offered to the imagination matter of quite different quality. The contrast Coleridge draws between the two religions in this respect presents a striking analogy to the usual distinction between the self-contained perfection of form in pagan classic art and the suggestive quality and striving spirit, often outswelling definite form, in Christian romantic art. To Coleridge the latter appears to be much more favorable to sublimity.

In other places Coleridge reveals an even more definite tendency to relate Christian belief to the sublime. Indeed, one may be reasonably certain that when he talks of contemplating the "infinite" in the experience of sublimity he often has in mind the Godhead of Christian theology. In the following passage, itself illustrative of sublime writing, religious concept and sublimity seem fused in a sort of inalienable union:

She [a young lady who had killed her mother] is recovered, and is acquainted with what she has done, and is very calm. She was a truly pious young woman; and her Brother, whose soul is almost wrapped up in her, hath had his heart purified by this horror of desolation, and prostrates his spirit at the throne of God in believing Silence. The Terrors of the Almighty are the whirlwind, the earthquake, and the Fire that precede the still small voice of his Love. The pestilence of our lusts must be scattered, the strong-layed Foundations of our Pride blown up, and the stubble and chaff of our Vanities burnt, ere we can give ear to the inspeaking Voice of Mercy, "Why *will* ye die?"[46]

One may compare the type of sublimity recorded here with what Santayana calls the "heroic reaction of the soul" to evil. When evil is irreparable, he says, when our life has been lived, "a strong spirit has the sublime resource of standing at bay and of surveying almost from the other world the vicissitudes of this."[47] And further:

The more intimate to himself the tragedy he is able to look back upon with calmness, the more sublime that calmness is, and the more divine the ecstasy in which he achieves it. For the more of the accidental vesture of life we are able to strip ourselves of, the more naked and simple is the

[46] To Benjamin Flower (December 1796), Griggs, Vol. I, pp. 64-5.
[47] George Santayana, *The Sense of Beauty*, New York, 1896, p. 236.

surviving spirit; the more complete its superiority and unity, and, consequently, the more unqualified its joy. There remains little in us, then, but
that intellectual essence, which several great philosophers have called eternal
and identified with the Divinity.[48]

Through thus piecing together scattered evidence we are able to
reconstruct, let us hope with fair accuracy, Coleridge's theory of the
sublime. This theory may be summarized as follows:

(1) Sublimity is in the mind of the observer not in the object; that is, it is
inherently subjective.
(2) Sublimity is an effect of infinity—of "unity as boundless or endless
allness"; or it is an impression of unfathomable greatness of power.
(3) An object cannot give both the effect of beauty (or grandeur, picturesqueness, prettiness, etc.) and sublimity in the same mind at the same time.
(4) Objects fitted to arouse sublimity are such as admit of no comparison:
that is, in the experience of sublimity, whatever the object, comparison
is always suspended.
(5) Such objects differ from those fitted to excite beauty in that they
present such greatness, such complexity, such variety, or such shadowy,
indefinite quality, that the form escapes successful apprehension.
(6) In certain cases, the effect of sublimity may be produced from a small
or otherwise physically unimpressive object through the peculiar action
of an individual mind in contemplation of this object as a symbol of
infinite quality or being (e.g. Plato's snake; Coleridge's dung-pellet).
(7) Literature and the other arts are sublime when they convey an impression of infinite power, or of obscure and undefined vastness of being.
(8) The finest examples of sublimity in literature are to be found in the
Hebrew Scriptures; next to them in Milton.

Coleridge's theory has much in common with Kant's, but presents
some differences. In general, one may say that, like Kant, Coleridge
regards sublimity as a species of contemplative activity in which moral
ideas are inextricably interwoven. Like Kant, too, he conceives of this
experience as a subjective thing in which the mind, baffled in its
attempts to grasp an infinite complexity, takes refuge in itself, and finds
its pleasure in an expansive exercise of creative energy in constructions
which have no boundaries fixed by the sensible world. In beauty, on
the other hand, the mind finds satisfaction in the object, whose form

[48] *ibid.*, p. 237.

it successfully apprehends, and whose charm and grace, or loveliness, invites to contemplation.

Kant's description of the experience of sublimity is more specific than is Coleridge's. In contemplating vast objects, Kant explains, the infinity presented is "for the imagination like an abyss in which it fears to lose itself," [49] but here reason asserts itself, holding before the imagination representations of the infinite of which man is a part, and inviting the mind to a survey of its inward might. In this act the soul becomes conscious of its own powers and their superiority to nature, even in its most overwhelming aspects, and of its own affinity with the eternal supersensible.[50] The result is that the initial momentary check or repulsion is succeeded by a liberation of spirit, a sense of freedom in escape from the dominions of physical reality that expresses itself in the unique "inspiriting satisfaction" of the sublime.[51] In contrast with beauty, which is characterized by repose, and is positive, this satisfaction is marked by agitation, and, because it springs from an impulse towards that which is unattainable—the infinite—it is negative; yet the experience as a whole is pleasurable, since it "expands the soul."[52] Kant's explanation is metaphysical; he refers the sublime to the supersensible, and finds for it an *a priori* basis, in universal, authentic, and necessary laws of reason.

How far Coleridge agreed or failed to agree with the elaborate Kantian metaphysical exegesis cannot be precisely told. We know that on certain points he openly dissented, but other differences can only be inferred. Coleridge seems not at all concerned as is Kant with defining sublimity in terms of transcendental philosophy, a fact somewhat surprising in view of the general trend of his thinking. He appears to be, on the whole, nearer the mystical-religious-psychological English tradition than to Kant. He is significantly silent on the subject of duality in the experience—pain or opposition followed by pleasurable release—an element which Kant regarded as basic.[53] It is true that this

---

[49] *The Critique of Judgment,* Bernard translation, Vol. I, i, No. 27.
[50] *ibid.,* No. 28.
[51] *ibid.,* Nos. 27, 28.
[52] *ibid.,* No. 29.
[53] Victor Bouillier ("Silvain et Kant," *Revue de Litterature Comparee,* Vol. VIII [1928], p. 253) notes this, indeed, as the most "tangible characteristic of the sublime,"

duality may be implied in certain passages in Coleridge, where, though the word is not used, the conditions for sublimity elsewhere prescribed are indicated. Thus the religious-sublime of the young woman and her brother described in the letter to Benjamin Flower (see page 211 above) postulates duality: calm after the purifying "horror of desolation," the "voice of Love" after the exhibitions of the "Terrors of the Almighty." It may be said, too, that duality is implicit wherever there is recognition of the recoil of the mind upon itself after vain attempts of the imagination to grasp the multiform details of objects of sublimity.[54] But, unless I have missed them, Coleridge fails to make definite statements or clear applications to this point. Perhaps this was deliberate. He may have felt, as does Professor Carritt, that sublimity is often as immediate as is beauty, with no initial negative stage.[55] It is certain that he shows little sympathy with Burke's idea that fear is the basis of the sublime.[56] Awe and reverence are frequently indicated, but seldom fear.

On the question of comparison in sublimity Coleridge is explicit. As we have seen, he takes outright exception to the principle, and in doing so is denying a fundamental tenet in Kant's theory. For with Kant comparison not only enters into the first negative phase, but is essential, through the agency of reason, to the soul's intuition of its own relative superiority, and the consequent sense of liberation and expansion, in the positive phase of the experience. To reject this explanation is to imply a quite different basis for the pleasure of the sublime. This basis Coleridge does not make entirely clear. He is content to say that in

and bases much of his argument against the thesis of Alfred Michiels ("La Theorie de Kant sur le sublime exposee par un Francais en 1708," *Revue Contemporaine* [September 15, 1852]) that Silvain had anticipated Kant in his theory on the fact that this characteristic is not recognized by Silvain.

Hume's statements for the theory of duality are important and basic, founded on rather elaborate psychological principle. They may be found in his *Treatise*, Book II, Part II, sections V-VIII (Selby-Bigge, pp. 421 *ff.*, esp. 423, 432, 435).

[54] See, for example, passages quoted on pages 197-8 and 201-2, above.

[55] E. F. Carritt, *The Theory of Beauty*, London, 1914, pp. 234 *ff*. The passages quoted on pages 196-7, 202, 206, and 207 above, indicate direct response with no moment of check.

[56] Coleridge did not care for Burke's esthetics. "Burke's Essay on the Sublime and Beautiful," he remarked, "seems to me a poor thing; and what he says upon Taste is neither profound nor accurate" (*Table Talk*, Oxford ed., p. 73).

sublimity the mind experiences a sense of "endless allness," or that it loses itself in contemplations of eternity.

Again, however, we may resort to inferences for a fuller explanation. It would seem logical, in view of Coleridge's general philosophic theory, to assume that, basically at least, apprehensions of infinity in the experience of the sublime are referable to reason and religion. According to this theory the mind must depend for its very idea of greatness on reason and religion—often quite indistinguishable in Coleridge. In *The Friend* he writes of the "elevation of spirit . . . to a world of spirit," to "life in the idea, even in the supreme and godlike,"[57] and of the "opening of the inward eye to the glorious vision of that existence which admits of no question out of itself, acknowledges no predicate but the I AM IN THAT I AM."[58] He also describes forms of "impressive experience" in which the mind seeks in "the invisible world alone for the true cause and invisible *nexus* of the things that are seen."[59] To Coleridge the loftiest of all possible intuitions is of "supremacy of being as it is."

Hast thou ever raised thy mind to the consideration of existence, in and by itself, as the mere act of existing? Hast thou ever said to thyself thoughtfully: It is! heedless in that moment, whether it were a man before thee, or a flower, or a grain of sand,—without reference, in short, to this or that particular mode of existence? If thou hast attained to this, thou wilt have felt the presence of a mystery, which must have fixed thy spirit in awe in wonder.[60]

May we not believe that in these passages we have the clue to the nature—if not to the specific content—of Coleridge's experience of the sublime? If so, reason is inalienably related, though Coleridge is not concerned to say so, to sublimity. So, also is religion; for such a revelation of absolute being is impossible, according to Coleridge, without the offices of reason, which gives to the mind an idea whose source and "manifesting power" is God.[61] The total experience, however, even so

[57] Section II, Essay xi, Shedd, Vol. II, p. 471.
[58] *ibid.*, p. 468.
[59] *ibid.*, p. 467.
[60] *ibid.*, pp. 463-4.
[61] *ibid.*, pp. 464-5.

far as reason enters in, would seem to differ materially from Kant's. With Kant sublimity has its genesis in comparison, and ends, through the special intervening offices of reason, in a sense of the relative majesty and dignity of the human spirit. With Coleridge, sublimity begins with a species of emphatic response to a great, complex, or otherwise inspiring object, or with promptings to lofty speculations from something in itself small and unimpressive, and culminates in an intuition of the mystery and greatness of the absolute one and all of Deity.[62]

Coleridge differs from Kant yet again in that, where Kant virtually limits sublimity to nature, Coleridge, as we have seen, pays considerable attention to sublimity in poetry. E. F. Carritt has said that Coleridge, Wordsworth, and their disciples follow Kant's ideas of the sublime in dealing with nature, but accept Hegel in dealing with literature.[63] Without entering into the question of whether this is generally true,[64] we may readily admit that Coleridge shows certain likenesses to Hegelian theory in his attitude on the sublime in literature. Thus, though he does not limit sublimity to divine idea and to God as he appears in Hebrew and Christian writings,[65] he does show a distinct preference for the sublimity of the Scriptures and for that which bears a resemblance to it.

Among modern poets, Milton, even above Wordsworth and Shakespeare, unquestionably exemplifies Coleridge's ideal of the sublime. "Sublimity," he says, "is the preeminent characteristic of Paradise Lost."

It is not an arithmetical sublime like Klopstock's. . . . Klopstock mistakes bigness for greatness. There is a greatness arising from images of effort and

[62] cf. Hegel; who found the truest sublimity in an "intuitive vision of the essence of God as absolutely Spiritual and apart from all image" ("The Art of Sublimity," *The Philosophy of Fine Art,* tr. by F. P. B. Osmaston, London, 1920, Vol. II, p. 97).

[63] *op. cit.,* p. 228.

[64] The statement seems far too sweeping. For example, most of the differences from Kant in Coleridge's theory noted in preceding pages apply to nature as well as to literature.

[65] As does Hegel. "We find as nowhere else this art of the sublime . . . in the religious conceptions of the Hebrew race and their sacred poetry . . . God is the creator of the universe. This is the purest expression of the sublime itself" (*The Philosophy of Fine Art,* tr. by Osmaston, Vol. II, pp. 99, 100).

daring, and also from those of moral endurance; in Milton both are united. The fallen angels are human passions invested with dramatic reality.[66]

The subjective quality of *Paradise Lost* is particularly favorable to sublimity. In the vast half world of dream in which its action is projected, externalities are subordinate, mind transcends its object.

In all modern poetry in Christiandom there is . . . a fleeting away of external things, the mind or subject greater than the object, the reflective character predominant. In *Paradise Lost* the sublimest parts are the revelations of Milton's own mind, producing itself and evolving its own greatness; and this is so truly so that when that which is merely entertaining for its objective beauty is introduced, it at first seems a discord.[67]

Reading this passage, we can better understand why Coleridge admits of no sublimity in the Greeks, who were objective rather than subjective, and finds little of it in the Germans, who were inclined to seek the sublime through mechanical and physical device. Klopstock failed in sublimity because he mistook mathematical bigness for spiritual power; his idea, as we have seen from a remark quoted earlier in this essay, was to make things seem great by comparison—not by absolute quality. Schiller fails because he attempts to secure his effects through externalities, tending toward the melodramatic. Coleridge says:

Schiller has the material Sublime; to produce an effect, he sets you a whole town on fire, and throws infants with their mothers into the flames, or locks up a father in an old tower. But Shakespeare drops a handkerchief, and the same or greater effects follow.[68]

In another place he writes (again with a favorable reference to Shakespeare as, by implication, a successful practitioner of the sublime):

Schiller had two legitimate phases in his intellectual character: the first as author of *The Robbers*—a piece which must not be considered with reference to Shakespeare, but as a work of the mere material sublime, and in that line

[66] *Coleridge's Miscellaneous Criticism*, ed. by T. M. Raysor, Cambridge, 1936, 164.
[67] *ibid.*
[68] *Table Talk and Omniana* (December 29, 1822), pp. 33-4. To Spinoza, however, Coleridge allows true sublimity. Of a passage from Browne's *Religio Medici*, he remarks, "This recalls a sublime thought of Spinoza. Every true virtue is part of that love, with which God loveth himself (Raysor, *Coleridge's Miscellaneous Criticism*, p. 263).

it is undoubtedly very powerful indeed. It is quite genuine, and deeply imbued with Schiller's own soul. After this he out-grew the composition of such plays as *The Robbers,* and at once took his true and only rightful stand in the grand historical drama—the *Wallenstein*; not the intense drama of passion—he was not master of that—but the diffused drama of history, in which alone he had ample scope for his varied powers.[69]

Such statements imply that sublimity in literature requires subjectivity, intensity and depth of passion, quiet and simple rather than highly wrought technique, spiritually significant rather than mechanically exciting incident.[70]

Coleridge's lofty conception of poetry of the sublime type is admirably set forth in a letter to Joseph Cottle. He is agreeing with Wordsworth that Southey writes too "much at his ease," and "that he seldom feels his burthened breast Heaving beneath th' incumbent Deity." To posterity, Coleridge says, Southey's poems are likely to appear unseemly: their beauties lost from the bad company of the "overfluently written" which they keep.

Besides I am fearful that he will begin to rely too much on *story* and *event* in his poems, to the neglect of those *lofty imaginings,* that are peculiar to, and definite of, the poet. The *story* of Milton might be told in two pages— it is this which distinguishes an *Epic Poem* from a *Romance in metre.* Observe the march of Milton—his severe application, his laborious polish, his deep metaphysical researches, his prayers to God before he began his great poem, all that could lift and swell his intellect, became his daily food. I should not think of devoting less than twenty years to an Epic Poem. Then to collect materials and warm my mind with universal science. I would be a tolerable Mathematician, I would know thoroughly Mechanics, Hydrostatics, Optics, and Astronomy, Botany, Metallurgy, Fossilism, Chemistry, Geology, Anatomy, Medicine—then the *mind of man*—then the *minds of men*—in all

[69] *Table Talk and Omniana* (February 16, 1833), p. 210. It should be recalled that Coleridge once wrote a poem on the sublime in Schiller.

[70] For other cases in which Coleridge indicates the kind of writing that he regards as sublime see: Letter to Benjamin Flower, Griggs, Vol. I, p. 66; To Thomas Poole, Griggs, Vol. I, p. 171; To Edward Coleridge, Griggs, Vol. II, p. 401; a note on Wordsworth's *Ode on Intimations* ("this sublime ode"), *The Friend,* Sec. III, Essay xi, Shedd, Vol. II, p. 461 n.; a note on Spenser's *Epithalamion* ("truly sublime"), *Table Talk,* Oxford ed., p. 64; a remark on Sir Thomas Browne ("a quiet and sublime enthusiast"), Raysor, *op. cit.,* p. 218; a note on Drayton's *Polyolbion, Table Talk,* p. 156.

Travels, Voyages and Histories. So I would spend ten years—the next five to the composition of the poem—and the five last to the correction of it.

This passage contains the substance of what Longinus must have meant when he said that "sublimity is the echo of a great soul": great conceptions greatly expressed.[71] There is also the suggestion, reinforcing the implication in the remarks on Klopstock, that the best poet is, and must be, a poet of the sublime. It is an intriguing—and illuminating—reflection that here is a passage, written by the high priest of the English romantic school, which, except for style and for certain phrases (e.g. "lofty imaginings," "then the minds of men"), might have come from the pen of any one of several so-called typical neo-classic critics: Boileau, Pope, Lessing. The ideas of wide and deep knowledge and of laborious preparation, of careful composition, and of meticulous correction and polish are all such as the critics of the previous age upheld. Here is an interesting testimony to the fact that in the hands of its wisest exponents sublimity, however "romantic" it may appear to certain minds, need in no way conflict with the solid qualities of great art—as it did not in Milton. It is evidence, too, of the essential homogeneity on fundamentals of great critical minds, of whatever generation or "school."

[71] I do not mean to imply that Coleridge regarded the Longinian treatise as properly an exposition of the sublime. On the contrary, like Wordsworth, he denied the validity of the title applied by Boileau and generally adopted by critics and translators. Of the idea of Sappho's ode as representative of the sublime, he writes:

"No such thing. Longinus was no very profound critic; but he was no blunderer. Of the energetic, of the language of high excitement, elevated from passion, in short, ὁψότητος παθητικῆς. Of this indeed it was, is, and probably ever will be, the most perfect specimen. But as to sublime you might as well call it blue or small-poxed" (*Coleridge's Miscellaneous Criticism*, ed. by T. M. Raysor, Cambridge, 1936, p. 320).

COLERIDGE IN GERMANY (1799)

EDITH J. MORLEY

•

•

*As Portrayed in the Journal of George Bellas Greenough and in Some
Unpublished Letters of the Poet**

GEORGE BELLAS GREENOUGH, the distinguished man of
science and first president of the Geological Society, died, a
bachelor, in 1854, leaving to his cousin, Mrs. Colthurst, his first and only
love, the disposal of all his scientific and other papers. Like so many of
his contemporaries, Greenough appears to have treasured every scrap of
written paper, even the exercise-books and verses of his childhood, until
his death at an advanced age. These papers include a great variety of
matter—receipts, account books, proceedings of the Geological Society,
the Royal Society, the British Association, the Graphic Society, Archi-
tectural Associations, the Society for the Diffusion of Useful Knowledge
and a number of other bodies in which he played a leading part. The
bulk of the material is scientific and much of it is certainly of great value
—for example, the annotated and corrected copies of his own and other
published works; his numerous unpublished geological and geographical
writings, notes, and journals, etc. It also comprises many volumes of
detailed and very excellent descriptive diaries of his adventures and
travels in different parts of the world, together with a vast and incom-
pletely sifted mass of correspondence extending over his whole life.
Among the diaries is one of his Harz-Reise in May 1799, when Coleridge
formed one of the party: among his letters are several from Coleridge,
and one, not of any interest, from Southey—to name only the poets. But
as Greenough seems to have been on friendly terms with most of the

* Reprinted from *The London Mercury*.

interesting people of his day, whatever their walk of life, it is not surprising that his correspondence includes autograph letters from very many writers who have left their mark on the world, e.g. the Duke of Wellington, Darwin, Buckland, Faraday, Humphry Davy, to select haphazard only a few of them. By the great kindness of Miss Peggie Bowen-Colthurst, the present owner of Greenough's papers, I have been permitted to spend some days examining them and especially those which relate to Coleridge. In spite of a fairly careful search, not all of those which are known to have been there before their removal from Ireland in 1922 can now be found, though it is probable that they will ultimately be discovered in a place of safety where some of the more valuable may have been stored by the late owner during the Sinn Fein troubles.

I have found (1) the full rough diary of the Harz-Reise, and of subsequent expeditions with Coleridge in June of the same year. This is scored through in many places, and has obviously been used as the basis of a fuller, better-arranged journal, now missing, (2) a copy, in the handwriting of the late Mrs. Bowen-Colthurst of the main part of this diary, (3) eight letters of Coleridge to Greenough, dating from 1799 to 1817, (4) a copy of the letter of Greenough to Coleridge in answer to his of July 6, 1799, (5) copies of certain verses of the poet. Miss Bowen-Colthurst is sure that there should be other letters, which she has read, one of them a long one written shortly before Coleridge's death in 1834. She also tells me that she has formerly seen correspondence about the tour which discussed the possibility of the Wordsworths joining the party. This did not happen because the young men refused to allow Dorothy to come on a journey they considered unsuitable for a female, and the poet would not go without her. On May 4 to 9, 1799, Greenough wrote to his aunt, Mrs. Greenough:

I am going to spend ye Whitsuntide week in a pedestrian tour over the Harz, one of ye principal forests in Germany. Our party will consist of 5 Englishmen and one German. As ye younger Parry has not strength enough to walk 30 miles a day, as we must occasionally, he is to ride on horseback as long as he can by our side. I fear however that he will not be able to see ½ what is to be seen as some of ye mountains are too steep to ride over.

The journal records later that his white pony was hired at the rate of a thaler (3s. 11d.) the first day, and half a thaler for every succeeding day:

We took with us as few clothes as possible, and these being packed up in a portmanteau were thrown over the horse's back and fastened to the back of the saddle. Coleridge being inspired by ye beauty of ye Country spake:

> We walk'd: the younger Parry bore our goods,
> On damn'd bad roads thro' damn'd delightful woods.

Six Englishmen actually took part in the expedition, the party consisting of Greenough, the two Parry brothers, Carlyon, Chester, Coleridge, and the German, Blumenbach. They set forth from Göttingen on Saturday, May 11, 1799, on what Coleridge chose to call their "Carlyon-Parry-Greenation." The Harz-Reise lasted only for a week, but Coleridge and his Göttingen friends were in close association until he and Chester returned to England at the beginning of July. Greenough's journal covers several of their expeditions, which I do not propose to keep separate in this article. Nor is there any need, for our purpose, to print the journal *in extenso,* since the localities described are nowadays well known and the adventures not remarkable.

It is, however, worth examination from the point of view of economic and social conditions, especially among the German peasantry. These Greenough divides into five classes, the fourth and biggest of which was composed of serfs whose lives and persons were completely subject to their lords, so that they were obliged to work under whatever conditions were imposed on them, and were not free to move or even marry without permission. The fifth, or lowest, class of peasantry was made up of slaves as in Mecklenburg, Pommerania, Holstein, Westphalia and some districts of Hesse:

Slavery in these countries is not confined only to the peasantry but comprehends tradespeople, etc., also—yet the situation of these last is often better than of some of the fore-mentioned classes, and there are to be met among them some who, notwithstanding their servitude, have property to the amount of ten, twenty, and even thirty thousand Guldens.

Greenough chronicles the gradual diminution of serfdom, and it is not clear how far he is describing contemporary conditions, but he is quite

explicit about the widespread existence of servitude, to which he ascribes
the coarse manners and lack of morality among the peasants. On the
whole, however, the travellers experienced no rudeness or ill-treatment,
though on one occasion, at least, they had a narrow escape. The description—from a letter of Greenough to his aunt, written from Göttingen
on July 26, i.e. after Coleridge's return—is worth quoting. We know
from Carlyon's *Early Years and Late Reflections,* Vol. I, pp. 34-7, that,
as we might guess from what we know of his conversational methods,
Coleridge was the indiscreet moralist who brought their woes upon
them. The party on this occasion had lost their way and been delayed by
a storm when on an expedition to the "romantic castle" of Count Bird-
lipsch, situated about fifteen miles from Göttingen. The inn described
was situated in Hesse-Cassel:

In a timber yard before the house were collected together several men,
with what view I know not for they appeared to be doing nothing at all. We
asked "if beds were to be had here"—"How should they know?" was the
reply. We went to the door of the house where we knocked and hollo'd
most lustily. No answer was returned—soon afterwards we found another
door half-open and entered. "Hallo! Hallo! can we have beds here?" still
no answer. We returned to the men in the timber yard and entered into
conversation with them, but they had suspicions about us which we found
it impossible to remove. They lett [*sic*] off some Gunpowder almost in our
faces without giving us any notice of what they were going to do. We took
this however in good part—laughed, said it was very pretty and asked
whether they would not lett off some more—but it was useless to stand
talking and our whole party agreed to go again to the house and holla there
with a crescendo vociferation. We had not been long at this work before
a woman made her appearance with a lamp. "You seem to have slept sound,"
said I: "we are sorry to disturb your slumbers, but can you give us a night's
lodging here?" The fair one rubbed her eyes and said "No." "You have at
least a room where we can sit?" "No," replied she, with a more than laconic
conciseness. "But sure you would not go to turn us out in the fields at this
hour of night?" "Then, there's for you," said she, opening a door. We
entered the room—It stunk so of filth and smoke and was already occupied
by three men who were snoring in straw beds upon the floor. "But my good
woman, have you no other room than this?" "No"—"Well then we must
make this do. You can get us something to eat, can't you?" "No." "Or make
us a little coffee?" "No." There was something so droll in the looks, the

manners and the *tout ensemble* of this poor one-syllable uttering female that, notwithstanding the unpleasantness of our situation, we all, with one accord, burst into the most violent roar of laughter. "I wish you a good night's rest," said one. "The woman will think we are laughing at her," said another—"Which to be sure we are not," added a third. "Upon my word, we had better be quiet," exclaimed a fourth: "it may fare still worse with us than it does at present." "Is that possible? O heavens!" and we laughed again. The woman seated herself very coolly at the end of the room. "But my dear, you can give us a little clean straw." "No, I tell you, I can't give you anything before to-morrow morning." "And then we shan't want anything," said we. "So much the better," replied the woman. Our muscles were all worked up into another laugh when a stout fellow, one of those who had been in the yard, entered ye room and putting aside some things that were lying on a chair, sat himself down with much composure to unbutton his breeches knees. "Friend," said I, "is it not possible to procure here a little clean straw?" "O yes Sir," replied the man, "you may have as much as you please." "That's something like," we all cried in a breath, "and we feel exceedingly obliged to you, but as to this woman I don't know what to make of her." "Damn them, what do they mean by kicking up a noise here at this time of night?" exclaimed a voice from an adjacent room, "turn them out, I say, immediately."

Notwithstanding this, one of my comrades was resolved to lecture the woman, and going up to her, said "How could you have the heart to turn poor strangers out at this hour? Surely the pastor of the village cannot have given you proper instructions. Hospitality, compassion, meekness, goodness, charity, brotherly love—these are the virtues which as a Xtian you are bound to practise, or am I to imagine from your conduct that ye Hessians are not Xtns?" The woman seemed affected with what was said and fixed her eyes on the ground: the man at first seemed wholly inattentive, but no sooner did he hear the concluding words, "the Hessians are not Xtns," than he sprang up on his feet, foaming at the mouth and shivering with ungovernable rage. "Hessians not Xtns," bellowed he, snatching up a butter churn that lay by his side, and aiming it at my companion's head, "but I will shew you that they are." Fortunately one of the men who had been sleeping on the straw, started up and arrested his arm. He then seized hold of cups and saucers to throw at us and declared if he had a knife he would stab us to the heart, he would teach us whether the Hessians were Xtians, that he would. The man who from the next room had before insisted on our being turned out, now rushed from his bed no less furious than the other, stamped his feet, struck at us with all his fury, swore at us, called us scoundrels, ordered his pistols to be brought and threatened to kill us. The men who

had been lying on the floor got up in a minute, the whole house was awakened and poured in upon us, the men rushed in from the timber yard and in
less than a minute we were attacked with fists and sticks from every quarter.
We had nothing for it but retreat and instinctively rushed towards the door.
After having left ye house we hoped to be permitted at least to retreat with
impunity, but on looking behind us, saw 13 or 14 fellows close at our heels,
hooting at and insulting us. Not one of us having even a stick by way of
defence, we ran off as you may suppose, like so many dogs with tin canisters
tied to their tails. Our pursuers followed us only to the end of the Village.
. . .

Apart from this incident, the travellers had to put up with nothing
worse than extremely primitive conditions, sharing beds, when they
were lucky enough to obtain them, sleeping in straw on the floor on
several occasions and the like. Yet Greenough records that when they
had the good fortune to secure beds, there was no difficulty in getting
clean linen. Food, too, seems to have been abundant and cheap: the
commonest drink was "Schnaps," but usually coffee was obtainable.
Thus, we learn that the first night of the Harz expedition was passed at
a village called Poelen where they

got a good room upstairs where we drank some good coffee, and supped on
raw ham, Metwurst, potatoes. We all slept upon bare straw in our sitting
room and rose next morning at 6 almost as much fatigued as on ye preceding
night: we had scarcely anything to throw over us so that, except Coleridge
and myself, no one pulled off his cloaths.

The cost of provisions and of the accommodation obtained by the
travellers is usually recorded and we learn that the "whole expences" of
the party "amounted to about Th. 100" (£16 13s. 4d.) for the week's
journey, including payment of guides and hire of pony. The following
is a specimen entry:

May 1799.
Price of Provisions at Clausthall.

	M.	G.
Geräucherte Speck	6	
Schincken	6	
Koch Schweine Fleisch	2	6
Rind Fleisch	3	0

	M.	G.
Frische Roth und Leber Wurst von reinem Schweine Gut	3	0
mit Zusatz	2	4
Geräucherte Roth und Leber Wurst von reinem Schweine gut	3	4
mit Zusatz	3	0
Frische Brat Wurst	3	0
Geräucherte Brat Wurst	5	0
Schlact Wurst	8	0
Reine Schweine Schmalz	6	0
Nurst Fett	4	0

The bill at Clausthall amounted to Th. 22 GG. 22 plus Th. ½ to the Waiter.

Other interesting details of prices are: at Blankenburg:

GG.

A carrier has ....4 ⎫
A postboy ....3 ⎬ p. German mile.
Price of labor ....6 p. day.
A Servt ....6 Th. p. Month.
Postillion ....30 Th. p. Ann.
A maid Servt ....from 12 to 15 Th. p. Ann.

Greenough also gives the following particulars:

Of the best Meal they make at Göttingen

Zweyback and Krangel

Of the 2nd. Meal
French bread ⎫
Raspen bread ⎬ with milk

Semel bread ⎫
Kreuz bread ⎬ with water

Of the 3rd. Meal   Luffen—Cakes, etc.

———————

Rye bread
Clare Bread
Middle bread
Black bread

Commission bread for the soldiers where all the different meals are jumbled together.

———————

Pumpernickel.

———————

It is, however, time to leave these general considerations and to come to particular references to Coleridge and his intercourse with his companions. We know from his letters to his wife and to Poole that, having recently heard of the death of his younger infant, Berkeley, he was desperately homesick at the time, and this is borne out by the verses he wrote in the Brocken Stammbuch (see below, p. 229). This does not appear to have made him unsociable or silent and he was commonly both in high spirits and loquacious. Thus being, as he said, "afraid of getting a wetting," he walked across a river, hand-in-hand with Parry, rather than mount the horse, which had stumbled with one of its riders into a part somewhat deeper than he intended. Like his friends, he enjoyed seeing the peasants climb a greasy pole, or waltz

in the true style, the man continually putting his leg between those of the woman and his arms round her neck, and yet these fellows were so Germanic, phlegmatic and lethargic that some of them had pipes in their mouths and smoked them in their partner's face. The women here appeared to be much superior to the men in their manners and form; and Col[eridge] thinks he has observed this throughout Germa[ny].

At Blankenburg, when the party is to be shown over the Duke of Brunswick's castle by a "very pretty girl," they all "felt much interested about Coleridge's coat which had an immense rent under ye arm." A similar and more distressing accident befell him on another occasion (Wednesday, June 12—a walk to Wilhelmsthal) when he

was to have accompanied us, but an unfortunate Vulgar Fraction took place in his breeches, the taylor was too drunk to mend them in time, and therefore he resolved to walk over to us in the course of the day. . . . Coleridge arrived this evening at Minden where he slept and proceeded from thence on the next morning to Cassel where he found very great difficulty in discovering us. Coleridge proposed to give the girl at Blankenburg a Th. in Saxon Sechsters; so that she would thus have a handful of money which would not be worth a penny—not one of us could keep a grave face from this time till we went out, when Blumenbach at our earnest entreaties gave her 12. G. Gros. The lady bowed with as much thankfulness as if the sum had been enormous.[1]

[1] Greenough's Diary, p. 67.

That the young poet was, at this stage in his career, vigorous and capable of great physical exertion, is proved by the length of his walks and the amount of fatigue he was willing to endure. On occasion he refused to accompany the rest of the party, but this was usually because their expedition, e.g. to explore the mines at Clausthal, did not attract him, rather than on the score of the exertion involved. Once we hear that he and Carlyon "had been long since complaining of their fatigue and doubting their inability [sic] to walk so far" as from Harzburg to Goslar, but even then the others carried their point and they arrived at their destination at 10 p.m.:

We were shown into a room where some of our fellow creatures had been drinking and smoking and which consequently stank pretty fairly: but we were not inclined to be nice and were glad to put up with everything. . . . Fred Parry slept close to the window in the same room with Chester. Parry and Blumenbach got single beds in ye large room, and Carlyon slept in the same room with Coleridge and myself, who, for want of another bed, lay together.

More often, it is Coleridge who urges his companions to further efforts, or undertakes extra sight-seeing on his own account. For instance, after sleeping in a kind of Black Hole, twelve persons in a room eight feet square, "Coleridge and Chester and Carlyon left the room with all haste" —as well they might—"and walked towards the top of the Brocken." Greenough, on the contrary, was very unwell as a result of his experiences, and when they arrived at Elbingerode, their next halting place,

Went to see the beds at 3 o'clock in the afternoon, but had no sooner found one that looked comfortable than I hurried into it, not regarding at all the fate of my companions whom I left to shift for themselves. I rather reproached myself afterwards with this conduct, but Coleridge told me that in such a situation not to have been selfish would have been the greatest selfishness, that in parties of this kind we always ought to pay most attention to him who most requires it and that that person was in this case myself.

Greenough tells us less about Coleridge's philosophizing on these expeditions than does Carlyon, but there are a few references to his opinions which are of interest. Thus:

While my eye ranged with delight over so many scenes of grandeur and beauty, it occurred very forcibly to my mind that as far as human observa-

tion has been able to go, the charms of nature are relished by man alone . . .
and I could scarcely suppose that man was a being of so much consequence
as that all these objects should have been formed simply and solely for his
gratification. This I mentioned afterwards to Coleridge, who directed me to
observe still farther that men were less durable than their works, which, as
far as we see, are formed for their pleasure only . . . from hence he wished
to draw a new argument for the immortality of the soul: for if this be
admitted, the means will be only adequate to the end.[2]

Of references to literature there are not many. On the first visit to
Clausthal in May: "We passed the evening very pleasantly in talking,
smoking and transcribing some of Coleridge's poetry: supped very
miserably at 10½ and sung till we went to bed." Among the lines
transcribed in the Diary are those from the Brocken Stammbuch, "composed and dictated to me by Coleridge," says Greenough, who adds that
they were written at Elbingerode. But they are included in a letter to
Poole of May 6 (i.e. nearly a fortnight earlier), beginning, "My dear
Poole, my dear Poole!—I am homesick."[3]

> 'Tis sweet to him who all the week
> Thro' city crowds must push his way
> To stroll alone thro' woods and fields
> And hallow thus the Sabbath Day.
>
> And sweet it is in Summer bow'r
> Sincere, affectionate and gay,
> One's own dear children feasting round
> To celebrate one's marriage day.
>
> But what is all to his delight
> Who, having long been doom'd to roam,
> Throws off the bundle from his back
> Before the door of his dear home.
>
> Home-sickness is no baby-pang,
> That feel I hourly more and more,
> There's healing only in thy wings
> Thou breeze that play'st on Albion's shore.

---

[2] Greenough's Diary, p. 56.
[3] *Letters,* ed. E. H. Coleridge, Vol. I, p. 295.

Greenough also copied out the thirty-three lines Coleridge inscribed in
an album at Elbingerode, which are printed on p. 215 of Vol. I, of his
Poems (ed. E. H. Coleridge) and begin:

> I stood on Brocken's sovran height and saw . . .

There are, further, transcriptions of the "War Eclogue, *Fire, Famine,
Slaughter,*" first published by Coleridge in *Sibylline Leaves,* p. 97, and
of the fable which begins

> Underneath a huge [*an old* E. C.'s *Poems*] Oak tree
> There was of Swine a large Company. . . .

—in all forty-one lines with slight variants from the final form. Apart
from the poems, there are three literary references of some interest, only
one of which deals with Coleridge's work, viz.:

Coleridge wrote his play [*Osorio,* not performed until 1812] wholly at ye
Instigation of Sheridan—gave up some emoluments wholly on that account—
delivered it to Linley who gave it to Sheridan—Sheridan said it was impos-
sible that anything could be better adapted for representation than ye two
first acts and that the whole was excellent for ye Closet. He lent it to Grey,
Grey to Whitbread, Whitbread to Sir Francis Burdett and so on till at last
Col[eridge] heard Miss de Camp act one of ye Scenes in a public company.
Meanwhile Sheridan will give no answer—will not even give audience to
Coleridge.[4]

The others are as follows:

Coleridge had one day been abusing Mrs. T. Robinson's[5] poetry more than
he thought it deserved—he therefore agreed with his friends that by way of

[4] Greenough's Diary, p. 198.

[5] Mary Darby (Perdita) 1758-1800, married T. Robinson secretly in 1774. She was an
actress who performed with Garrick; the author of songs, plays and novels, but is
chiefly remembered as the mistress of George IV and by the Romney portrait of her.
Four poems to Perdita were written by Coleridge—one "an exceedingly silly copy of
verses," apparently sent to Mrs. Robinson in a letter first published in *Modern Language Notes,* February 1930 by E. L. Griggs, whose whole article on *Coleridge and
Mrs. Mary Robinson* should be consulted by those interested in the subject. The verses,
entitled *A Stranger Minstrel,* together with the poems *Perdita, Alexus to Sappho, The
Snow Drop* and a four-line fragment *O'er her piled grave the gale of Evening sighs*
are printed in E. H. Coleridge's edition of *The Complete Poetical Works of Samuel
Taylor Coleridge.* It is not possible to be sure which, if any of these, is the "sonnet" referred to by Greenough.

atonement he should publish a sonnet[6] in praise of that lady in the public papers. He filled his sonnet with the most extravagant eulogy. A few days later he received a most highly complimentary letter from Mrs. Robinson in which she begged his acceptance of all her works, handsomely bound and printed on wire-woven paper.[7]

I asked Coleridge's opinion concerning the authenticity of Chatterton's works. He mentioned Mill[e]s's[8] argument—viz. In Chatterton's Glossary many words are so explained as to make sense of the text, but not so much sense as Chatterton might have pointed out if he had been better versed in the ancient poets.—Now in answer to this we may observe first that if Mill[e]s had learning enough to find some passages falsely illustrated in the Glossary—so perhaps Chatterton might have had wit and sagacity enough to foresee that some Mill[e]s or other would arise and would purposely mis-render some passages in order that his story might hereafter appear more probable. Again—when Coleridge wrote his Greek ode, he first conceived the idea and afterwards hunted thro' the several poets for words in which to cloth[e] those ideas. It would be the same with Chatterton, supposing his book to be a forgery—and in this case Chatterton would no more fully com-prehend his own writing than Coleridge does ye Greek—hence Mill[e]s' argument rather confirms than refutes ye idea of Rowley's not being the Author.

At the end of June, Coleridge became impatient to return home and finally decided to leave Göttingen with Chester on Midsummer Day[9]

but had not determined whether to go in one of Brandes' Carriages, by the Extra Post, or by the Post Waggon to Hanover, to Brunswick, or to the Brocken! Their bills were not yet paid, their cloaths not yet packed nor had the Carpenter yet made the box according to the directions they had given.

A little persuasion induced them to take a carriage, add Carlyon and Greenough to the party, and proceed via the Brocken "in order to see the setting and rising Sun," on foot thence to Blankenburg, and then "travel extra Post to Helmstadt and Wolfenbüttel and Brunswick." This plan was carried out, Wolfenbüttel being included in the itinerary

[6] The sonnet is not among his published poems, and the date being unknown, I have not succeeded in finding it.

[7] Diary, Thursday, June 27, 1799.

[8] Jeremiah Milles, 1714-1784, maintained the authenticity of the Rowley poems.

[9] Diary, p. 184.

"to enable Coleridge to make some inquiries after Lessing" whose Life he proposed to write.

We wrote a letter to Prof. Lange who succeeded Lessing as secretary to the Library intreating the honor of being allowed to call upon him. The answer we received was that "the Library would be open at 2 o'clock." There's civility for you! We knew very well that the library was open all day. . . . At 2 precisely we went to the library, certain of meeting, as we thought, with Prof. Lange. Even then however to make up the measure of his rudeness, he did not appear. This incivility appeared to us all the more heinous because there is nothing which so much strikes a stranger on coming to Germany as the wonderful liberality with which the professors and learned men are willing to pour upon you their information. . . . Chester and I abhorred staying at Wolfenbüttel but Coleridge and Carlyon were desirous of avoiding exercise and easily proved that by this delay [of a night] we should not lose a moment of time. We therefore lounged away our time, listless, restless and uncomfortable. I scarce ever remember being so terribly hipped.[10]

The last entry which concerns us is on the following day, June 30, at Brunswick:

One evening when drinking tea in Parry's rooms, Coleridge had proposed all of a sudden to form a party to walk over Denmark, Norway and Sweden —I offered immediately to join it, but Parry would not. However, said he, if you are serious in your intention, I will write home and ask whether my father has any objections. This he did and Coleridge promised to wait 3 weeks for the answer. The answer did not arrive in time. Coleridge was impatient to return to his wife and family and as none of us thought it possible that Dr. Parry would consent on account of Frederic, he would wait no longer. The event turned out contrary to our expectations. Parry received a letter yesterday approving the plan. . . . The moment he received it he ordered one of Brandes' carriages and set off with Frederic. . . . They had arrived this morning. . . . The table d'hôte at the hotel d'Angleterre is very good but not so sumptuous by any means as its general magnificence led us to expect. What most engaged our attention was the great care with which some of the company combed their hair with the fork. . . . We bought a Map of Norway, Sweden and Denmark, calculated the time and distance and after giving the subject a very full discussion, Coleridge declared it impossible for him now to be of the party—but promised to take the tour with us during the next Spring. After this Coleridge, Carlyon and myself walked to Richmond, a palace of the Duchess of Brunswick's.

[10] Diary, Saturday, June 29.

Coleridge and Chester terribly disconcerted by the non arrival of their boxes.[11]

The friends parted on the following Wednesday, July 3, as we learn from a delightful letter of Coleridge to Greenough (dated July 6, 1799) which I am unfortunately not at present permitted to print in full. It contains a most amusing account of the poet's interview at Helmstadt with one Beireis, a virtuoso collector and a gentleman whose vanity was almost incredible. Coleridge tried "the Experiment whether I could not rise above Beireis's Self Praises—in Vain! My most extravagant compliments were as German Mustard to Cayenne Pepper!"

He went strai[gh]t to work—asked no questions—offered no Civilities—but full of himself ever, and Retching began instantly—"You wish to see my Things—what do you wish to see?—To see all, or half or quarter is impossible in one or two days—name the collection—Pictures or Coins or Minerals or Anatomical Preparations, or, or, or, or, or, etc., etc., etc." Now I had heard that his Coins and Minerals were really admirable, so I would *not* see them. I was afraid of too much Truth that Poisoner of Imagination! . . . So I chose his Pictures—O Lord! It was a Treat.

The letter concludes with a vivid description of the straits to which the travellers were reduced by the non-arrival of their boxes:

I should hear a cry of Stop Thief close at my ears with a safe Conscience—but if I caught only the echo of a Tally Ho! I should climb up into a Tree! You know me too well to suspect Hyperbole—I stink damnably—and that's the Truth! . . . Marry—and my Books—I shall be ruined—on the Debtors' Side in Newgate, Just 5 Yards distant from Sodomy, Murder and Housebreaking. Soul of Lessing! Hover over my Boxes! Ye Minnesänger! Fly after them!

Our next information about his movements comes from an extract copied from a letter in answer to the above from Greenough, dated July 18, 1799:

Your interview with the son of the Burgomeister [Beireis] at Mühlhausen [*sic*] must indeed have been a treat.

Apparently there had been a second letter from Coleridge sent off from Cuxhaven which greatly pleased the recipients but "gave us scarcely any

[11] *ibid.*, p. 212.

information—none respecting what after yourselves most interested us, your books and cloaths":

> However I am inclined to hope that they came to Hamburg in good time and that in spight of all your misfortunes, poor Chester and yourself were each on your return to England master of a clean shirt and a Guinea! . . . Blum[enbach] talks of you often and affectionately. He never sees us without lamenting your modesty in never having as yet shewn him any of your poetical writings. . . . I took leave of you without copying out your description of the Rosstrap—however as soon as it is finished you will still be able in case of a dearth of news to cram it into some sly corner of ye third page of a letter.

A gap of eighteen months now took place in the intercourse between the poet and his Göttingen friends. The next reference I have found is in Greenough's Journal written at Nether Stowey on Friday, January 9, 1801. It is sufficiently important to be included in full:

> Called on Chester. . . . With regard to Col[e]ridge I learned that on his arrival in England he repaired forthwith to Stowey, only stopping at Bath long enough to change horses, and having seen his family and friends there and corresponded for some time with Wordsworth who had taken his sister down to the North of England to settle there, he returned to London last April, stayed there 6 weeks and then wrote to his wife to pack up all his goods and chattels and follow him as soon as possible since he had determined to leave Stowey and go to live in Cumberland. During these 6 weeks he got introduced to a number of booksellers of whom Longman in Paternoster row proposed to him the translation of Schiller's *Piccolomini* which he at first declined. The offer however having been very handsome and liberal, he afterwards accepted it and having written to Schiller an account of his intention, received from him the MS. copy. He got a good deal of money by writing for the Newspapers and more particularly the *Morning Post* of which paper he procured by these means so extensive a sale that the proprietor of it in gratitude offered to take him into partnership which he refused.
>
> In order to make himself known he made his appearance 4 times a week in the 3rd row of the pit at Drury Lane. He was introduced to Godwin, to Horne Tooke whom he likes very much, to Sheridan whom he detests and several others of the great men of the Age. What conversation passed between him and Sheridan on the subject of his *Osorio* I cannot learn—He is reconciled to Southey.[12]

12 See *Letters*, Vol. I, pp. 303-4, July 29, 1799.

Wordsworth shewed *his* play to Linley who proposed several alterations. Wordsworth said he would not submit to having one syllable altered, that if in its present form it was not fit for the stage, he would try the experiment whether it was adopted for the closet.

As yet however it has not been published.

Coleridge and Wordsworth have now taken an house between them.[13] Their direction is Greta Hall, Keswick, Cumberland. Since his arrival there, he has been blessed with another boy, whom he has christened Derwent in honor of his favorite lake in that neighbourhood.

He always speaks kindly of his countrymen at Göttingen and expressed to Chester his intention of writing to us as soon as he reached London. He told him that he had remitted to Carlyon the amount of his debt.

He now seldom or never writes to his friends at Stowey—not even to Poole. The intelligence received of him is contained in a letter from Mrs. Coleridge to Miss Chester from which it appears that the wife is not so partial to her new residence as the husband and it is the general opinion that sooner or later they must return to Stowey.

C. Lloyd lives in the North at no great distance from Keswick.

On Monday, April 13, of the same year, Coleridge writes that he heard lately with a deep emotion that you had visited Stowey and wrote immediately for your Address. This evening I received it.

He exonerates himself from blame because he had appeared neglectful:

I should calumniate myself most vilely, if I should admit that I had really been forgetful or had felt one symptom of a cooling and alienated mind. Your name is familiar with all whom I love yet where I have spoken of you once, I have thought of you a thousand times—aye, with the Heart's thoughts.

His silence had been due to pecuniary and domestic perplexities, to ill-health, ignorance of Greenough's whereabouts, to his own removal to Greta Hall. He goes on to speak of his ill-health and his belief that he is likely soon to die.

I wish to live, but I have kept my *best* hope so unprofan'd by Ambition, so pure from the love of Praise and I have so deep an intuition that *to cease to be* are sounds without meaning, that though I wish to live, yet the Thought of Death is never for a moment accompanied by gloom, much less terror in my feelings or imagination.

13 This was a mistake, Southey and Coleridge shared Greta Hall. Wordsworth was at Dove Cottage.

The remaining letters are of less interest, but all of them are worth publication, as well as the two from which the above passages are cited. It is to be hoped they may be printed *in extenso* before long, together with all the passages in Greenough's Diary which refer to Coleridge. For he never appears in a more attractive light than in these early years. It is therefore of real value to obtain more first-hand information about him and his doings at this period of his life.

PART TWO

PROFESSOR HARPER: AN APPRECIATION

J. DUNCAN SPAETH

•

•

HAVING been intimately associated with Professor Harper for more than thirty years at Princeton, I find it a particular pleasure to accede to the request of the editor of the present volume to contribute a brief sketch to this series of studies by his friends and former pupils. It is a privilege and an honor to associate myself with this group of scholars who wish by their contributions to put on record their devotion to him.

George McLean Harper took his Bachelor of Arts degree in Princeton in 1884, in an era when the holders of that degree could still claim to have been graduated "not in entire forgetfulness and not in utter nakedness" so far as the masterpieces of classical antiquity are concerned. Already, as an undergraduate, he had shown his literary talent by winning the Class of 1859 Prize in English, and by his contributions to the *Nassau Literary Magazine,* one of which, entitled "With Romeo and Little Nannie," the story of a circus elephant and his offspring, has become a classic of American school-readers.

Though by native temperament inclined to

> The love of learning, the sequestered nooks
> And all the sweet serenity of books,

his years immediately after graduation were spent in active journalism, first as a staff reporter on the New York *Tribune* and later as assistant editor of *Scribner's Magazine.* The desire to solidify and broaden the foundations of his scholarship sent Harper, like so many ambitious students of his generation, to Germany where for nearly two years he heard lectures in German history and literature, first at Göttingen and later in Berlin. There he familiarized himself with German life and letters. Later travel and study in Italy and France prepared him for the instructorship in Romance Languages and Literature to which his alma mater called him in 1889. It was the day when preparation for the Ph.D. degree was still thought compatible with active teaching, and in 1892 young Harper, who in the previous year had been promoted to an assistant professorship in French, took his doctor's degree at Princeton. Two years later he became professor of Romance Languages and Literature. His *Masters of French Literature,* 1901, and his *Life of Sainte-Beuve,* 1909, are among the fruits of his studies in this field.

In 1900 he joined the English Department as Holmes Professor of Belles Lettres and English Language and Literature. He soon became one of the most versatile teachers in the Department, giving courses at various times in every period from Shakespeare and the Elizabethan Drama to the Victorian Age. In latter years his favorite courses have been in Milton and the seventeenth century, and the period of Wordsworth and Coleridge, in which he is a recognized authority, at home and abroad.

The introduction of the preceptorial system gave Professor Harper an opportunity to increase his hold upon his students by his rare gift of inspiring them and guiding them to an appreciation of what is enduring and great in literature; many Princeton men who have won their laurels in the field of letters owe the awakening of their powers to contact with his richly stored mind and his unaffected delight in the great masters.

In his guidance of graduate students, Professor Harper, while demanding exact scholarship and industrious investigation, never allowed attention to literary problems to deaden the sense for literary values. Always himself master of the literature of his subject, he constantly impressed upon his students the fact that intimacy with the subject is more important than command of the literature of the subject, and that the discovery of literary values is as essential a part of literary scholarship as the determination of literary origins.

His own work as a productive scholar is a brilliant exemplification of his critical faith. His *William Wordsworth* (1916) is much more than a biography. It is a fresh and vital reinterpretation of the work and influence of Wordsworth, epoch-making for Wordsworth scholarship both in its factual revelations and its critical expositions. In England and America, indeed wherever Wordsworth is seriously studied, Harper's name is known and honored, and Princeton has her place in the sun.

When in 1926, through the generosity of Edward Bok, a Woodrow Wilson Professorship of Literature was endowed at Princeton, the donor expressing the hope that the incumbent of the chair should himself be an exponent of the liberal and humane faith of the great President, and should, like him, be a master of English prose, the choice fell upon Professor Harper by acclamation. He had been a loyal supporter and warm friend of President Wilson, had edited the President's addresses, had been a consistent and outspoken liberal, and had in his writings shown himself a master of English prose.

Although Professor Harper was nominally retired in 1932, he continued for two years to conduct graduate courses in Literary Criticism and in Coleridge and Wordsworth. It should be noted, too, that he has continued his literary labors to the present time, and his most recently published volume, *Literary Appreciations,* was issued in 1937.

Professor Harper has not only made solid contributions to literary criticism and biography, but is the author of delightful essays and stories. His *Dreams and Memories* and his *Spirit of Delight* are redolent of a rare personal charm; in his vivid sketch of Clovelly, entitled "New Wine in an Old Bottle," in spite of his professed disdain of "mere philology," he makes some very sound and philologically pertinent observations on the Devonshire dialect.

Professor Harper's literary and scholarly pursuits never tempted him to withdraw into an ivory tower where he could evade the challenge of contemporary political and social conflicts, or contemplate them with oriental detachment. Robert Frost writes somewhere of a politician who was

> "a democrat in principle if not at heart."

George Harper has been not only a democrat in principle, but a democrat at heart, in the best sense of that much abused word; he not only sympathized vicariously with the revolutionary hopes of the young Wordsworth for a freer and better world for all men; but also he never hesitated to express by word and deed his political and social convictions. He advised his students to familiarize themselves with the life and problems of the majority of their countrymen by spending part of their vacations at work in field or factory. In his own community it has been not only academic problems that engaged his interest, but he has been active in every movement that had for its aim the improvement of living conditions in the town. He has combined, with his love of books and music and his enjoyment of "the simple life" and country joys, a passion for social justice that made him an uncompromising opponent of oppression and impatient of the distinctions created by wealth and social caste. But even his deep ingrained antipathies were softened when he discussed them with a congenial friend in an atmosphere mellowed by the smoke of his briar pipe.

On the eve of his retirement from active teaching his colleagues and graduate students in the English Department tendered him a complimentary dinner by way of expressing their affection and respect. It may not be inappropriate to conclude this brief sketch with words spoken on that occasion by the present writer, who was privileged to act as spokesman for his colleagues.

"We do not bid him farewell. We congratulate him on his well earned leisure, and we indulge the hope that freed from the heavy and weary weight of departmental meetings he may again enjoy what he happily phrased 'the grin and fling of animal spirits,' recalling the time when long ago he first read Burns in his grandfather's library. It is a pleasant exercise of hope and joy to imagine his autumn brightening into a long Indian summer of mellow fruitfulness in which his pen will continue to glean his teeming brain and garner the full ripened grain of reflection, reading, and experience.

"And we rejoice with him that his fellow-Wordsworthian, Mrs. Harper, the partner of his studies and travels, the maker of his home, is still at his side, and that the happiness is his of seeing a son and a daughter follow their father's footsteps and win honor in a profession the best traditions of which they saw exemplified in their home. For his colleagues in the Department he will continue a beloved companion. Princeton will be a better place to live in because he is our neighbor and friend, with whom we can share our common loyalties to the masters of the imagination who have irradiated human experience with the light that never was on sea or land, a friend who in moods of despondency and seasons of depression will help us recapture the Spirit of Delight he has found in the Love of Books. Like his own best-loved poet we shall always think of him as 'a man of cheerful yesterdays and confident tomorrows,' and in the quiet strength of his well knit character and the serenity of his unspoiled mind he will be to us a living proof of Wordsworth's faith that in the spirit of man a power abides

> to feed
> A calm, a beautiful and silent fire
> From the encumbrances of mortal life
> And sometimes, so relenting justice wills
> From palpable oppressions of despair.

"When in a charming paper once delivered before the English Club, he spoke of Dorothy Wordsworth as an unspoiled child of nature and yet a finely finished product of civilization, we perceived that he had unconsciously revealed the secret of the unique impression he has made on all whose privilege it is to know him. We salute him as 'an unspoiled child of nature and yet a finely finished product of civilization.'"

BIBLIOGRAPHY OF THE WORKS OF
GEORGE McLEAN HARPER

EVELYN GRIGGS

•
•

BOOKS

Charles-Augustin Sainte-Beuve, Philadelphia and London, 1909.
Dreams and Memories, Princeton and Oxford, 1922.
John Morley and Other Essays, Princeton and Oxford, 1920.
The Legend of the Holy Grail, Baltimore, 1893.
Literary Appreciations, New York, 1937.
Masters of French Literature, New York, 1901.
Spirit of Delight, New York and London, 1928.
William Wordsworth, His Life, Works, and Influence, 2 vols., New York and London, 1916; second edition, 1923; third edition (in one vol.), 1929.
Wordsworth's French Daughter, the Story of Her Birth, with the Certificates of Her Baptism and Marriage, Princeton, 1921.

WORKS EDITED

Contes de Balzac; edited with introduction and notes by George McLean Harper and L. E. Livingwood, New York, 1894.
Seven Causeries du Lundi (Sainte-Beuve); with an essay on the author and notes by George McLean Harper, New York, 1897.
Émile Augier and Jules Sandeau: La Pierre de Touche; edited, with notes and an introduction by George McLean Harper, New York, 1912.
President Wilson's Addresses; edited by George McLean Harper, New York, 1918.
Victor Hugo: Hernani; edited with notes and an essay on Victor Hugo by George McLean Harper, New York, 1894.
Wordsworth's Poems; selected and edited with an introduction by George McLean Harper (Modern Student's Library), New York, 1923.

William Wordsworth: Complete Poetical Works; edited by Thomas Hutchinson, and with an introduction and notes by George McLean Harper, Oxford, 1933.

ARTICLES IN BOOKS

"An Account of the Sesquicentennial Celebration," in *Princeton University: Memorial Book of the Sesquicentennial Celebration*, Princeton, 1898.

"La Fontaine," in *Warner's Library of the World's Best Literature*, New York, 1896.

"Froissart," in *Warner's Library of the World's Best Literature*, New York, 1896.

"Gems of Purest Ray," in *Coleridge: Studies by Several Hands*, edited by E. Blunden and E. L. Griggs, London, 1934.

"The Legend of the Holy Grail," in *Warner's Library of the World's Best Literature*, New York, 1896.

"Literature in the United States," in the new *Enciclopedia Italiana*, translated into Italian, 1937.

Several biographies in the *Dictionary of American Biography*, viz., "John McLean," "Francis Landey Patton," "James Ormsbec Murray," "Charles W. Shields."

ARTICLES

"Across the Dead Line in Belgium," *Youth's Companion*, XCIII (May 8, 1919).

"Anglo-American Entente," *Yale Review*, n.s., IX, 484-99 (April 1920).

"Balzac," *Scribner's Magazine*, XXVII, 617-26 (May 1900).

"Children's Appeal to the Sun" (a poem), *Texas Review*, I, 247 (April 1916).

"Coleridge and the Susquehanna," *Nation*, XCV, 330-1 (October 10, 1912).

"Coleridge's Conversation Poems," *Quarterly Review*, CCXLIII, 284-98 (April 1925).

"The Crisis in Wordsworth's Life and Art," *Queen's Quarterly*, XL, 1-13 (February 1933).

"Declaration of Dependence: an American View," *Quarterly Review*, CCLXXI, 233-44 (October 1938).

"Did Wordsworth Defy the Guillotine?", *Quarterly Review*, CCXLVIII, 254-64 (April 1927).

"Émile Legouis," *Quarterly Review*, CCLXX, 15-27 (January 1938).

"The Encouragement of Serious Reading," *Library Journal*, XXVIII, 217-21 (May 1903).

"Eugénie de Guérin and Dorothy Wordsworth," *Atlantic Monthly*, CXXXI, 649-57 (May 1923).

"Face of Paris," *Scribner's Magazine*, LXII, 693-7 (December 1917).

"Fame of Victor Hugo," *Atlantic Monthly*, LXXXIX, 236-49 (February 1902).

"Flemish Question," *Unpopular Review*, X, 43-55 (July 1918).

"French Fiction of Today," *Outlook*, LXXXII, 28-32 (January 1906).

"George Herbert's Poems," *Quarterly Review*, CCLXVII, 58-73 (July 1936).

"Grandpère and Family," *Yale Review*, n.s., VII, 819-26 (July 1918).

"Hardy, Hudson, Housman," *Scribner's Magazine*, LXXVIII, 151-7 (August 1925).

"Honor Bright," *Youth's Companion*, XCIII, 115-16 (March 6, 1919).

"If Dante Were Alive," *Sewanee Review*, XXIX, 258-67 (July 1921).

"In a Paris Hospital," *Scribner's Magazine*, LXIII, 34-7 (January 1918).

"John Morley," *Atlantic Monthly*, CVIII, 805-17 (December 1911).

"Katherine Mansfield," *Quarterly Review*, CCLIII, 377-87 (October 1929).

"Mars' Hill and the Parthenon," *Virginia Quarterly Review*, I, 338-49 (October 1925).

"Matthew Arnold and the Zeit-Geist," *Virginia Quarterly Review*, II, 415-31 (July 1926).

"Milton's 'Two-handed Engine'," (*London*) *Times Literary Supplement*, 424 (June 16, 1927).

"More's Shelburne Essays," *Atlantic Monthly*, XCVIII, 561-70 (October 1906).

"Mycenae" (written in collaboration with Belle Westcott Harper), *Sewanee Review*, XXXIII, 49-56 (January 1925).

"New Program of Studies at Princeton," *Educational Review*, XXIX, 141-50 (February 1905).

"New Wine in an Old Bottle," *Scribner's Magazine*, LI, 684-90 (June 1912).

"Orderly Wanted," *Youth's Companion*, XCII, 603-4 (November 14, 1918).

"Place of French Literature," *Atlantic Monthly*, LXXXV, 360-70 (March 1900).

"Poet of the Rural Scene," *Saturday Review of Literature*, IX, 352 (December 31, 1932).

"Robert Burns's Country," *Scribner's Magazine*, XLIV, 641-55 (December 1908).

"Rousseau, Godwin, and Wordsworth," *Atlantic Monthly*, CIX, 639-50 (May 1912).

"Samuel Taylor Coleridge," *Quarterly Review*, CCLXIII, 94-110 (July 1934).

"Scotch-Irish in America," *Nation*, CIV, 45-6 (January 11, 1917).

"Scott's Novels. An American View," *Quarterly Review*, CCLIX, 344-51 (October 1932).

"Seeing Americans First," *Scribner's Magazine*, LXXXVI, 649-55 (December 1929).

"Tempest in a Swiss University," *Nation*, LXXXVI, 443 (May 14, 1908).

"U.S. General Hospital No. 9," *Scribner's Magazine*, LXIV, 410-15 (October 1918).

"Vino di Orvieto," *Sewanee Review*, XXXIII, 291-9 (July 1925).

"Was Wordsworth Ever a Mystic?", *Discovery*, 348-50 (November 1928).

"W. C. Brownell," *Atlantic Monthly*, CV, 481-90 (April 1910).

"Wordsworth at Blois," *Nation*, XCVI, 354-5 (April 10, 1913); also *Texas Review*, I, 6 (July 1916).

"Wordsworth-Coleridge Combination," *Sewanee Review*, XXXI, 258-74 (July 1923).

"Wordsworth in France," *(London) Times Literary Supplement*, 370 (May 1, 1930).

"Wordsworth's Lines to Hartley Coleridge," *(London) Times Literary Supplement* (August 31, 1922).

"Wordsworth's Lucy," *(London) Times Literary Supplement*, 797 (November 11, 1926).

"Wordsworth's Vast City," *Modern Language Notes*, XLII, 464-5 (November 1927).

TRANSLATIONS

Rein's *Japan*, Vol. II, from the German (in collaboration), New York, 1888.

Gabriele d'Annunzio's "San Pantaleone," in *Stories by Foreign Authors*, New York, 1898.

PAMPHLETS (privately printed)

"Viewed from Afar" (on the "Quad" question), Princeton, 1908.

"The Profession of Teaching," 1913.

INDEX

INDEX

.
.